THE SUPPER

The Supper

New Creation, Hospitality, and Hope in Christ

RONALD P. HESSELGRAVE

WIPF & STOCK · Eugene, Oregon

THE SUPPER
New Creation, Hospitality, and Hope in Christ

Copyright © 2019 Ronald P. Hesselgrave. All rights reserved. Except for brief quotations in critical publications or reviews, no part of this book may be reproduced in any manner without prior written permission from the publisher. Write: Permissions, Wipf and Stock Publishers, 199 W. 8th Ave., Suite 3, Eugene, OR 97401.

Wipf & Stock
An Imprint of Wipf and Stock Publishers
199 W. 8th Ave., Suite 3
Eugene, OR 97401

www.wipfandstock.com

PAPERBACK ISBN: 978-1-5326-7576-8
HARDCOVER ISBN: 978-1-5326-7577-5
EBOOK ISBN: 978-1-5326-7578-2

Manufactured in the U.S.A.   SEPTEMBER 6, 2019

Unless otherwise noted, Scripture is taken from the Holy Bible, New International Version. NIV®. Copyright © 1973, 1978, 1984 International Bible Society. Used by permission of Zondervan Bible Publishers.

Scripture translations labeled ESV® are from the Holy Bible, English Standard Version. Copyright © 2001 by Crossway Bible, a publishing ministry of Good News Publishers. Used by permission. All rights reserved.

Scripture quotations marked (TLB) are taken from The Living Bible copyright © 1971. Used by permission of Tyndale House Publishers, Inc., Carol Stream, Illinois 60188. All rights reserved.

Revised Standard Version of the Bible, copyright 1952 [2nd edition, 1971] by the Division of Christian Education of the National Council of the Churches of Christ in the United States of America. Used by permission. All rights reserved.

In memory of my father,
Dr. David J. Hesselgrave
(January 3, 1924—May 21, 2018),

and my mother,
Gertrude E. Hesselgrave
(January 5, 1920—February 4, 2019),
in gratitude for their lives and support

Contents

List of Illustrations and Tables | viii
Preface | ix

    1   The Supper and its Historical Context | 1

Part One—Old Testament Preparation | 23

    2   The Worldview Story | 25
    3   The Jewish Roots of the Last Supper | 38
    4   The Divine Bridegroom and the Song of Songs | 54

Part Two—New Exodus and New Creation | 63

    5   The Exodus Motif in the Gospels and Pauline Epistles | 65
    6   Feeding of the Multitude and Manna in the Wilderness | 74
    7   The Meaning of Servanthood and the Last Supper | 88
    8   Eating Unworthily | 102

Part Three—Eucharistic Hospitality | 121

    9   Connecting Hospitality to the Lord's Supper | 123
   10 Fellowship with Sinners at Festal Meals | 139
   11 Outcasts as Honored Guests at the Great Banquet | 154
   12 Fellowship, Breaking Bread, and Sharing Possessions | 171

Part Four—The Wedding Supper | 187

   13 The Wedding Supper and the Biblical Hope | 189
   14 The Wedding at Cana | 202
   15 Revelation and the Wedding Supper of the Lamb | 216

Conclusion—The Lord's Supper and the Life of the Church | 235

   16 How Should We Define the Gospel? | 237
   17 The Church as a New Covenant Community | 250

Bibliography | 265

List of Illustrations and Tables

Illustrations

Figure 1. The Cosmos, Garden, and Tabernacle/Temple | 30

Figure 2. Adam's Story as a Mirror of Israel's Story | 36

Figure 3. God's Covenant with Israel | 44

Figure 4. Feeding of the Multitude, New Exodus, and Last Supper | 75

Figure 5. Israel, Jesus, and the Church | 173

Figure 6. Jesus' Glory as the Divine Bridegroom (Jn 2:11) | 205

Tables

Table 1. Symbolism of the Tabernacle/Temple | 32

Table 2. Jesus as the Bread of Life and the New Creation in John's Gospel | 78

Table 3. The Theme of Luke 14:1–24 | 156

Table 4. The Cana Wedding and Jesus' Passion | 211

Preface

"Dinner's ready!" is a familiar call heard in many households across America. When those words are heard, family members know that they are to drop whatever they are doing and come together for the family meal. Though family meals are becoming less and less common in our postmodern, fragmented, and harried society, traditionally they have been viewed as a symbol of togetherness and solidarity. As the well-known saying goes, "The family that eats together stays together." All of us need to eat. But meals with others around a table play an important role in each of our lives. Meals are times when memories are created. Specific meals take place in conjunction with significant events—with various holidays, such as Christmas or Thanksgiving; birthdays that mark significant milestones in our lives; weddings and anniversaries, and even the passing of loved ones and close friends.

In both the Old and New Testaments, meals are at the heart of the story of redemption. The deliverance of the Israelites from slavery in Egypt is celebrated with a Passover meal. Following the exodus, God's covenant with Israel is ratified when Moses and the other leaders of the Israelites feast in God's presence on Mt. Sinai. "They saw God, and they ate and drank" (Exod 24:11). The prophet Isaiah describes the final day of salvation in terms of a great banquet, which God prepares for all of the nations of the world—a banquet of the richest food and the finest wine (Isa 25:6). During his ministry, Jesus regularly shares truths about the kingdom of God in the context of meals with his followers, social outcasts and those at the margins, and even his adversaries. He predicts his death during a final meal with his disciples. Following his resurrection, he then meets two of his disciples on the Road to Emmaus and reveals himself as the risen Christ while eating with them around the table (Lk 24:13–30). Various biblical texts indicate that the first-century Christians remembered Jesus' sacrificial death in the context of community meals (Acts 2:42, 46; 1 Cor 11:20–21; and Jude 12; cf.

2 Pet 2:13). Finally, in the book of Revelation the Apostle John describes human history as headed toward the "wedding supper of the Lamb," when the great multitude will celebrate the coming of God's reign in the new heaven and new earth (Rev 19:1–8; 21:1–4).

Why these many connections between meals and the biblical story? In their insightful book, *Friendship at the Margins: Discovering Mutuality in Service and Mission*, Christopher Heuertz and Christine Pohl help to fill the gaps in our understanding by showing the importance of friendship as a Christian vocation. Eating a meal with others around a table is one of the most powerful demonstrations of mutuality and friendship. We tend to eat meals with those persons we like and with whom we have things in common. But shared meals also help to break down social boundaries and promote reconciliation between people. In Scripture, communal meals represent God's presence. They are important times of healing and restoration. So, when our practices of Communion (or Eucharist) are closely connected to our common meals, we catch glimpses into the nature of God's kingdom.[1]

The association of shared meals with friendship, reconciliation, healing, and restoration is important for grasping the meaning of the gospel as well as the purpose of the church and its mission. Several times in Scripture, Abraham is described as being God's friend (2 Chron 20:7; Isa 41:8; Jas 2:23). Abraham's life is transformed by his faith in God. But the story of Abraham in Genesis links his election and blessing to keeping the way of the Lord "by doing righteousness and justice" (Gen 18:18–19). James is also clear that Abraham's status as a "friend of God" involved a demonstration of saving faith through his works, which most certainly included the hospitality he showed to three strangers by welcoming them into his home and providing a meal (Jas 2:23–24; Gen 18:1–15).[2]

Jesus is the ultimate source and model of friendship, because he loves without limits or boundaries. When he eats and drinks with tax collectors and sinners he is called their "friend" by his enemies—a description which is in no way intended to be complimentary (Lk 7:34). During the Last Supper with his disciples, which takes place in the Upper Room (Jn 13:1–17:26), Jesus calls his disciples friends rather than servants; and he defines friendship in terms of love (15:12–17). "Greater love has no one than this," he explains, "than someone lays down his life for his friends." Jesus' linking of friendship with sacrificial love finds ultimate expression on the cross. This intimacy between Jesus and his disciples is most clearly demonstrated in the foot-washing ceremony (13:1–17), which is a "sacrament of friendship."

---

1. Heuertz and Pohl, *Friendship at the Margins*, 80–83.
2. See Jipp, *Saved by Faith and Hospitality*, 5–6.

First, Jesus' "laying down his robe" anticipates his "laying down his life" in friendship (13:4). Second, Jesus makes it clear in his exchange with Peter that one's relationship with Jesus is dependent upon his or her willingness to accept his act of sacrificial love (13:8). Jesus' disciples are therefore asked to both receive what Jesus offers and participate in his ultimate act of friendship. His modeling of true friendship means that if we really want to be called "friend" by Jesus we must also be willing to give ourselves freely in friendship without worrying who is on the receiving end of our love.[3] In the words of Heuertz and Pohl:

> Jesus offers us friendship, and that gift shapes a surprisingly subversive missional paradigm. A grateful response to God's gift of friendship involves offering that same gift to others—whether family or strangers, coworkers or children who live on the street. Offering and receiving friendship breaks down the barriers of "us" and "them" and opens up possibilities of healing and reconciliation.[4]

My purpose in writing this book largely grows out of my work as a home-based missionary—most recently with a team called the Marginal Mission Network, which is an arm of EFCA ReachGlobal in Europe. Although I am retired, I am still actively involved with this team, which has the goal of mobilizing the church *to* the margins and growing and inspiring the church *from* the margins. The Marginal Mission Network engages with people whom society tends to overlook and even denigrate—including persons with disabilities, the poor, immigrants, and other vulnerable people, such as trafficked persons, who are victims of injustice. The unfortunate reality is that the church often mimics society. Both covertly and overtly, the marginalized are often targets of an "Us versus Them" mindset which betrays our oneness in Christ and goes against the grain of what God is working to accomplish in the world. Even in our evangelism and efforts to help, the marginalized tend to be treated as objects or projects rather than fellow recipients of God's friendship. True friendship is not possible when various people or people groups are considered to be "other" than us.

We tend to forget that Jesus identified himself with the marginalized and was himself marginalized. When Philip tracked down Nathanial and exclaimed that he had found the Messiah spoken of by Moses and the prophets and that he was "Jesus of Nazareth," Nathanial asked rhetorically, "Can anything good come out of Nazareth?" (Jn 1:1:45–46). This was a perfectly natural question to ask. After all, Nazareth was a poor, nondescript town,

3. O'Day, "I Have Called You Friends," 23–24.
4. Heuertz and Pohl, *Friendship at the Margins*, 30.

far removed from the centers of religious, political, or economic power and influence. Philip's response is as transformative for us as it was for Nathanial and the other disciples: "Come and see." Jesus healed the sick, lame, and the blind. He shared the table of friendship and fellowship with social outcasts, and he instructed his disciples to do the same. Seeing Jesus at the margins means identifying with the least of these. It involves experiencing his healing presence in places of weakness and vulnerability rather than in centers of religious, political, or economic power. This does not mean that God has a "preference for the poor." Most certainly, God's grace is for *everyone*. But one of the underlying themes of this book is that the embodied grace which we celebrate in the Lord's Supper gravitates toward the most unlikely and unseen places in ways that run counter to our worldly preoccupation with wealth and power.[5] Two other writers, Kris Rocke and Joel Van Dyke, describe God's creative work of grace in this way: "Grace is like water—it flows downhill and pools up in the lowest places."[6]

Nowadays, in our Western culture, the meals that we share with family members, friends, or coworkers rarely have the depth of meaning that they had in the social world of Jesus' day. When our practice of the Lord's Supper is divorced from an awareness of its original cultural and historical context, it is therefore difficult for us to fully understand why Jesus chose a meal as the occasion to describe his ultimate sacrifice. Ironically, the Lord's Table, which celebrates our common experience of God's grace, is often a source of controversy and disagreement over how to interpret and practice it. While some of these disagreements over details such as the meaning of the elements are important, the real tragedy is that the Jesus meal itself has become a sign of division rather than our unity in Christ.[7] It is essential that we recover the Lord's Supper as a community celebration. Most significantly, when we break the bread and drink the wine (or juice) together we are asserting the reality of the new creation in Christ, affirming God's forgiveness, grace, and cruciform love which is to be embodied in the Christian community, and anticipating the day when God's present and ongoing work of restoration, justice, and reconciliation will ultimately prevail. "The Supper," then, is basically a condensed summary of the story of God's redemption. Rightly understood, it embodies the radical countercultural nature of the gospel.

Meals are an essential part of our daily lives. This is why, in the Christian community, meals are a central symbol of God's kingdom. Jesus gave

---

5. See Leong, *Race and Place*, 143–44.
6. Rocke and Van Dyke, *The Geography of Grace*, 1
7. See Wright, *The Meal Jesus Gave Us*, 39.

the Last Supper to announce the coming of the kingdom through his death and resurrection. Our community meals are therefore connected to Jesus' meal(s), just as the Lord's Supper, or Eucharist, remembers his ultimate sacrifice and anticipates the final festive banquet, which celebrates God's healing presence through all of creation. When we pray, "Thy kingdom come" followed by "Give us each day our daily bread" (Lk 11:1–2), we are asking for the blessings of God's future kingdom to be partially realized in the present. We are not only praying for our needs as symbolized in the bread. We are also praying *for* and *with* those in the wider Christian and human family who are in desperate need. As N. T. Wright reminds us, we cannot pray for God's kingdom to come unless we ourselves are prepared to live this way.[8] God's grand story of redemption has to motivate and inform our particular stories, both individually and corporately. This, I would suggest, is, in large part, what it means to proclaim, or "perform," the Lord's death until he comes (1 Cor 11:26).[9]

This book explores these and other concepts, which are rooted in Jesus' Last Supper with his disciples—and subsequently in the church's practice of the Lord's Supper, or Eucharist. As the subtitle indicates, my focus is on the three interrelated themes of "new creation," "hospitality," and "hope" in Christ. These three themes comprise the "new covenant," which is anticipated in the Old Testament and realized in the New Testament community through Jesus' death and resurrection. This has significant implications for the life of the church.

In writing this book I have benefited greatly from my ongoing dialogue with Jim Baker and other members of the Marginal Mission Network. My wife, Kathi, and I are also grateful to be part of a multicultural church body (Christian Neighbors Church) which, in both its practice of the Lord's Supper and its community life, strives to live out the New Testament principles of fellowship, mutual love, and hospitality discussed in this book. I have enjoyed and learned from various conversations with our pastor, Rev. Luke McFadden, on the meaning and significance of the Eucharist. My brother, Dennis Hesselgrave, and Dr. Michael Cooper have also read portions of the manuscript and given valuable feedback. My thanks to John McFadden for doing the painstaking work of editing the manuscript. I am also deeply indebted to Kathi for putting up with my long hours at the computer. She has read every chapter and offered helpful insights. Without her support and

---

8. Wright, *The Lord and His Prayer*, 13–33.

9. As Gorman points out, the "proclamation" of Christ's death means that in *both* its life and preaching the church must reflect the cruciform love of the Lord. In this sense, the church embodies or "performs" the gospel (*Cruciformity*, 234; and *Apostle of the Crucified Lord*, 269, 589).

constant encouragement, this book would not have been possible. Finally, I have dedicated this book to the memory of my parents, Dr. David and Gertrude Hesselgrave, who recently passed into glory. Their lives of sacrificial service to God and others made an indelible impression on me and my two siblings, their grandchildren, and the wider church family. They are deeply missed.

1

The Supper and its Historical Context

IN recent years, there has been a great deal of interest in what is often referred to as the "historical Jesus." Since the heart of the gospel message concerns Jesus' death and resurrection, it is natural that much of the attention should be given to these central aspects of the Christian faith. This is particularly the case when Easter approaches and there are many media portrayals of the life and death of Jesus. No one denies that Jesus ate a final meal with his disciples. His words about the cup, the bread, his body and blood are among the most secure and established elements of our tradition about Jesus.[1] However, many secular Jesus scholars view these events through the category of myth rather than true history. Christians, of course, believe otherwise—that Jesus died and rose again so that all of his followers could eventually do the same (1 Cor 15:12–58). This is what Jesus predicted when he told his disciples in the Last Supper: "I will not drink of this fruit of the vine from now on until that day when I drink it anew with you in my Father's kingdom" (Matt 26:29). Yet, I often wonder whether we as Christians really grasp the full meaning and significance of Jesus' words. If we did, I believe it would revolutionize our lives.

Not too long ago, my wife Kathi and I took a trip to Springfield, Illinois where we visited the Lincoln Monument and the Lincoln Museum. We also toured reconstructions of the houses and communities where Abraham Lincoln lived during his early years as a child and then as a young adult. Visiting these various sites helped us to put the life of this great president into historical perspective. Such historical monuments, reconstructions, and museums help us to mark key turning points in our nation's history.

---

1. See Keener, *The Historical Jesus of the Gospels*, 296–99.

We also remember these events through the celebration of holidays such as President's Day, Memorial Day, and the Fourth of July. In these celebrations we commemorate the sacrifices that were made; and through various means such as symbols, parades, and speeches we even in some sense relive or re-enact the great historical events which have impacted us both individually and collectively as a nation.

The Lord's Supper (also called "Communion," "the Lord's Table," and the "Eucharist"[2]) is such a commemorative event in the life of the church. In this ordinance we remember, both individually and collectively, Jesus' sacrificial death on the cross. One author has observed, however, that for many Christians the Lord's Supper, or Eucharist, is an isolated event that is barely connected with Jesus' ministry. Although we repeat Jesus' words which were first uttered in the Last Supper, we "pay little attention to [their] context in the story of the passion, let alone the whole gospel. Isolated in our perception of its origins, the Eucharist becomes equally isolated in the life of Christians today. And the New Testament, which should help us integrate the Eucharist into our lives, ends up reinforcing its isolation."[3]

While these words might seem to some to be an overstatement, I agree with this author that the Lord's Supper is often divorced from its historical context. The main point is that the Lord's Supper is rooted in Jesus' "Last Supper" with his disciples, which was essentially a Passover meal.[4] The ante-

---

2. The word *Eucharist* come from the Greek *eucharistia*, which means "thanksgiving." While not commonly used in evangelical circles, it fittingly conveys the significance of this ordinance and therefore will be employed throughout this study along with the term the "Lord's Supper."

3. LaVerdiere, *Dining in the Kingdom of God*, 2–3.

4. Some downplay the connection between the Lord's Supper and the Passover or Last Supper. Witherington, for example, argues that, "There seems to be no historical evidence that early Christians used the Lord's Supper as an occasion to dramatize either the Passover or the Last Supper" (*Making a Meal of It*, 61). Wright, however, disagrees. "Many people today, including many Christians," he argues, "don't realize where the central Christian act came from, or what it meant to begin with . . . But the basic fact of the matter is this: what Christians do today when they meet to break bread and drink wine together is the central Christian action, which links us in an unbroken line . . . ultimately . . . to Jesus and his friends in the Upper Room on the night he was about to be betrayed (and denied, forsaken, arrested, tried, mocked and execute." Furthermore, the "Jesus-meal" was "woven into the heart of Christian living by the time Paul wrote to Corinth in the mid-50s, twenty years or so after Jesus' death and resurrection. It held such a strong place in Paul's own thinking that he could speak of the very action of the meal as proclaiming the death of the Lord until he comes. *Doing* it *said* it" (*The Meal Jesus Gave Us*, 37, 43). Since there is some question as to exactly when the Last Supper occurred, some have argued that it may not have been a Passover meal proper, but a Passover-like meal. Either way, the connection of the Lord's Supper or Eucharist to the Last Supper and exodus has the same significance.

cedent of the Lord's Supper is therefore the Jewish celebration of the deliverance of the Israelites from their captivity in Egypt. Why is this important?

Let's back up for a moment and consider why the Gospels were written in the first place. The underlying message of the separate gospel accounts is that Jesus' life, death, and resurrection comprise the central event of cosmic and human history and provide the key organizing principle for our lives as Christians.[5] The Last Supper, which forms the basis for our practice of the Lord's Supper, points to this reality. Of further importance is the fact that the Gospels connect Jesus' *identity* as King over all things with his *purpose* in dying on the cross.[6] For various reasons, Christians have tended to separate the kingdom and the cross. On one hand, there are "kingdom Christians" who have a social-gospel agenda; on the other, there are "cross Christians" with a "saving-souls-for-heaven" agenda. Each of the four gospels, however, brings these two viewpoints together into a unity that is much greater and more comprehensive than the sum of their parts.[7] N. T. Wright and others have alerted us to the tendency of Christians to split off what philosophers call the "problem of evil" from what theologians think of as the "atonement"—"as though the cross of Jesus were not, in the New Testament, God's ultimate answer to the 'problem of evil.'" According to Wright, this is a dangerous mistake.[8]

For Wright, this myopic understanding of the gospel can be corrected only by seeing the story of Jesus as climax of the story of Israel. In other words, the story of Israel—and indeed the whole story of the world to which the story of Israel is a response—is most clearly and fully understood through the story of Jesus. In *Mere Christianity* C. S. Lewis conveys this sense of divine redemption as a "story" when he states that "in Christianity God is not a static thing . . . but a dynamic, pulsating activity, a life, almost a kind of drama." Moreover, this drama is played out in each one of us as believers; or (putting it the other way around) each one of us has to enter into the pattern of this drama.[9] From this perspective, the Last Supper is itself a divine "drama" that we as followers of Christ participate in through the observance of the Lord's Supper. That is a central theme that I intend to develop in this book.

---

5. Keller, *King's Cross*, x.
6. Ibid., xiv.
7. See Wright, *How God Became King*, 159.
8. Ibid.
9. Lewis, *Mere Christianity*, 171.

The Last Supper as Embodied Drama

Before going into the details of the Last Supper, let me further clarify the approach I am taking in this book. What do I mean when I describe the Last Supper (and therefore the Lord's Supper or Eucharist) as a "drama?"

A Nexus of Issues

There is a nexus of issues which confronts any reader of the Bible.[10] Often, they are not directly addressed in our "plain" reading of the Bible. But they are always lurking under the surface. First, what is the relationship between the Old Testament and the New Testament? One biblical scholar, Craig Bartholomew, has observed that, "Utterly central . . . must be the question of the Old Testament—New Testament relationship, and this needs to be carefully nuanced."[11] I agree with those who argue that the Bible must be approached in terms of "completion and development." In explaining this concept, Ben Witherington argues that while there is considerable continuity between the Old Testament and New Testament, "the Christian experience of things, particularly of the life, death, and resurrection experiences of Jesus . . . have caused a rather clear and dramatic reconfiguration of even the basic lineaments of Old Testament thought."[12] When, for example, the New Testament writers talk about a new covenant this is not merely a renewed form of the old covenant but a new relationship with God—a "new creation" and "new birth"—which is possible only through the person and work of Christ.[13]

A second, and related, question is how we should understand the content of Scripture. In other words, should we stress the diversity or unity of the Bible's content? It is obvious to any discerning reader of the Bible that there are different perspectives, contexts, and literary genres in the pages of Scripture. This might lead some to stress the Bible's diversity. Yet, there are others who maintain—and I would agree—that there is an overarching unity of the Bible and that specific passages or books should be understood as part of the biblical story line.[14] According to Witherington, "the Bible itself encourages both the conveying and reading of its theology and ethics in the context of a narrative."[15] What he calls the "symbolic universe" of

---

10. See Klink and Lockett, *Understanding Biblical Theology*, 17–20.
11. Bartholomew, "Biblical Theology and Biblical Interpretation," 11.
12. Witherington, *New Testament Theology and Ethics, Vol. Two*, 47
13. Ibid., 47–8.
14. Klink and Lockett, *Understanding Biblical Theology*, 18.
15. Witherington, *New Testament Theology and Ethics, Vol. Two*, 102.

the biblical writers—the "mental furniture" of concepts such as God, sin, salvation, Israel, faith, heaven, hell, love, forgiveness, truth, etc.—is expressed in the context of narrative, particularly the "grand narrative" of the Bible.[16]

A final question that needs to be addressed is whether the story line of the Bible is descriptive or prescriptive. That is, does the Bible simply narrate or describe an ancient story that has little relevance for us today; or is this story to be understood as both speaking to our modern world and as authoritative for Christian life and practice?[17] Again, I would suggest that it is the latter. Specifically concerning the events of the Passover and subsequently the Last Supper, I would argue that the Bible is not simply describing *what* happened. These events also have particular relevance for revealing God's purpose for the church and the world today.

The Last Supper/Lord's Supper and the Story of the Bible

To be more specific, the overall perspective that I am adopting in this book approaches the Bible as a "worldview story." That is, there is a "story shape," or continuous and interconnected narrative running throughout the Bible that connects the Old and New Testaments and expresses the Bible's theology of redemption.[18] This means that we have to understand individual episodes or passages of Scripture from the perspective of the overarching story line. The Bible's unified and interconnected story is the key "hermeneutical lens" through which individual passages or books find their theological meaning and significance.[19] The interpreter takes into account the relation between the "plot" and the larger "story." The plot is the discrete sequence of interconnected actions or episodes narrated by an individual author, where story is the overarching shape of reality.[20]

---

16. Ibid., 59; 102 This raises the question of the relationship between "narrative" and "drama." Vanhoozer describes the "story of Scripture" as drama in his thought provoking *The Drama of Doctrine*. Witherington, however, is critical of Vanhoozer's characterization of biblical theology in terms of "theodrama." He argues that it "seems better to talk about narrative rather than the drama." He maintains that narrative can be just as dramatic as drama, particularly since in the cultures of the biblical writers the biblical story was narrated or "performed" orally (*New Testament Theology and Ethics, Vol. Two*, 49–51). In my view, it is still useful to retain the concept of "drama," which better conveys the idea that believers are active *participants* in the divine love story.

17. Klink and Lockett, *Understanding Biblical Theology*, 20.

18. Ibid., 93.

19. Ibid., 101.

20. Ibid., 97.

This narrative approach to biblical theology involves discerning the historically grounded "worldview" of the biblical authors. Also, an important part of discovering the overarching story of Scripture is seeing how the New Testament authors use the Old Testament. This further necessitates that we avoid lifting specific passages out of their historical context. N. T. Wright is particularly critical of approaches which read the Bible without reference to the early Christian origins. The result is that readers often tend to hear a particular church tradition, or worse, their own voices, instead of those of Jesus or Paul.[21]

N. T. Wright further shows how a "dramaturgical" understanding of the overarching biblical narrative makes it relevant for modern readers. The biblical metanarrative, he argues, is a story of what the Creator of this world has done and is doing to redeem his people and ultimately to restore his creation. Using the analogy of a play or drama in which God's authority is rendered through the overarching story line, he goes on to argue that "'the authority of scripture' is most truly put into operation as the church goes to work in the world on behalf of the gospel, the good news that in Jesus Christ the living God has defeated the powers of evil and begun the work of new creation."[22]

One of Kathi's and my favorite movies is *The Mission*, which was nominated as Best Picture in the 1987 Academy Awards. In the opening scene, a Jesuit missionary is strapped to a cross–shaped raft and then sent down the river and over the vast Iguazu Falls in South America. Throughout the rest of the movie, the cross is displayed as a powerful symbol of sacrificial love. As director Roland Joffe exclaimed, "[*The Mission*] is a movie about love, and it's a movie about what love is. It's a movie about the pain of love, about the vulnerability of love; about the longing for peace that love can bring or that the lack of love can take away." The Bible likewise views salvation history as a *divine love story* that comes to its final climax in the bloody wood of a Roman cross.[23] It is this story that is at the heart of the Last Supper and our practice of Communion, or the Lord's Supper.

Various authors have pointed to the dramatic characteristics of the Last Supper and Eucharist as a "summary" of the overarching story of redemption in the Bible. David Gushee and Glen Stassen describe this meal as "embodied drama." In the account of the Last Supper, Jesus did not simply tell a story about giving his life for others. He incarnated it in his own body and blood—both as a private act and as a community drama that included

21. Ibid., 110
22. Quoted in Ibid., 97; 111.
23. Pitre, *Jesus the Bridegroom*, 3.

the disciples, the Jewish community and authorities, and the Roman power structures. Furthermore, it is embodied *now* through the life and worship of the church. And it will be incarnated in the future kingdom, which Jesus portrays as a banquet, or "love feast."[24]

Kevin Vanhoozer makes a similar point when he argues that the Lord's Supper (or Eucharist) does not simply express a doctrine; it is also a theater for presenting Christ and the gospel. In its observance of the Lord's Supper the church serves as a microcosm, an embodied summary of the whole drama of redemption. "The Lord's Supper is the conspicuous display not only of the high point of the drama, the death of Jesus, but also of the drama's end, the perfection of God's kingdom on earth as it is in heaven."[25]

Another way of describing the approach I am taking in this book is to use the analogy of a camera lens.[26] Throughout the history of eucharistic theology, emphasis has been placed on the theological significance of the elements. In this "zoom lens" approach, theological debate has focused on two main issues: First, what does or does not happen to the bread and wine? And second, what benefit does participation in the Eucharist or Lord's Supper bring to the individual participant?[27] Over the past five-hundred years, many books and articles have been devoted to disputes between Protestants and Catholics over transubstantiation and to intramural debates between Protestants over how grace is conveyed through the elements of the sacrament. Among evangelicals, in particular, this question is treated almost exclusively in the context of individual soteriology or salvation. The issues raised by the "zoom lens" approach are important, as we will soon see. But this approach needs to be supplemented by another approach, one which examines the Eucharist through a wide-angle lens. In the wide-angle view, the Eucharist becomes the focal point for the relationships of church members to one another, creation, and God. The central question is what does this ordinance of the church express about the church's understanding of itself and her place in the world? From this perspective, the Lord's Supper is not just a means of grace to individual participants; it is also formative of the church's communal ethos and interpersonal relations of those who are "in Christ."[28] To again use the language of drama, the Supper is the church's

---

24. Gushee and Stassen, *Kingdom Ethics*, 78–9.
25. Vanhoozer, *Faith Speaking Understanding*, 166.
26. See Leithart, *Blessed Are the Hungry*, 157–62.
27. Ibid., 157–58.
28. Ibid., 160–62

"role-play," or performance, which fills not just a few minutes of worship but all of life.[29]

Sharing in Jesus' Story

We get a sense of the deeper significance of Jesus' Last Supper as a drama by reading and interacting with the post-resurrection story of the Road to Emmaus (Lk 24:13–35). As you read this story, try putting yourself in the shoes of these two disciples. Cleopus and his companion (who is probably his wife, Mary) are walking down the road to the village of Emmaus when a stranger joins them. Observing their obvious dejection, he asks, "What have you been talking about?" They explain how their dreams had been dashed by the crucifixion of the person they hoped was the Messiah who would redeem Israel. The stranger then explains from the Scriptures why these events had to take place. As they near the village, the couple convince the stranger to come at stay overnight at their house. The turning point in the story comes when they are seated at the dinner table. Jesus prays, breaks the bread, and gives it to them. At that point they suddenly recognize him and he vanishes. Amazed, the couple then run back to Jerusalem and tell the other disciples what they experienced.

Now the question we must ask is this: Why did the disciples recognize Jesus when they did? The obvious similarity between Luke's description of Jesus' actions in this account ("he took the bread, gave thanks, broke it, and gave it to them") and the words in his and other accounts of the Last Supper (Lk 22:19; cf. Matt 26:26; Mk 14:22; 1 Cor 11:23–24) cannot be accidental. Luke, in effect, is saying that the disciples came to "know" Jesus in the "breaking of the bread."[30] The same echoes of the Last Supper can be seen in Acts 2 where the disciples' fellowship is described in terms of "breaking bread" together. "When the disciples met together to break bread, they also met with Jesus in the bread."[31] This is known as the "real presence" of Jesus in the elements of the Lord's Supper.

In their emphasis on the "symbolic" nature of the Lord's Supper, evangelicals have often missed the larger significance of this ordinance. The Lord's Supper is more than the memory of Christ's death and a reminder that he is with us. To begin with, the words of Jesus "do this in remembrance of me," (Lk 22:19–20) which Paul repeats (1 Cor 11:24–25) do not simply mean "to recollect," "recall," or "remember" Jesus' death at the intellectual

---

29. Ibid., 186.
30. Wright, *The Meal Jesus Gave Us*, 68.
31. Bird, *Evangelical Theology*, 789.

level. For the Jew in the first century it meant recalling the significance of his death on the cross and *experiencing* it once again. "To remember Christ's self-giving death is to participate in it as a present reality, to live faithfully and appropriately in the shadow of the cross."[32] In 1 Corinthians 10:16 Paul teaches that there is a real encounter and "participation" with Christ's blood and body in the elements. The word for "participation" that Paul uses is *koinonia*, meaning "fellowship" or "sharing." That is, through the Holy Spirit, we actually "commune" with Christ in the elements.[33] Some are reticent to take Paul's words here literally.[34] But, as Michael Bird argues, Paul is not speaking metaphorically or symbolically. "One can only fellowship with Christ's body and blood if Christ is somehow present in the bread and wine. You cannot fellowship, partake, share, or commune with one who is entirely absent."[35]

Furthermore, if union with Christ is the fundamental reality of salvation and if the Supper is communion with Christ, then the Supper must mean everything that union with Christ means. In the words of one author, "The significance of the Supper is as high and deep and wide as salvation itself. . . . The whole history of Scripture is the history of Jesus Christ, and in the Supper we are inserted into this Christ and this history."[36] In a very real sense, then, as we participate in the Lord's Supper we are privileged to *share* in Jesus' story. "This is God's play," says N. T. Wright, "and you are privileged to take part in it. You are not at liberty to muck around with the plot. It isn't a service made up of odd bits and pieces tied together with a few hymns and prayers, at the end of which you just happen to share bread and wine. It is God's drama, not yours, rooted in scripture and in the events of which scripture speaks."[37] When we break the bread to share in the body of Christ, "we become for a moment the disciples sitting around the table at the Last Supper." But, even more than that, since the risen Christ gives himself to us as food and drink, the Eucharist is the arrival of God's future in the present. "It is the future coming to meet us in the present."[38]

Seldom do we think (much less act) in these terms. We generally think of God as the Creator of our lives. But it is not very often that we think of

---

32. Gorman, *Apostle of the Crucified Lord*, 269.

33. Bird, *Evangelical Theology*, 789.

34. See, for example, Morris, *The First Epistle of Paul to the Corinthians*, 146; and Johnson, *I Corinthians*, 166.

35. Bird agrees with Calvin that one cannot divorce the sign (bread and wine) from what it signifies (Christ). Bird, *Evangelical Theology*, 785, 791–92.

36. Leithart, *Blessed Are the Hungry*, 13–14.

37. Wright, *The Meal Jesus Gave Us*, 68.

38. Wright, *Surprised by Hope*, 274.

God (and the risen Christ) as the Author of our lives, the one who writes the story of our lives and calls us to share or participate in his divine story.[39] But this is exactly what the story or drama of the Last Supper teaches us!

The Significance of the Shared Meal

During my early years as a child, the dinner table was one of the central features of our family life. Mom was a consummate homemaker and cook. It was always expected that we would eat at least the evening meal together. And despite my father's busy schedule, he made every effort to see that nothing would interfere with this regular family gathering. We also had family devotions after each evening meal. For both Kathi and me, reconnecting over a shared meal, particularly on special occasions, has been an important part of our family traditions.

Sadly, for the most part, the image in the Norman Rockwell painting of a family eating together around a table is a thing of the past. Americans often do not eat together. The average American eats one in every five meals in their car, one in four eats at least one fast food meal every single day, and the majority of American families indicate that they eat a single meal together less than five days a week.[40] This practice of not eating together takes its toll, physically, socially, and psychologically. Studies have shown that students who do not regularly eat with their parents are significantly more likely to be truant at school; and children who do not eat dinner with their parents at least twice a week are 40 percent more likely to be overweight compared to those who do. Alternatively, children who do eat dinner with their parents five or more days a week have less trouble with drugs and alcohol, eat healthier, show better academic performance, and report being closer to their parents than those who do not.[41]

There are two big reasons why the failure to eat together is associated with these negative effects. First, of course, is the obvious fact that eating out (especially inexpensive fast food) is less healthy. Even food eaten in restaurants generally has higher fat, salt, and caloric content than meals eaten in the home. Secondly, while the dinner table creates a sense of community, eating alone is often alienating. In fact, as Alice Julier argues in her book *Eating Together*, dining together can radically change people's perceptions of people from other groups, races, genders, and socioeconomic backgrounds.

---

39. See Allender, *To Be Told*, 3.
40. Delistraty, "The Importance of Eating Together," 26.
41. Ibid., 35–6.

Alternatively, lack of access to shared food reinforces differences and often means exclusion of people from important social and economic resources.[42]

Recently, two researchers at Cornell University analyzed 52 of the most famous paintings of *The Last Supper* and found that the sizes of the portions and plates in the artworks have grown by between 23 and 69 percent over the past millennium. In this illustration of the principle that "art imitates life," these researchers conclude from their study of history's most famous diner that: "The last thousand years have witnessed dramatic increases in the production, availability, safety, abundance and affordability of food."[43] The tragic irony is that while in rich countries like ours the phenomenon of serving bigger portions on bigger plates often pushes people to overeat, in the poorest countries of the world millions of people suffer from malnutrition and starvation. Even in our own country about one in every five children goes to bed hungry at some point during the year.

In light of these facts it is significant that in the early church the Lord's Supper was celebrated in conjunction with a common meal, as was the Last Supper that Jesus held with his disciples (Acts 2:42–46; 1 Cor 11:20–21).[44] This indicates that the practice of the early church should serve as a model for how the Lord's Supper ought to be practiced by Christians today. In other words, when we share in God's story of redemption, we do so not simply as individuals, but collectively as members of Christ's body. And an important, indeed crucial, part of this ordinance in which we collectively participate is the context of a shared meal. For Paul, two elements are inseparable: 1) fellowship with Christ in the partaking of the bread and the cup (his "real presence"); and 2) the experience of solidarity or fellowship with one another—including "those who have nothing" (1 Cor 11:22)—around the table as the body of Christ (the church).[45] Yet, in our individualistically oriented culture, seldom is the Lord's Supper celebrated in this fashion. In the remainder of this chapter I want to show why it is so important that we recover the ancient tradition of the Lord's Supper as a shared meal.

Setting the Last Supper in Its Historical Context

Many of us are so familiar with the Lord's Supper that it has become a "routine." In fact, our very familiarity with the Lord's Supper may cause us to overlook some central features of this ordinance. It is necessary that we see

---

42. Julier, *Eating Together*, 2.
43. Fahmy, "Super-sizing the 'Last Supper.'"
44. See Gehring, *House Church and Mission*, 84.
45. See Gorman, *Apostle of the Crucified Lord*, 268.

it with fresh eyes. And in order to do this we again have to put ourselves in the "drama" of the original Last Supper that Jesus shared with his disciples before his death on the cross.

The Passover Context of the Last Supper

Imagine that you are a Jew living in the city of Jerusalem. The city is teeming with people who have come from every part of the Roman Empire to celebrate the most popular and important holiday on the Jewish religious calendar—the Passover. This, of course, is the meal that for hundreds of years the Jews have celebrated to commemorate God's rescue of the Israelites from their slavery in Egypt. This special day is called "Pesach," which means to "pass over."[46] The Passover is the event of the year for Jews "to remember God's faithful ransoming, rescuing, saving work."[47]

We are all familiar with that ancient story. The Israelites were instructed to take a perfect lamb and kill it on the fourteenth day of the month. That evening they were to take some of the blood and put it on the tops and sides of the door frames. And they were to roast the lamb and eat it along with unleavened bread and bitter herbs. The bread was eaten without leaven because of the haste with which they had to leave Egypt; and the bitter herbs symbolized the sorrow they experienced in Egypt. The blood from the Passover lamb was a "sign" that protected the Israelites from the plague of death that God sent on the Egyptians. To this day, when Jews take part in this meal they sit sideways in a "reclining" position to indicate that they are a "free" people. Slaves stand; free people recline. So, the whole meal defines who they are and who they will be. It also describes who God was, is, and will be.[48]

Following Jewish custom, Jesus and his disciples had come to Jerusalem to observe the Passover. According to John's Gospel, it was on Sunday (the 10th day of Nissan) that Jesus, in fulfillment of Zechariah's prophecy (Zech 9:9), entered Jerusalem riding on a donkey with throngs of people proclaiming him as the "King of Israel" (Jn 12:12–15). The next day he cleansed the temple, prophetically citing the words of Isaiah and Jeremiah— "'My house shall be a house of prayer,' but you have made it 'a den of robbers'" (Lk 19:45; cf. Isa 56:7; Jer 7:11). Because he knew that he was a wanted man, Jesus made arrangements for the observance of the Passover to take place in a private room. The disciples were instructed to have a clandestine

---

46. Wright, *The Meal God Gave Us*, 9.
47. McKnight, *A Community Called Atonement*, 85.
48. Wright, *The Meal Jesus Gave Us*, 12–13.

rendezvous with a man carrying a jar of water who leads them to the Upper Room. There they made preparations for the Passover meal (Mk 14:12–16). Although there is some question as to when the Last Supper took place, Mark and Luke indicate that it was on the afternoon of Nissan 14 (Thursday), the time when the Passover Lamb was being sacrificed.[49] The ancient historian Josephus records that on the Passover week of one year, 255,000 lambs were bought, sold, and sacrificed in the temple courts.[50] Some think that the disciples' "preparation" may therefore have involved the acquiring of a Passover lamb that was both sacrificed in the temple and prepared for consumption in accordance with Jewish custom in the first century (Mark 14:12; Lk 22:7–9).[51] Others, however, disagree, noting that none of the gospels specifically mention the eating of a roasted lamb in their accounts of the Last Supper.[52]

The Meal Itself

We are now ready to look in greater detail at the meal itself. While Jesus and his twelve disciples "recline" at the table, he states that this event is the fulfillment of a longstanding desire to eat the Passover meal with them before he suffers. (Lk 22:14–15) In the traditional Passover meal there were four courses or points at which the presider would hold up the glass of wine and explain the feast's meaning. These four cups represented the four promises made by God in Exodus 6:6–7. These promises were: 1) rescue from Egypt; 2) freedom from slavery; 3) redemption by God's divine power; and 4) a renewed relationship with God.[53] The third cup came at a point near the end of the meal. The presider would quote from Deuteronomy 26 to bless the elements—the bread, herbs, the lamb—and explain how they were reminders of God's deliverance.[54] It is probably at this point where Jesus states that he will not eat the meal or drink of the fruit of the vine again until it finds fulfillment in the kingdom of God. (Lk 22:16–18; cf Matt 26:29; Mk 14:25).[55]

49. Pitre, *Jesus and the Last Supper*, 391.

50. See Keller, *King's Cross*, 156

51. Pitre, *Jesus and the Last Supper*, 395–96.

52. Keller, *King's Cross*, 167. McKnight argues that this was most likely a "Passover-like" meal which took place the night before the Passover meal proper. It should be noted, however, that these differences of interpretation are not crucial, since the Passover was an eight-day event, and not simply a one-night meal (*A Community Called Atonement*, 84}.

53. Keller, *King's Cross*, 164–65.

54. Ibid., 165.

55. See Bock, *Luke*, 551.

In ancient times when someone announced "I'm not going to eat or drink until I _____," they were making a solemn oath. It was like signing a contract.[56] One can imagine what was going on in the disciples' minds. "It's all very well for us to sit here as though it's just another Pesach," they may well have thought, "but how is this all going to bring about God's kingdom?"[57]

Jesus makes some further startling statements. First, after giving thanks, he distributes the unleavened bread among his disciples and identifies it with his own body. He also describes the cup of wine as "the new covenant in my blood, which is poured out for you" (Lk 22:19–20). Jesus further instructs his disciples, "Do this in remembrance of me." Again, one can imagine the disciple's amazement at these words. What could Jesus have meant? Since the Old Testament not only links the unleavened bread with the redemption from Egypt but also with eating the flesh of the Passover lamb, it is likely that Jesus is drawing a parallel between the sacrifice of the Passover lamb and his own suffering and death.[58] Said in another way, the gospel writers make no mention of eating a lamb at the Last Supper because the Lamb of God was *at* the table. Jesus was the main course.[59] This is why John the Baptist describes Jesus as the Passover lamb (Jn 1:29); and why the Gospel of John records that this Lamb was being slaughtered at the very time that the Jews were preparing their Passover lambs (Jn 19:14; cf. Exod 12:5–6). This same connection is also made by the Apostle Paul when, twenty years after Jesus' crucifixion he describes Christ as "our Passover lamb, [who] has been sacrificed" (1 Cor 5:7).

Some Questions

This brief reenactment of the Last Supper raises some questions which are often not addressed in discussions of this ordinance that Jesus gave to his followers.

First, in each of the Synoptic Gospels, Jesus describes the cup as "the new covenant in my blood" (Lk 22:20) or "my blood of the covenant" (Mk 14:24; Matt 26:28). Why does Jesus describe the cup (and his death) in this way? What is the significance of Jesus' reference to the "new covenant?" Often, this question is given little attention. Yet, it seems to be obviously important for understanding the meaning that Jesus attached to his death.[60]

---

56. Keller, *King's Cross*, 165–66.
57. Wright, *The Meal God Gave Us*, 15–16.
58. Pitre, *Jesus and the Last Supper*, 405–16.
59. Keller, *King Jesus*, 167.
60. See Gorman, *The Death of the Messiah*, 14–15.

Second, during Jesus' giving of the Last Supper, apparently the breaking of the bread and drinking from the cup was separated by the sharing of a meal, or "supper." The key action that Jesus took in the week of his death was to organize a meal with his followers. When he wanted to explain what his death was about "he did not give them a theory, a model, a metaphor, or any such thing; he gave them a *meal* . . ."[61] Why did he do this? What is the significance of the shared meal as a context for the breaking of bread and drinking the wine?

This last question leads directly to the next one. The meal that Jesus celebrated was, as we have observed, the Passover—or Passover-like—meal. The many books on the "atonement" seldom highlight the fact that Jesus chose to go to Jerusalem and (so it seems) force a showdown, not on the Day of Atonement, the Festival of Tabernacles or any other special day on the sacred calendar, but at the Passover.[62] Again, what are we to make of this?

Finally, all of the Synoptic Gospels place the Last Supper within the context of the kingdom. This is most explicit in Luke, which makes a double allusion to the kingdom (Lk 22: 15-17; cf. Matt 26:26-29; Mk 14:22-24). Nonetheless, in all three gospels Jesus indicates that there would be a "gap" in time between his death and the final Passover in the kingdom that would "fulfill" all preceding Passovers.[63] What is the significance of these references to the kingdom?

Multiple Meanings of the Last Supper

Again, it is important to note that these questions can best be answered if we situate Jesus' Last Supper within its historical context. Since Jesus was a Jew living in the first century, we must interpret what he said in the light of ancient Jewish beliefs and expectations regarding the coming Messiah. Many of these expectations at the time of Jesus were in varying degrees tied to the celebration of the Passover meal.

It should be emphasized, however, that the Passover is not the only source for understanding the Last Supper. Jesus' last meal with his disciples also connects backward into his public ministry, which was often distinguished by shared meals of one sort or another.[64] Furthermore, while many connections to the Passover are implicit, what Jesus makes most explicit is the connection of the elements to his death. *This is radically new.* Thus,

---

61. Wright, *The Day the Revolution Began*, 182.
62. Ibid., 170
63. Byme, *The Hospitality of God*, 172-73.
64. See Borg and Crossan, *The Last Week*, 113.

while the Last Supper that Jesus performed has many points of continuity with the old Passover sacrifice and meal, he also radically reinterprets it around his own impending sacrificial death.[65]

It is apparent that Jesus' final meal has multiple levels and nuances of meaning. In this book I will highlight three meanings which make allusions to the Passover and exodus, and also reflect the messianic hopes of many Jews at the time of Jesus. The following is a brief summary of these meanings which I will describe in greater detail in the following chapters.

New Exodus and New Creation

For many Jews living under Roman domination there was the hope for a "new exodus" and a "new covenant." As the Roman Catholic theologian Brant Pitre observes, this Jewish hope for a new exodus involved "the expectation that the God of Israel would one day save his people in much the same way that he had saved them centuries before, at the time of Moses, the time of the first exodus. It was the hope that when the age of salvation finally dawned, God would recapitulate (or 'recap') the events that had transpired during the flight from Egypt."[66]

Jesus' statement, "This is the new covenant in my blood" (or words to that effect) thus reflected these sentiments of many Jews of his day. In later chapters, we will look at the meaning and significance of this phrase in greater detail as it relates to the Old Testament. Basically, in the Last Supper Jesus is saying that a primary purpose of his death is to create a transformed people, a (new) people living out a (new) covenant relationship with God together (see Rom 6:3–6; 2 Cor 5:15–21; and Titus 2:14).[67] The new covenant (which Paul also refers to in 1 Corinthians 11:25) is a key concept which connects the Passover, the Last Supper and the Eucharist. The Passover meal was a time of remembering God's act of grace, of mercy, and of liberation which marked the birth of the people of the covenant. As a re-enactment of the Passover meal, "the Last Supper is really the First Supper, the first celebration of the new covenant. By Jesus' sacrificial and covenant-making death, the community of the new covenant . . . is born."[68] God's purpose is to form a people or community that becomes more and more Christlike (or

---

65. Pitre, *Jesus and the Last Supper*, 420.
66. Pitre, *Jesus and the Jewish Roots of the Eucharist*, 23–4.
67. Gorman, *The Death of the Messiah*, 3.
68. Ibid., 38.

Godlike)—a new humanity, or new creation, where the image of God will be restored, not just in individuals, but within the community as a whole.[69]

Hospitality and Forgiveness of Sins

The second basic concept that the Jews of Jesus' day associated with the Passover was the forgiveness of sins. A great many Jews of the first century were aware of the pronouncements of the great prophets such as Isaiah and Jeremiah that Israel's disasters and the pagan oppression that continued to their day were the result of her own idolatry and sin. If there was to be a fresh act of liberation that would undo this long exile, it would necessarily involve a divine act of "forgiveness of sins." In the time of Jesus, then, many Jews were looking for a great event of restoration consisting of *both* a "new Passover" *and* the forgiveness of sins, as Jeremiah had prophesied many years before (Jer 31:31–34).[70]

Again, this provides the framework for understanding the words and actions of Jesus himself. In the Last Supper he explicitly connects the "new covenant" of his blood with the "forgiveness of sins," as Matthew makes clear (Matt 26:28). Outside of the Christian movement, the first-century Jews did not, of course, have this understanding of Jesus' death. There were those who hoped for a Messiah or prophetic leader like Moses who would lead Israel out of its present troubles. But they did not think that such a leader would suffer.[71] Some Jewish traditions tied the Passover feast to the coming of the Messiah and the dawn of the age of Salvation. That is, the future redemption would take place on the same night as the original redemption—the night of the Passover.[72] Jesus seems to be deliberately altering this tradition by indicating that it is *his* blood—not the blood of the Passover lamb—through which there is forgiveness of sins and final redemption.[73]

It is critical that we keep in mind the fact that in the Jewish covenantal tradition, forgiveness of sins indicated both a personal resolution of one's relationship to God *and* the restoration of Israel (the corporate sense of forgiveness).[74] In the historic context of a *shared* (Passover) meal, the Last Supper is a therefore a celebration of the *divine hospitality*, of acceptance and forgiveness of sins—*both* individual and corporate—through Christ. This is

69. Ibid., 30.
70. Wright, *The Day the Revolution Began*, 64, 115.
71. Ibid., 65.
72. Pitre, *Jesus and the Jewish Roots of the Eucharist*, 67–8.
73. Ibid., 73.
74. McKnight, *A Community Called Atonement*, 85.

what can be referred to as "eucharistic hospitality."[75] The cross is the ultimate manifestation of the hospitality of God toward us as sinners. This divine hospitality, which portrays God as a compassionate God who is always welcoming, accepting and forgiving, is the source of *human hospitality*, or the hospitality that *we* extend to others (Matt 6:12). The theme of divine and human hospitality in the Last Supper is simply a continuation and culmination of the meal practice of Jesus during his public ministry (which itself is rooted in the Old Testament concept of hospitality and the experience of the exodus)—his eating with "tax collectors and sinners" (Mk 2:16) and with the marginalized and outcasts in a society in which the people with whom one shared a meal was of utmost importance. The idea of hospitality is also reflected in the common meals which accompanied the fellowship, prayer, and sharing of possessions by believers following Pentecost (Act 2:42–47).

Messianic Banquet

A third idea or concept that the Jews associated with the Passover is that of a banquet. When Moses and the Israelites sealed their covenant relationship with God on Mount Sinai following the exodus, they celebrated with a banquet—a heavenly meal (Exod 24:11).[76] A closely related idea or picture of the covenant within Jewish thinking, and particularly within the Old Testament, is that of a wedding feast or banquet in which God is the bridegroom and Israel is the bride. In the period between the Old and New Testaments (including Judaism at the time of Christ) there were similar notions of feasting in the future time of salvation.[77]

It is in this context that we must understand Jesus' references to the kingdom of God. When he says, "I will not drink again of the fruit of the vine until the kingdom of God comes" (Lk 22:16; cf. 1 Cor 11:26), he is looking forward to the eschatological banquet, the final act of the drama of redemption. In his public ministry Jesus describes the fulfillment of the kingdom in terms of a wedding feast. In the book of Revelation, the angel likewise describes this completion of God's plan of salvation in terms feasting with the risen Lord at the wedding supper of the Lamb (Rev 19:9). The Last Supper is therefore a foretaste of the redemptive power of God's kingdom, which was inaugurated through Jesus' death and resurrection and

---

75. Boersma, *Violence, Hospitality, and the Cross*, 215.

76. Pitre, *Jesus and the Jewish Roots of the Eucharist*, 30.

77. Pitre, *Jesus and the Last Supper*, 452–58; also Wainwright, *Eucharist and Eschatology*, 21–25.

will come in its fullness when Christ returns in glory.[78] It is a place where the past (Jesus' death and resurrection), present (life in Christ and in community), and future (the fulfillment of God's kingdom) all come together.

Method and Organization of the Book

The basic argument of this book is that the above theological motifs or levels of meaning which are associated with the Last Supper are crucial to a proper understanding and practice of the Lord's Supper or Eucharist. While these meanings or concepts are closely interrelated and overlapping, each is deserving of separate treatment. This book's structure is developed around these three themes.

Recovering Biblical Imagination

We as Christians are often seriously lacking when it comes to developing a biblically informed imagination. Many of us do not see the relevance of the biblical drama of redemption, which reaches back to the story of Israel and the early church, for our everyday lives. There is an ever widening "gap" between what we believe cognitively as Christians and our vision of the "good life." We are often so captive to culturally conditioned pictures of the good life that we are unable to "connect the biblical and cultural dots." We fail to see," says Kevin Vanhoozer, "how the biblical story of what God has done and is doing in Christ relates to the modern world of climate change, stock market fluctuations and mass immigration."[79]

This book represents a modest effort to recover a biblical imagination—to see "as in the mind's (and heart's) eye" how things fit together in Christ. It encourages what Vanhoozer describes as "faith imagining God's imaginings after him," or "[imagining] God, the world and ourselves in light of the biblical story of salvation."[80] Our actual practice of the Lord's Supper reflects our understanding of the "good news" of the gospel. In fact, as I have suggested, the Lord's Supper (or Eucharist) is an enacted summary or "performance" of the gospel. My hope is that this book will stimulate you into thinking and reflecting on how you, both individually and as part of a local congregation, can better "embody" or "live out" the deeper meaning and significance of this ordinance in your particular context.

---

78. Pitre, *Jesus and the Last Supper*, 511–12
79. Vanhoozer, *Pictures at a Theological Exposition*, 20.
80. Ibid., 26–27.

Approach and Outline

With this goal in mind, I have selected passages from Scripture which describe in some way the divine drama portrayed in the Last Supper. These passages either: 1) foreshadow or look forward to the Last Supper in some way; 2) describe or directly refer to the event of the Last Supper; or 3) describe future eschatological events to which the Last Supper points. I begin with several key passages in the Old Testament which are foundational to understanding the meaning of the Last Supper. Then I discuss passages in the New Testament that specifically relate to the previously mentioned themes of: 1) new exodus and new creation; 2) hospitality and forgiveness of sins; and 3) the messianic banquet. Inasmuch as stories are one way of enlightening what Paul calls the "eyes of your hearts" (Eph 1:18), many of the passages I examine are in the form of a story. While my approach is largely exegetical in nature, my concern is not simply descriptive. Wherever possible, I try to make practical applications to everyday life and show the relevance of the passage under discussion to contemporary issues that are (or should be) of concern to us, both as individual followers of Christ and collectively as his corporate body, the church. With this in mind, I have written this book not only for pastors and other church leaders, but also for educated lay persons who are concerned about the meaning and significance of the Lord's Supper for the church.

My focus in treating selected passages that are related in some way to the Last Supper is to understand them within the larger biblical, theological, and historical context. Specifically, I draw upon the disciplines of biblical, systematic, and pastoral theology to relate the theology of the Lord's Supper or Eucharist to the three biblical concepts or themes discussed above.[81] In the first part of *The Supper* I describe the Old Testament background to the Last Supper. Part two of the book looks at the Last Supper and Eucharist in relation to the biblical themes of the new exodus/ new creation. Part three addresses the theme of eucharistic hospitality. Part four centers on eschatology (or the doctrine of "last things") and the theme of the messianic banquet or the wedding supper which is anticipated in the Last Supper and Eucharist. In the final two chapters I make some summary observations

---

81. Other titles related to this topic include Witherington, *Making a Meal of It*; LaVerdiere, *Dining in the Kingdom of God*; Wright, *The Meal God Gave Us*; Wainwright, *Eucharist and Eschatology*; Leithart, *Blessed Are the Hungry*; and several books by Pitre (*Jesus and the Last Supper*; *Jesus and the Jewish Roots of the Eucharist*; and *Jesus the Bridegroom*). I have benefited from all of these works. But while these books may treat separate aspects of the theology of the Eucharist, none examine all three of these motifs systematically as they relate to the larger theme of redemption in the Bible. The present study is unique in that respect.

on what all of this means for the church, particularly evangelicalism in America. In chapter sixteen, I address the question: How should we define the gospel? I briefly critique two popular conceptions of the gospel among evangelicals—first, what is often referred to as "the emerging church;" and, secondly, the individualistic gospel of personal salvation. In chapter seventeen I conclude with a discussion of the church's "political presence," or corporate life and witness within the theological context of the Eucharist. Specifically, I summarize what it means for the church to be a community of the "new covenant" in the world.

Part One

Old Testament Preparation

2

The Worldview Story

Our Western culture is permeated by the "power of story." According to some, it has become the dominant means through which we understand the world, ourselves, and each other.¹ But for Christians, there is one story that is totally unique, and is the dominant story by which we are to understand human history and the meaning of human life.² That is the story of God's redemption through Christ. It is this redemption through Christ's death on the cross which Christians commemorate and celebrate through the ordinance of the Lord's Supper.

With respect to the practice of the Lord's Supper, I have argued three things. First, this ordinance is a drama, or "performance" of the gospel. As Eugene LaVerdiere puts it, "To know and live the Eucharist [is] to know, live and be the gospel of Jesus Christ, our Lord and Lord of all."³ Secondly, as such, it cannot be properly understood or practiced apart from an understanding of the event of the Last Supper which Jesus celebrated with his disciples prior to his crucifixion. Third, there is a close connection between the Last Supper and the events of the Passover. This requires that we have a clear understanding of the Old Testament and its connection to the New Testament. More specifically, while in some respects the Old Testament

---

1. Fulford, *The Triumph of Narrative*, 151-54.

2. For a helpful discussion of the vision of ultimate reality implicit in the biblical narrative relative to other worldview stories see Olson, *The Essentials of Christian Thought*. Olson points out that contemporary Western society is awash is competing worldview stories, or visions of ultimate reality. Christians often unwittingly absorb beliefs about reality from worldviews that are completely alien to the Bible. It is therefore essential that Christians know and understand the basic philosophy—or vision of ultimate reality—of the Bible (13).

3. LaVerdiere, *Dining in the Kingdom of God*, 198.

needs to be treated independently of the New, we must also see how the two Testaments exist on a continuum. We have to therefore consider how God's revelation through Christ is the climax of his plan of redemption which began with his covenant with Israel in the Old Testament.[4] In this chapter my purpose is to give a summary of the overarching story of God's redemption in the Bible.

Three Theological Tendencies in the Church Today

In my view, there are three tendencies among many Christians today which hinder a full understanding of this biblical story of redemption. This, in turn, undermines our ability to fully appreciate the significance of the Lord's Supper and its linkage to the Old Testament.

First, there is a tendency to "atomize" biblical texts and strip passages out of their literary and historical context. This often results in a failure to see the big picture. To use an old adage, we tend to "lose the forest for the trees." With some notable exceptions, for the most part, Bible scholars and teachers have not clearly articulated major themes in the Bible and shown how they fit together to form a larger mosaic or picture. Seeing this big picture helps us to better understand and appreciate the details, and it may significantly alter our reading of individual books or passages.[5] As I suggested in chapter one, the worldview story of the Bible as a whole serves as a "hermeneutical lens" for understanding and interpreting the different parts.

A second and related short-coming is that Christians in America are inclined to separate the Story of Jesus (or the story of the gospel) as told in the New Testament from the Old Testament. This is largely due to the fact that much of the Old Testament is foreign to many people in the American church. However, as Scot McKnight and others have pointed out, the Story of Jesus brings the Story of Israel as found in the Old Testament to its completion or final resolution. The two stories are necessarily connected. The Old and New Testaments *together* make up the Bible's story. What we call the "gospel" only makes sense in the context of this larger story or "metanarrative." If we ignore this larger biblical story the gospel inevitably gets distorted.[6]

Finally, it is customary in America (particularly within more conservative denominations) to reduce the gospel, or what is often referred to as the

---

4. Walton, *Old Testament Theology for Christians*, 20–22.
5. See Alexander, *From Eden to the New Jerusalem*, 11.
6. McKnight, *The King Jesus Gospel*, 36.

"Plan of Salvation,"[7] to individualist terms of "being saved." This individual salvation is usually cast in terms of praying the sinner's prayer, receiving forgiveness based on God's grace, and having the assurance of going to heaven through faith in Christ. This is indeed a crucial *part* of the story. The usual evangelical declaration that "it is well with my soul" (to quote a popular hymn) because of forgiveness of sins through Jesus' shed blood on the cross is an important and profoundly biblical expression of the Christian faith. But while this is *a* central confession, it is not the *full* expression of biblical story of redemption. The gospel cannot be *reduced* to these terms. Richard Mouw reminds us that the God who declares here and now that it is "well" with my soul is the same God who once looked at the world he created and declared it to be good. This God wants once again to say that "it is well" with his entire creation.[8]

Rightly understood, the Plan of Salvation in Scripture flows out of and is founded upon the Story of Israel and the Story of Jesus. Both of these stories culminate in the day when King Jesus sits on the throne and pronounces, "I am making everything new" (Rev 21:5). We should, as Mouw argues, share in God's restless yearning for the renewal of his creation.[9] Unfortunately, the Plan of Salvation as generally presented is given so much weight that it tends to drown out this larger story of God's redemptive purposes. This has massive implications for the gospel itself.[10]

A Cliff Notes Summary of the Biblical Story

In this section I will give a very brief sketch of the biblical story, which will be filled in with more details as we proceed. This worldview story gives us a larger context for understanding and applying the individual narratives that relate more specifically to the Last Supper and Eucharist.

There Can't be an End Without a Beginning

At the end of Revelation, the Apostle John gives vivid description of a "new heaven and a new earth" which some day will be a reality. This new creation is pictured as a holy city that comes from heaven. A voice from the throne announces that God has come to live with human beings, so that his glory

---

7. Ibid., 37.
8. Mouw, *When the Kings Come Marching In*, 110–111.
9. Ibid., 111.
10. For a fuller discussion of this, see McKnight, *The King Jesus Gospel*, 37–43.

fills the earth (Rev 21:1–3, 11, and 23). "With this remarkable vision of God coming to dwell with humanity on a new earth the biblical story comes to an end."[11]

But, as every good storyteller knows, there can't be a dramatic ending without a beginning. The biblical metastory begins with the creation account in the opening chapters of Genesis. Unfortunately, most Christians skip over the first three chapters of the Bible when describing God's story of redemption. Treatments of the creation account in the first chapters of Genesis are usually mired in the "creation–evolution" controversy. Roger Olson observes that when it comes to Genesis, "many people either throw the baby of theological meaning out with the bathwater of literalism or focus so much on attempting to take everything literally that they miss the points the passages are making."[12] One of the great tragedies of Christian and secular thought about the biblical account is this false polarization between literalism and myth. Our concern as Christians, however, should be with "the metaphysical implications of Genesis, not how literally or historically to interpret its narratives of origins." The purpose of Genesis 1–3 is not about the mechanics of origins. Rather, this narrative is *primarily* about the nature of the world as creation, God's relation to the world as Lord over all creation, and what was lost due to human disobedience.[13]

To the extent that Christians describe the creation account in relation to God's plan of redemption, emphasis is usually placed on the fall of Adam and Eve and the entrance of sin into the world. From this perspective, the culmination of the plan of redemption is the final defeat of Satan, who is thrown into the lake of fire (Rev 20:10). But I would argue that this is not the best way to frame the biblical story. Various commentators have noted how the first three chapters of Genesis and the last three chapters of Revelation seem to "speak" to each other, like the first and last chapters of a novel. These parallels, or biblical "echoes," are, as I will show in greater detail, no coincidence. The biblical writers intend to communicate that God's original purpose for creation is to demonstrate his glory and have humans share in that glory. The first earth is designed to be a divine residence or sacred space where God coexists with his people. In the Old Testament, God's presence and glory are associated with *shalom*, or human peace, flourishing,

---

11. Alexander, *From Eden to the New Jerusalem*, 14.

12. Olson, *The Essentials of Christian Thought*, 186.

13. Ibid., 186–87. For a helpful and highly readable dialogue between two Christian scientists—a creationist and theistic evolutionist—over how to interpret the creation account in Genesis 1–3 in relation to the scientific data, see Wood and Falk, *The Fool and the Heretic*, 29–50; 105–62. See also Walton, *The Lost World of Genesis One* and *The Lost World of Adam and Eve*.

fulfillment and joy (Ps 85:8–9). But because of the sin of Adam and Eve, this plan is thwarted. The couple is banished from the garden and driven from God's presence. The long and complex story that follows focuses on how the earth can be renewed or restored to once again be a sacred dwelling place for God and humanity.[14] The biblical story of redemption, then, is basically the story of "sacred space established, sacred space lost, and sacred space about to be regained."[15] Stated differently, God's plan of redemption or salvation is a "*shalom* project."[16]

Christ the Hinge of History

Throughout this story as it unfolds in the Old and New Testaments, God uses various representatives or "mediators" (Abraham, Moses, David, etc.) to achieve his purposes. But the final mediator or Messiah to which the entire Old Testament points is, of course, Christ. His death and resurrection is the "hinge" of history. Through him sin and death are defeated. As the "new Adam," Christ is the head and source of the cosmic restoration, which is the culmination of redemptive history. We should bear in mind that what we have at the end of human history as we know it is not simply a "re-creation" of God's initial creation. It is a "new creation." The garden into which God places Adam and Eve is not the ideal condition. As Scot McKnight points out, "The ideal condition is a flourishing, vibrant, culture-creating, God-honoring, Jesus-centered city."[17] Redemption through Christ brings creation to its final goal—which Adam was intended, but unable, to achieve. It brings the initial creation to full glory in Christ. The end of the Bible is therefore the beginning of the Bible glorified.

In the process of communicating this grand story we should further resist the all-too-common tendency to separate theology from ethics. This is emphasized by Ben Witherington in his massive and groundbreaking two-volume work, *New Testament Theology and Ethics*. God originally created humans not only with the capacity for relationship with him but also with the capacity to reflect his moral character on earth. Christ, who perfectly bore the image and nature of God, is the culmination of God's reclamation project which was initiated after the fall. As the last Adam, he is "the means of the renewal of [God's image] in human beings through divine action but also through belief, behavior, and more specifically the behavior called

---

14. Alexander, *From Eden to the New Jerusalem*, 24.
15. Walton, *The Lost World of Adam and Eve*, 51.
16. See Ott, *God's Shalom Project*, 9–10.
17. McKnight, *The King Jesus Gospel*, 36.

imitation—the imitation of Christ."[18] Ethics in the New Testament is primarily the application of God's moral character and behavior (pre-eminently his love) to human beings, who are enabled by his Spirit to become imitators of Christ and so of God. For this reason, theology and ethics can never be severed. In the New Testament we are urged to look to Christ, first to adore and praise him as the author and finisher of our faith, and then to imitate him and be conformed to his image through the internal work of God.[19]

Filling in the Details

Biblical scholars have often been puzzled by the fact that in his final vision of the Apocalypse John does not describe the full panorama of the new heaven and earth with the many features of a worldwide "new creation." Instead, he focuses on a city that is garden-like, and in the shape of a temple.[20] Why?

The answer seems to lie in the fact that the Old Testament writers often picture Eden as a temple-garden. In fact, the entire cosmos is described as God's "resting place," or temple. The biblical writers also create important visual or symbolic links between the garden of Eden and the creation of the cosmos, particularly as depicted in Genesis 1–3, and the tabernacle of the exodus and Jerusalem temple. In the Old Testament, then, there is a trifold linkage between the garden, cosmos, and tabernacle/temple—a linkage which is reflected in prophetic expectations of a "new creation," and, finally, in John's depiction of the new heaven and new earth.

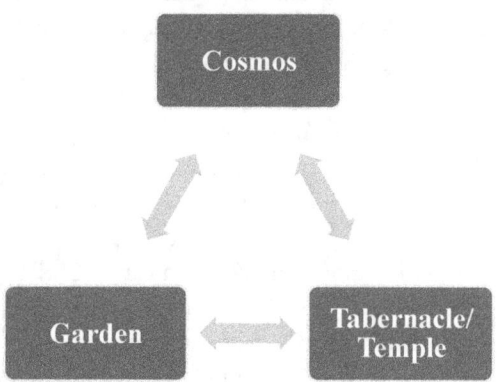

Figure 1: The Cosmos, Garden, and Tabernacle/Temple

18. Witherington, *New Testament Theology and Ethics, Vol. One*, 21.
19. Ibid., 22–23.
20. See Beale, *The Temple and the Church's Mission*, 23.

Let's look in greater detail at these pieces of the puzzle.

The Cosmos/Garden as a Temple

In the Old Testament, the cosmos is often associated with the temple. Isaiah 66:1–2 is the clearest example of this:

> This is what the Lord says:
> "Heaven is my throne
> and the earth is my footstool.
> Where is the house you will build for me?
> Where will my resting place be?
> Has not my hand made all these things, and so they come into being?"
> declares the Lord.

Here we are given a picture of a cosmos-sized temple. The prophet Isaiah also draws a close connection between: 1) the temple and God's rest; and 2) creation and the temple.[21] In the creation story, God "rests" on the seventh day (Gen 2:2). Since the temple is elsewhere described as God's "resting place" and also identified as the residence from which he rules (Ps 132:7–8, 13–14), the idea is that following the activity of the first six days God rests in his cosmic temple and rules from his residence.[22] The garden of Eden is also described as sacred space. The biblical writers speak of God walking in Eden as he later does in the tabernacle (Gen 3:8; cf. Lev 26:12; Deut 23:15; 2 Sam 7:6–7).

This imagery is particularly significant given the role of the tabernacle and temple for the Israelites. In the first exodus, the worship of God was centered in the tabernacle of Moses, or portable "temple" that was used by the Israelites while traveling in the wilderness. This temple was the prototype of the far grander temple, which was constructed during the reign of Solomon. Reading the detailed descriptions of the tabernacle (Exod 25–40) and the temple (1 Kings 6:1–8:10) causes eyes of even the most serious reader to glaze over. Like the ceremonial rules in Leviticus, we are inclined to skip over these passages. They are often viewed as part of the Old Testament "law" which has little relevance for us today.

But behind the painful detail lies a divine pattern. God designed the earthly temple to correspond in some significant manner to his creation of the heavens and the earth (Gen 2:4). As G. K. Beale argues, Israel's temple

---

21. Walton, *The Lost World of Genesis One*, 83–84.
22. Ibid., 74.

as well as the tabernacle, were composed of three main parts, each of which symbolized a major part of the cosmos:

- the outer court represented the habitable world where humanity dwelt;
- the holy place was emblematic of the visible heavens and its light sources; and
- the holy of holies symbolized the invisible dimension of the cosmos, where God and his heavenly hosts dwelt.[23]

Thus, the Old Testament sanctuaries functioned as a microcosm of the entire heaven and earth, as partially described in Genesis 1 and 2.[24] The table below shows some of the symbolism of the temple and earlier tabernacle.

Outer Court: Habitable World	
Altar	Bosom of the earth (Ezek 43:14; cf. Exod 20:24–24; 27:1)
Wash Basin	The sea (1 Kgs 7:23–26)
Outer Court	Where all Israelites (representing all humanity) could enter and worship
Holy Place: Visible Sky	
Lampstand and Olive Oil	Light of celestial bodies (Gen 1:14; cf. Exod 27:20; Rev 1:20)[25]
The Veil	Firmament separating the place of God's presence from the place of human habitation (Gen 1:6)[26]
Holy of Holies: God's Dwelling Place	
Cherubim	Guardians of God's heavenly temple (Exod 25:18; 1 Kgs 6:23–28; 2 Sam 6:2; Rev 4:7–9)
Ark	Footstool of God's heavenly throne (Ex 25:10–16; 1 Chr 28:2; Ps 99:5)

Table 1. Symbolism of the Tabernacle/Temple

23. Beale, *The Temple and the Church's Mission*, 32

24. Psalm 78:69 states: "He built his sanctuary like the heights, like the earth that he established forever." In other words, God designed Israel's tabernacle/temple to be comparable to the heavens and to the earth (Ibid., 31–32).

25. Genesis 1:14 uses the unusual word "lights" instead of "sun" and "moon." This is the word used throughout the remainder of the Pentateuch for the "lights" on the tabernacle lampstands. Walton, Gene*sis*, 148.

26. In the words of Walton, "If we transpose from the horizontal axis to the vertical, the veil separated the earthly sphere, with its functions, from the heavenly sphere, where God dwells . . . . Thus the veil served the same symbolic function as the firmament" (*The Lost World of Genesis One*, 82).

The New Creation as a New Eden/Temple

We now come to the manner in which the Old Testament prophets, and later John, picture the new creation in terms of a new Eden or new temple.

Following the exodus out of Egypt, the Israelites set out on their journey to the promised land, the land of Canaan, which had been promised to Abraham many years before. This is described in Exodus as a "spacious land, a land flowing with milk and honey" (Exod 3:8). Much of the story of the Israelites is taken up with the account of how they conquered this land and then lost it when they were again taken into captivity. But the hope for a return to the land was sustained by the Old Testament prophets.

What is fascinating about this biblical hope, however, is that this *future* promised land is not always pictured as being identical to the earthly land of Israel.[27] Isaiah, for example, envisions Jerusalem as part of a "new heaven and a new earth," or an entirely new creation (Isa 65:17–25; 66:22). Many of the Old Testament prophets further describe this new creation in terms of a future "new temple" that God will build in the age of salvation (Mic 4:1–2; Isa 56:6–7; 60:1–7; Ezek 37:24–28; Hag 2:6–9).[28] The prophet Ezekiel describes the future promised land as "like the garden of Eden" (Ezek 36:33–35). It is further significant that Ezekiel alludes to "Eden, the garden of God" as Israel's first sanctuary, or temple, which was desecrated (Ezek 28:13–14, 16, 18; cf. 7:24). And he describes the future eschatological temple as having garden-like features, with water flowing out from under the holy of holies (Ezek 47:1).[29]

John's vision in Revelation 21 and 22 represents the fulfillment of these expectations. There are some striking resemblances between his description of the New Jerusalem and the garden of Eden and temple as pictured in the Old Testament.

- The New Jerusalem in Revelation is pictured like the original garden, with the river of water of life flowing through it. "On each side of the river stood the tree of life, bearing twelve crops of fruit, yielding its fruit every month . . ." (Rev 22:1–2; cf. Gen 2:8–10) Some of the natural resources (gold and onyx) that flourish in the garden (Gen 2:12) are put to use in the New Jerusalem in the construction of the city's streets and foundation (Rev 21:18–21).

- Just as sculpted cherubim are placed on the ark of covenant in the holy of holies of the earthly temple (2 Kgs 6:23–28; cf. 2 Sam 6:2), so

---

27. Pitre, *Jesus and the Jewish Roots of the Eucharist*, 39.
28. Ibid., 35–36.
29. Beale, *The Temple and the Church's Mission*, 74.

the angelic cherubim guard God's throne in the heavenly temple (Rev 4:7–9).
- The precious stones forming the foundation of the city (Rev 21:18–21) reflect the description of Solomon's temple (1 Kgs 6:20–22; 7:9–10) and the jewels of the priestly attire (Exod 28:17–20).
- Most importantly, the shape and dimensions of the city in Revelation 21:16 ("its length and width and height are equal") are based on the description of the holy of holies in 1 Kings 6:20 (where the length, breadth, and height are of equal measurement).[30]

But the new creation, while similar to the old, is not a carbon copy.[31] There are also some significant differences:

- The natural bodies of sun and moon are no longer needed, for their functions of illumination have been replaced by the glory of God (Rev 21:11; 22:5). Moreover, no longer will there be any curse (Rev 22:3).
- There is no temple in the city, because the Lord God Almighty and the Lamb are its temple (Rev 21:22).
- Because the temple curtain was torn at Christ's death, there is no veil in the heavenly temple (Heb 10:20). In fact, in the end-times temple there will be only one section—the holy of holies, the dimensions of which will cover the whole cosmos. The glory of God will fill every part of the new creation (Rev 21:23).[32]

Adam and Eve—the Image of God and the Effects of Sin

Adam and Eve are the apex of God's creation. Their total uniqueness as humans is expressed by the statement in Genesis that "God created man in his own image; in the image of God he created him, male and female he created them" (Gen 1:27). Theologians have pondered the meaning and significance of this verse. The context suggests that the human couple are appointed as human viceroys to govern the earth on God's behalf (Gen 1:26).[33] Richard Middleton states:

> The writer of Genesis 1 portrays God as king presiding over "heaven and earth," an ordered and harmonious realm in which

---

30. Ibid., 23.
31. See Crouse, *Culture Making*, 165.
32. Beale, *The Temple and the Church's Mission*, 392.
33. Alexander, *From Eden to the New Jerusalem*, 76.

each creature manifests the will of the creator and is thus declared "good." Humanity is created *like* God, with the special role of representing or imaging God's rule in the world.[34]

Humans are essentially given a royal task to develop all aspects of culture, technology, and civilization and transform the earth's environment into a sociocultural world that glorifies the creator. This is "a holy task, a sacred calling, in which the human race as God's image on earth manifests something of the creator's own lordship over the cosmos" (Ps 8:1, 3–8).[35]

Since the garden is viewed by the biblical writers as a temple, Adam and Eve are also given what is essentially a "priestly" role of tending or caring for this "sacred space." The description in Genesis 2:15 that God put Adam into the garden to "work it and take care of it" is generally understood to mean that he is given landscaping and agricultural responsibilities. But the terms used here are more commonly used in the Old Testament to describe service to God. The verb "take care of" is used in the contexts of Levitical responsibilities of guarding and caring for sacred space.[36]

When these concepts are combined with God's blessing to be fruitful, multiply, and fill the earth (Gen 1:28), the idea is that God's authority and rule will be extended throughout the earth as people increase in number and spread outwards. In *The Screwtape Letters*, C.S. Lewis' satirical portrayal of human life from the vantage point of the underworld, Screwtape, the experienced demon, writes to his inexperienced nephew, Wormwood:

> [God] really does want to fill the universe with a lot of loathsome little replicas of Himself—creatures, whose life, on its miniature scale, will be qualitatively like His own, not because He has absorbed them but because their wills freely conform to His.[37]

This is God's "blueprint" for the created order. "Taken in conjunction with their holy status, Adam and Eve are to be fruitful so that their descendants may, as priest-kings, extend God's temple and kingdom throughout the earth."[38]

But Adam and Eve sinned by disobeying God—and, as the saying goes, the rest is history. This is not the place to get into the ongoing theological debate over "original sin." The main point is that instead of reflecting God's

---

34. Quoted in Ibid., 77.
35. Middleton, *A New Heaven and a New Earth*, 43.
36. Walton, *The Lost World of Adam and Eve*, 105–6.
37. Lewis, *The Screwtape Letters*, 41.
38. Alexander, *From Eden to the New Jerusalem*, 78.

wise ordering of the world, the human couple chose to make themselves the center of wisdom apart from God. They sought to elevate themselves to God's role.[39] As a result, Adam and Eve, and therefore all of humanity, became "cracked Eikons," or distorted image bearers. Sin is fundamentally rebellion against God. But it spreads to other relations. "Sin is the hyperrelational distortion and corruption of the Eikon's relationship with God and therefore with self, with others, and with the world."[40]

God has not abandoned his creational purpose. The next stage in God's redemptive plan is taken up in the story of Israel. In fact, in one sense the story of Adam and Eve can be read as a precursor to the story of Israel. In some significant ways the story of Adam mirrors the story of Israel from exodus to exile:[41] The story of Adam and Eve is therefore, in part, a story of Israel's origins.[42]

Israel's Story	Adam's Story
• Exodus: creation of Israel's story • Commands through Moses • Promises of the Land of Canaan • Disobedience leads to exile/death	• Creation of Adam and Eve • Command not to eat of the tree • Garden and blessing to be fruitful • Disobedience leads to exile and death

Figure 2: Adam's Story as a Mirror of Israel's Story

39. Walton, *The Lost World of Adam and Eve*, 143.

40. McKnight, *A Community Called Atonement*, 23.

41. I am indebted to Enns for this observation. The following chart is adapted from his description of the relationship between Adam's story and Israel's story (*The Evolution of Adam*, 66). Excerpt from *The Evolution of Adam* by Peter Enns, copyright © 2012. Used by permission of Brazos Press, a division of Baker Publishing Group.

42. Ibid. This view assumes that the Pentateuch was not authored by one person (Moses) but is rather the end product of a complex literary process—written, oral, or both—that came to a close in the post-exilic period (Ibid., 23). Walton argues that "it would be remiss to engage in a flat reading that considers all of the Old Testament as a reflection of Israelite thinking in the postexilic period." But, he agrees that it is "obvious" that "there are layers and theological development." So in his approach to Old Testament theology, he assumes that "there is older material embedded in texts that have been edited over time or that have been pulled together in a later period." With respect to books such as Exodus, he continues, we can say that "the ancient perspectives were preserved, even as they were passed down and subject to editing" (*Old Testament Theology for Christians*, 14).

Conclusion

In summary, the story of the Bible is essentially the progressive unfolding of God's redemptive plan. Key events in the story of Israel foreshadow the ultimate fulfillment of God's redemptive purposes through the true image-bearer, Jesus the Messiah. This is what we celebrate in the Lord's Supper. Viewed from the perspective of the end of history, the Lord's Supper is a condensed summary or summation of the final climax of the drama of redemption. It also signifies the creation of a new, unified body of Christ which is (or ought to be) the prime exhibit of God's kingdom on earth and a preview of things to come.[43] In chapter three we will look in greater detail at how the story of Israel sheds light on Jesus' Last Supper with his disciples, and therefore on the church's practice of the Lord's Supper.

---

43. Vanhoozer, *Faith Speaking Understanding*, 160.

3

The Jewish Roots of the Last Supper

CHRISTIANS are generally aware that Jesus used unleavened bread and wine to dramatize his own death. Less known, however, is the fact that Jesus' words of explanation over the bread and wine ("This is my body . . . this is my blood") are very similar to the words spoken by the head of the Jewish household over the Passover food ("This is the bread of affliction which our fathers had to eat as they came out of Egypt"). Thus, Jesus modeled his sayings after the ritual of interpreting the Passover. As John Stott states: "The central importance that Jesus attached to his death is underlined by the fact that he was actually giving instructions for the annual celebration of the Passover to be replaced by his own supper."[1]

The significance of Jesus' allusion to the Passover in the Last Supper can be illustrated by reference to a contemporary analogy. When a new episode of the Star Wars saga comes out in theaters it becomes the talk of moviegoers everywhere. Each episode builds on the previous episodes, and cannot be fully understood or appreciated apart from reference to what has come before. When it was initially released in 1977, the first Star Wars movie only bore the title *Star Wars*. Later the subtitle *A New Hope* was added. This was a not so subtle indication of what the series was all about. "The Star Wars saga," writes one movie critic, "explores lots of ideas, but one it keeps coming back to is the idea of hope. Where does it come from? Why? And when it looks like the last glimmer of hope has been extinguished, is there any reason to go on?" For the past several decades each Star Wars installment has explored and built on these ideas, moving from hope to despair, and back again as the war wages between the dark side with its immense

---

1. Stott, *The Cross of Christ*, 74.

power and a scrappy band of rebels who dare to think that everyone and everything matters.[2]

For the Israelites, the greatest symbol of hope was the exodus, after which God made a covenant with the people of Israel. It is this great event that for centuries was recounted in the Passover meal. As one author has noted, "In the stories of the OT there is no more central event than the exodus, by which God rescued his people, delivering them from bondage, covenanted with them, and thereby identified them as his own, all the while promising them a final Messiah to come."[3] In the last 600 years before Christ, the vision and hope for the return of God's reign and restoration of his people—a new Passover and new exodus—was the constant refrain of the prophets.[4] Jesus views his ministry and especially his death (and resurrection) as the fulfillment of this prophetic expectation of a future salvation. For us to understand why Jesus so closely identifies his impending death with the events surrounding the Passover we have to become familiar with the story line of the Old Testament and its completion in the New Testament. We must immerse ourselves in this story as fully as those Star Wars enthusiasts who immerse themselves in the Star Wars saga. We have to become People of the Story.[5]

The Covenant in the Story of Israel

I have noted that in his Last Supper with his disciples, Jesus specifically refers to his death as "the blood of the covenant" (Mk 14:24; Matt 26:28) or "the new covenant in my blood" (Lk 22:20). With this expression he directly connects his impending death with the covenant—or sacred bond—that God had made with his people in the Old Testament. Put in another way, Jesus' story is a culmination or completion of Israel's story. "The 'event' of Jesus Christ," says Kevin Vanhoozer, "stands as the culmination of a series of . . . revelatory and redemptive events, recorded in the Old and New Testaments, which *together* recount a single drama of redemption which is both covenantal in its focus and cosmic in its scope."[6] Therefore, what God was doing in Christ ultimately makes sense *only* if we place the person and work

---

2. Wilkinson, "The Last Jedi," 1.
3. Pennington, "The Lord's Last Supper in the Fourfold Witness of the Gospels," 48.
4. Ibid., 48–49.
5. McKnight, *The King Jesus Gospel*, 153.
6. Vanhoozer, *Drama of Doctrine*, 38–39.

of Christ within the Old Testament context of creation and covenant. There is a cosmic stage and covenantal plot.[7]

We need to begin, then, with the meaning of the covenant and the central role that it plays in the story of Israel. But since the story of Israel is part of a larger cosmic drama, we need to take a few steps back to see that the covenant is connected with God's purpose for creation as a whole. Again, to use Vanhoozer's way of describing this relationship, the plot, or story line, is the covenant; but the larger "stage" is cosmic in scope. Let's further draw out the implications of this way of picturing the biblical metastory.

Covenant of Vocation

Believers often view the end goal of the Christian life as "going to heaven." Our ultimate purpose, in other words, is to escape this body and find our rest or completion in some future state or existence outside of space, time, and matter as we know it. Later, I will discuss further how this is a highly misleading picture of heaven. For now, I would simply argue that our true goal as believers is not heaven as it is usually depicted but a renewed human vocation *within God's renewed creation*. From the book of Genesis onward, the Bible points us towards a "covenant of vocation."[8] As N. T. Wright puts it, what the Bible offers is the "vocation" of

> being a genuine human being, with genuine human tasks to perform as part of the Creator's purpose for his world. The main task of this vocation is "image-bearing," reflecting the Creator's wise stewardship into the world and reflecting the praises of all creation back to its maker. . . .
>
> Within this narrative, creation itself is understood as a kind of Temple, a heaven–and–earth duality, where humans function as the "image-bearers" in the cosmic Temple, part of earth yet reflecting the life and love of heaven. This is how creation was designed to function and flourish: under the stewardship of the image–bearers. . . . According to Genesis, this is what humans were made for.[9]

From this perspective, the human predicament or plight is not simply that humans have broken God's moral law. The much more serious disease is that "humans have turned their God-given vocation upside down, giving

---

7. Ibid., 39.
8. Wright, *The Day the Revolution* Began, 74.
9. Ibid., 76–77.

worship and allegiance to forces and powers within creation itself."[10] In other words, sin at its root is idolatry, or worshipping and serving forces *within* creation rather than the God *of* creation. The result is sin and death.[11]

Abrahamic Covenant

We have seen how the task that God gave Adam and Eve of representing and governing his garden temple was radically distorted by their rebellion. What Adam was to do in the garden is therefore given to subsequent representatives with whom God enters into a covenantal relationship. For our purposes, the next central event in the biblical metastory is God's choice of Abraham, and then through him one people, Israel, to act on his behalf.

In the Genesis account, the bridge passage between chapters 1–11 (often called "primeval history") and chapters 12–50 (the history of the patriarchs of Israel—Abraham, Isaac, and Jacob) is God's promise of blessing to Abraham in Genesis 12:2–3:

> I will make you into a great nation
> and I will bless you;
> I will make your name great,
> and you will be a blessing,
> I will bless those who bless you,
> and whoever curses you I will curse;
> and all peoples on earth
> will be blessed through you.

Much has been written about this passage. It is not possible to treat it in detail here.[12] It is worth noting, however, that this promise takes the form of a covenant. It conveys the essential strategy that God is going to pursue to restore his creation. Abraham and his progeny will be blessed and made into a great nation *so that through him* all the nations on the earth will be blessed.[13]

Various commentators on this passage have noted that the word "blessing" has a rich meaning which implies the reversal of sin's curse and

---

10. Ibid., 77.
11. Ibid.
12. For a detailed treatment of different interpretations of this passage see Hesselgrave, *The JustMissional Church*, 204–207.
13. Goheen, *A Light to the Nations*, 26–7.

the restoration of creation to its intended goodness and fullness.[14] It may not be a coincidence that the word "bless" is used five times in Genesis 12:2–3, while the word "curse" is used the same number of times in Genesis 1–11. God's blessing through Abraham annuls the curse brought about by Adam's sin. In the words of Michael Goheen, "Blessing restores all the good that God had generously bestowed on the creation in the beginning (e.g., Gen 1:22, 28) and thus anticipates his subsequent redemptive work for the flourishing of human beings, in relationship with God, with one another, and with nonhuman creation."[15]

It is further significant that in the Old Testament, eating and drinking (particularly in a ceremonial or cultic setting) is associated with divine blessing.[16] The psalmist pictures God's unfailing love and care for him using the image of a meal:

> You prepare a table for me
> in the presence of my enemies
> You anoint my head with oil;
> my cup overflows.
> (Ps 23:5)

The prophet Isaiah sees the nations coming to Israel (55:5) to share in the blessings of the "everlasting covenant" (55:5):

> Come, all you who are thirsty,
> come to the waters,
> and you who have no money,
> come, buy and eat!
> (Isa 55:1)

In the Gospels Jesus also pictures the future salvation under the image of feasting and feeding:

> I say to you that many will come from the east and the west, and will take their places at the feast with Abraham, Isaac, and Jacob in the kingdom of heaven. (Matt 8:11)

> People will come from east and west and north and south, and will take their places at the feast in the kingdom of God. (Lk 13:29)

---

14. Ibid., 31,
15. Ibid.
16. Wainwright, *Eucharist and Eschatology*, 19.

These passages reflect the Old Testament expectation that God would bless the world through Abraham's progeny out of which would come the promised Messiah. This expectation is fulfilled in the person of Christ through his work on the cross. This association of God's blessing and salvation through Christ with feasting is fundamental to our understanding and practice of the Lord's Supper.

The promise to Abraham in Genesis 12:2–3 can therefore be seen as the "gospel in advance" (Gal 3:8). But the blessing to Abraham is *restorative* as well as *redemptive*. In other words, in addition to the *ultimate* purpose of Abraham's blessing there is also a more *immediate* or *proximate* purpose in God's commissioning of Abraham. He and his descendants are a blessing to the nations in the sense that they are called to be an *example*—religiously, morally, and ethically—to all the peoples of the earth.[17] The close parallels between Abraham and Adam suggest that Abraham and his progeny are chosen to be the "true Adamic humanity." In their personal and social lives they "are to exhibit God's creational design for human life and the goal toward which his redemptive purpose is moving."[18]

The Exodus, Passover, and God's Covenant with Israel

We now come to what was the central event in Israel's history—the exodus. It was particularly through this event that the Israelites viewed their collective life as a nation. The episode in which God redeemed the Israelites from Pharaoh's fury was so awesome that it became for them and their progeny the dynamic of their entire national and spiritual existence.[19] In the book of Exodus God tells Moses how this mighty act of liberation relates to his plans for them as a people:

> You yourselves have seen what I did in Egypt, and how I carried you on eagle's wings and brought you to myself. Now if you obey me fully and keep my covenant, then out of all nations you will be my treasured possession. Although the whole earth is mine, you will be for me a kingdom of priests and a holy nation (Exod 19:4–6).

This passage, along with God's promise to Abraham in Genesis 12:2–3, serves as the interpretive lens through which we see the role and identity of

---

17. See Wright, *The Mission of God*, 358.
18. Goheen, *A Light to the Nations*, 32.
19. Johnson, *A History of the Jews*, 26.

God's people in the Old Testament.[20] Both passages talk about God entering into a sacred family relationship with his people by means of a covenant.

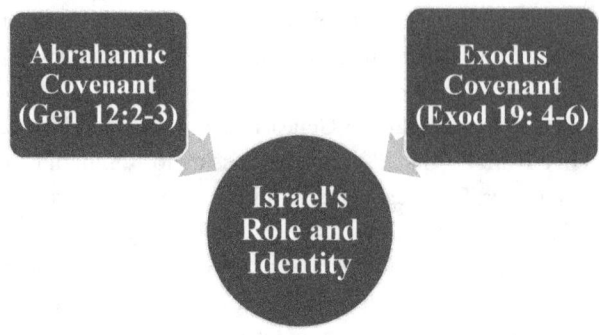

Figure 3: God's Covenant with Israel

The description of Israel as a "kingdom of priests" conveys the idea that *collectively* the Israelites are to be a "royal priesthood," or a body of priests ruling as kings. The heart of God's plan for Israel is that it would become a nation of "priest-kings." Israel is to "fulfill the role originally allocated through Adam and Eve to all human beings."[21] The term "holy nation" further signifies that the Israelites are to be ethically distinctive and given wholly to God as a nation. They are to be holy as God is holy (Lev 20:26)—an expression which involves both correctness in religious ritual and living with integrity, righteousness, and justice in every area of life. Israel is also set apart in the sense that that it has a distinctive purpose—to serve and represent God as a light or showcase to the nations. As a holy nation, then, the Israel is to be a societal model religiously and ethically, a paradigm of what God intends for the world as a whole.[22]

20. Goheen, *A Light to the Nations*, 49.

21. Alexander, *From Eden to Jerusalem*, 84.

22. Goheen, *A Light to the Nations*, 39. While arguing that Israel as a society was called to be a light to other nations, I also affirm what is often referred to as "progressive revelation." As Kaiser states, "there can be little doubt that the Old Testament is a series of successive divine revelations leading up to the grand disclosure in Jesus Christ." Vos describes this as an "organic progress is from seed–form to the attainment of full growth." It is also important that we "distinguish between what is described and what is being prescribed in the character, actions, and judgments of men, nations, and events in the Old Testament." Kaiser, *Toward Old Testament Ethics*, 60–67. When we look at the big picture or Big Story, we see how there is a direction or trajectory from the Old Testament to the New Testament, whereby God adapts his ideals to a people whose attitudes, structures, and actions are flawed because of the fall and there is a progressive step-by-step growth in the knowledge and understanding of God's healing strategy. This

Connected with this whole constellation of ideas is, as we have seen, the emphasis that the book of Exodus places on the construction of the tabernacle following the exodus (Exod 25-40). The specific purpose for this tent is that it is to be a dwelling for God in the midst of his people (Exod 25:8-9). The most significant item in the tabernacle is the Ark of the Covenant, a rectangular box placed in the inner sanctum or holy of holies, which serves a double function as a chest and footstool of a throne. As a chest it contains the documents of the covenant. As a footstool it extends the heavenly throne to the earth and therefore is the place where the divine king's feet touch the earth. Consequently, the tabernacle links heaven and earth.[23] This association of the tabernacle (and later the temple) with God's presence prefigures Jesus' own description of himself as the final temple (John 2:19) and Paul's description of the church as a temple in which God's Spirit dwells (1 Cor 3:16).

There is one final element which is critical for understanding the relationship of the events of the exodus to the Last Supper—and that is the sacrifice of the Passover lamb. The original Passover took place in the context of God's final judgment on the Egyptians, the slaying of their firstborn males (Exod 12:12-13). The Israelites are instructed to slay a lamb or young goat as a sacrifice, smear its blood on the doorposts, and eat of its meat (Exod 12:6-11; 21-22). In this way, the Passover lambs become a substitute for Israelite firstborn who are protected from the angel of death. Subsequent performances of the Passover ritual are a means of consecrating the people of Israel as a nation of "priests." As Desmond Alexander states:

---

raises the difficult issue of the Israelite conquest of Canaan, which seems to promote genocide. In *The Lost World of the Israelite Conquest* the Waltons argue that the key word *herem* (Joshua 2:10, 6:17-18) which is usually translated "utterly destroy" should be rendered as "remove from use" (169-211). In offering this helpful interpretation, however, the Waltons make some other arguments that are more problematic. First, they maintain that the conquest narrative is concerned with establishing "cosmological order" and creating space in which God can dwell in covenantal relationship with his people, not with divine judgment for sin. But, as Bailey responds in his review of the book, one wonders why it cannot be both. Furthermore, the Waltons maintain that "covenantal holiness" does not have to do with "moral character" but is rather a status granted by God (103-17). Again, however, this argument seems to create too much of a discontinuity between morality and the covenantal relationship. As Bailey asks, does not the covenant reveal something about the moral character of God? Harbin similarly states that while the term "holy" in the OT does denote a sphere of God's being or activity, it also has a communal moral dimension. (See his review in JETS.) For a very helpful discussion of the Israelite conquest narrative and violence in the Old Testament generally, see also: Copan, *Is God a Moral Monster? Making Sense of the Old Testament God*.

23. Alexander, *From Eden to the New Jerusalem*, 33.

> The sacrifice of the animal atones for the sin of the people, the blood smeared on the doorposts purifies those within the house, and the sacrificial meat sanctifies or makes holy all who eat it. Understood in this way, the Passover ritual enables all of the Israelites to obtain holy status, an important prerequisite to becoming a royal priesthood (Exod 19:6).[24]

The author of Hebrews makes essentially the same point when he states that "without the shedding of blood there is no forgiveness of sins" (Heb 9:12). In this sense, Jesus is our Passover sacrifice.

The Exodus, the Gospel, and the Last Supper

When it comes to the relationship between the Old and New Testaments, there are many Christians who think that the difference between the two can be summed up by saying that in the Old Testament people were saved by obeying the law, whereas in the New Testament people are saved by grace through faith. But this is a distortion. To quote Chris Wright, for Paul "salvation had always been, even in the Old Testament, a matter of God's promise and grace, received by faith (like Abraham)."[25] In this respect, there is the obvious point of continuity as well as development between the inauguration of the new covenant through the blood of Christ (which is highlighted in the Last Supper) and the Mosaic covenant following the exodus (Exod 24:8). As will become clearer in later chapters, we can see the exodus in the gospel and the gospel in the exodus. But before we explore in greater detail some key Old Testament passages which are foundational to a proper understanding of the Last Supper, we need to look at the Old Testament roots of a term that is regularly employed by Christians (particularly evangelicals) but is often misunderstood—the word "gospel."

Gospel in the Old and New Testaments

The words "evangelical" and "evangelize" derive from the Greek word *euangelion*, which means gospel or "good news." In both the Old and New Testaments the words "gospel" and "salvation" are closely related. They naturally belong together.

Historically, the relationship between these terms is rooted in the time of exile in Babylon when the Israelites had lost their land, city, and temple.

---

24. Ibid., 129.
25. Wright, *The Mission of God's People*, 117.

In that time of despair and hopelessness, Israel was in desperate need of "good news."[26] This is provided in the prophecies of Isaiah, who jubilantly proclaims the good news that God will deliver Israel from exile with these words:

> How beautiful on the mountains
> are the feet of those who bring good news,
> who proclaim peace,
> who bring good tidings,
> who proclaim salvation,
> who say to Zion,
> "Your God reigns!"
> Listen! Your watchmen lift up their voices;
> together they shout for joy.
> When the Lord returns to Zion,
> they will see it with their own eyes.
> Burst into songs of joy together,
> you ruins of Jerusalem,
> for the Lord has comforted his people,
> he has redeemed Jerusalem.
> The Lord will lay bare his holy arm
> in the sight of all the nations,
> and all the ends of the earth will see
> the salvation of our God.
> (Isa 52:7–10)

In this passage, good news and salvation are characterized in terms of the reign of God, which brings *shalom* or peace. Chris Wright puts it well: "God's reign will bring wholeness and fullness of life, when all things are as God intended them to be, when we are at peace with God, with ourselves and with the world."[27] Ultimately, the fulfillment of this vision involves the restoration, not just of individuals, but of God's entire creation. In other words, it takes the focus off personal salvation and includes the concept that God is working to restore the entire cosmos (including us) to what he

---

26. Ibid., 180.
27. Ibid., 182.

originally intended it to be.[28] "When God reigns over all creation and over all humanity, it will be good, for God is good."[29]

Another key term in this passage and a concept that is repeatedly used in reference to God in Isaiah is the word "redeem." The term itself is rooted in the exodus—that other great event of liberation when God powerfully acted to "redeem" the Israelites out of Egypt (Exod 6:6–8). As I have indicated, in the story of Israel the exodus is the central component to a much larger paradigm or model of God's redemptive activity. The return from exile is a re-enactment of the exodus. But in Isaiah's vision, God's promise of redemption pertains not just to the people of Israel. It is universal in scope and power. Israel's gospel is a gospel for "all nations" (Isa 52:10).[30]

This Old Testament background helps us better understand the meaning of the gospel in the New Testament. The message of the Gospels and the rest of the New Testament is that in Christ the good news of Isaiah is realized (Mk 1:1, 14–15; Lk 4:16–19). This celebration of the "good news" of God's saving activity is rooted in the covenant that God ratified with Israel following the first exodus.

When we speak of "the gospel" we generally have in mind what is referred to as "justification," or being made right with God through forgiveness of sins. This is indeed a critical element of salvation which we dare not neglect. For there to be restoration to a right relationship with God there must be atonement for sins. This is what Christ accomplished through his death on the cross; and what we celebrate in the Lord's Supper.

However, this emphasis on justification is limited by its almost exclusive focus on the individual and its fixation on deliverance from the judgment of sin.[31] To speak *only* in these terms leaves a "hole in the gospel."[32] In *Evangelical Theology* Michael Bird notes that, "In the Scriptures salvation can mean deliverance from enemies, physical danger, death, disability, demonic powers, illness, poverty, injustice, social exclusion, false accusation, shame, and of course sin and its consequences." The Scriptures affirm God's desire to save people in both their current physical state and their future eternal state.[33] Salvation is fundamentally *deliverance* from that which impedes well-being and *restoration* to wholeness in one's relationship to God, others, and the world. Moreover, what we might refer to as "redemption

---

28. See Walton, *Old Testament Theology for Christians*, 8.
29. Wright, *The Mission of God's People*, 182.
30. Ibid., 184–85.
31. Middleton, *A New Heaven and a New Earth*, 79.
32. Richard Stearns, *The Hole in Our Gospel*, 2.
33. Bird, *Evangelical Theology*, 493.

history" or "salvation history" is bigger than our own personal salvation. It is not just about us.[34] Wholeness or well-being is God's original intention for creation. In this respect, the exodus—God's deliverance of the Israelites from bondage, their restoration through a covenantal relationship with him, and their call to be a light to the nations—serves as the most important paradigm or model for salvation.[35]

Intertwined with this concept of wholeness or flourishing of the redeemed is God's presence among them. A good case can be made that the primary theme that progresses throughout the Old Testament, and in fact throughout the entire Bible, is the establishment of God's presence among his people.[36] The promise that God will be present among his people is why so much emphasis is placed on the building of the tabernacle and temple. It is reiterated in Jeremiah's famous oracle of a new covenant ("I will be their God, and they shall be my people") which is quoted by Hebrews as being fulfilled in Jesus (Jer 31:33; Heb 8:10). And it culminates in John's vision of God sitting on his throne in the New Jerusalem:[37]

> And I heard a loud voice from the throne saying, "Now the dwelling of God is with mortals, and he will live with them. They will be his people, and God himself will be with them and be their God." (Rev 21:3).

God's presence and relationship as expressed through the covenant are the Bible's plot line and theological focus from the opening chapters of Genesis to the closing chapters of Revelation.[38]

Christ as the Climax of the Old Testament

When speaking of the relationship between the Old and New Testaments, it is best to refer to Christ as the climax of God's redemptive plan, which is initiated by God's covenant with Israel. John Walton states that "all of God's revelation reaches a new plateau in Christ, so all of it can be seen as heading in that direction. In that way we can talk about the Old Testament as pointing to Christ."[39]

---

34. Walton, *Old Testament Theology for Christians*, 8.

35. Middleton, *A New Heaven and a New Earth*, 79. See also Wright, *The Mission of God's People*, 182.

36. Walton, *Old Testament Theology for Christians*, 26–27.

37. Middleton, *A New Heaven and a New Earth*, 90.

38. Walton, *Old Testament Theology for Christians*, 28.

39. Ibid., 5–6.

It is from this vantage point that we should understand three key Old Testament passages which have a special connection to the Last Supper: Exodus 24:1–18; Jeremiah 31:31–34; and Isaiah 25:6–9. The Mosaic covenant described in Exodus 24 is the climax of the covenant-making experience which was initiated when God descended on Mount Sinai (Exod 19). What is central in this covenant is the divine presence, which is pictured in various ways throughout the book of Exodus (3:8; 13:18–22; 15:17). In this chapter, God and humanity meet in communion on the cosmic mountain. God is worshiped, and he in response provides the rest and life of his presence (cf. Exod 33:14: "My presence shall go with you, and I will give you rest."). The manner of worship in Exodus 24 thus "reflects a pattern inherent in the divine ordering of creation. It reveals the framework of God's design for the ideal universe."[40]

This passage concludes with Moses drawing near to God to receive the stone tablets and the instructions for building the tabernacle. But he first waits for six days on the cloud-covered mountain and receives the covenant stipulations on the seventh day when God calls him from within the cloud (vs 16). Here the writer intends to describe the creation of the covenant community after the pattern of God's creation of the cosmos in Genesis 1 and 2.

Two other features of this text stand out. First, the covenant ratification begins with two sacrifices—a burnt offering to make atonement for sin and a peace sacrifice or fellowship offering which expresses the well-being (or *shalom*) between the parties in the covenant (vss 5–7). But the covenant-making process does not end with these sacrifices. At the end of the covenant ceremony Moses and the other worshipers have a "communal meal" in God's presence (vs 11). These aspects of the Mosaic covenant point to the blood of the new covenant (Lk 22:20) and the heavenly banquet (Rev 19:9) which Jesus alludes to in the Last Supper.

Unfortunately, the celebration of the covenant described in Exodus 24 is short-lived. Shortly thereafter, the Israelites break their covenant with God by worshiping the golden calf (Exod 32). This disobedience is repeated by subsequent generations. Ultimately, it results in God's judgment, the defeat of Israel by foreign powers, and the exile. The prophets view the exile as necessary. It is a means by which God will refine and purify the nation and from which a renewed, faithful people (the "remnant") will emerge.[41] Jeremiah is among the prophets who proclaim that God is going to make a "new covenant," which will be even greater than the covenant with Moses

---

40. Hilber, "Theology of Worship in Exodus 24," 177, 186.
41. See Routledge, "Replacement or Fulfillment?," 144.

(Jer 31:32). This "new covenant" has been described as a fulfillment of Israel's hope for restoration which would bring about a "transformed people of God"[42] and "generate a new day for the whole human race."[43]

We have seen that the prophet Isaiah describes the hope for exiles in terms of a "redeemed Jerusalem" (Isa 52:9; cf. 65:17–25). In 25:6–9 he pictures God's heavenly city in the final day of salvation. The reference to "elders" in Isaiah 24:23 looks back to the Mosaic covenant with Israel which was celebrated in a meal with the elders (Ex 24:11). But now in the envisaged messianic banquet the emphasis is placed on the universality of God's blessing—it will include *all peoples* or ethnic groups (Isa 25:6–7) and all *nations* or political entities (25:7).[44]

Thus, a central feature of God's covenant with Israel and subsequently the new covenant in Christ is a desire for human flourishing or *shalom*. Nicholas Wolterstorff describes *shalom* in this way:

> The state of *shalom* is the state of flourishing in all dimensions of one's existence: in one's relation to God, in one's relations to one's fellow human beings, in one's relation to nature, and in one's relation to oneself. Evidently justice has something to do with the fact that God's love for each and every one of God's human creatures takes the form of God desiring the *shalom* of each and every one. Not merely the freedom from violation of one's property, but flourishing of each and every one.[45]

Conclusion: God's Victory Over Evil

Evil is a reality of the world that no one can ignore. When we think of evil, our minds conjure up images of the horrors of Auschwitz or the 9/11 terrorist attacks. We are shocked by stories in the news of child sex abuse, mass murder, and genocide. The reality of evil belies the naïve belief in human progress. In *People of the Lie*, the well-known psychotherapist M. Scott Peck goes against the standard psychiatric model that there is no such thing as a darker evil power in the world. He came to recognize the existence of a force or forces of evil which are supra-personal, supra-human, and which appear to take over individuals and, in some cases, entire societies. Postmodern

---

42. Gorman, *The Death of the Messiah*, 27.
43. Wright, *The Day the Revolution Began*, 115.
44. Motyer, *Isaiah*, 192.
45. Quoted in George and Toyama–Szeto, *God of Justice*, 22.

nihilism acknowledges that evil is a real and powerful force in the world, but it gives us no clue as to what we should do about it.[46]

The Old Testament wasn't written simply to "tell us about God" in some abstract way. Rather, it was written to tell a story about how chaos in the world is the result of rebellious created spirits and what God has done, is doing, and will do about evil.[47] In various passages, reference is made to the literary chaos monsters of Rahab and Leviathan to portray God's absolute sovereignty over creation and the ultimate defeat of evil.[48] The psalmist, for example, declares:

> But you, O God, are my king from of old;
> you bring salvation on the earth.
> It was you who split open the sea by your power;
> you broke the heads of the monster in the waters.
> It was you who crushed the heads of the Leviathan
> and gave him as food to the creatures of the desert.
> (Ps 74:12–14)

The prophet Isaiah similarly proclaims:

> Awake, awake! Clothe yourself with strength,
> O arm of the Lord;
> awake, as in days gone by,
> as in generations of old.
> Was it not you who cut Rahab to pieces,
> who pierced that monster through?
> Was it not you who dried up the sea,
> the waters of the great deep,
> who made a road in the depths of the sea
> so that the redeemed might cross over?
> (Isa 51:9–10; cf. Hab 3:8–15)

---

46. See Wright, *Evil and the Justice of God*, 19–41.

47. Ibid., 45. See also Oswalt, *The Bible among the Myths*, 66.

48. The monster called Leviathan is frequently found in Canaanite literature; and Rahab appears to have been used by the Egyptians. They are most commonly used in the ancient mythical story of a god who defeats the chaos monster in primeval time and brings order into the world. The biblical writers appropriate these mythical figures for literary purposes to make a point about God's sovereignty over evil. This does not mean that the biblical writers adopt the mythical worldview of the Egyptians or Canaanites. As Oswalt states: "That you might call someone a Hercules does not prove that your view of the world is the same as that of the ancient Greeks from whose myths that personage comes" (Ibid., 93).

In these passages the biblical writers directly allude to the story of the exodus. As John Oswalt observes, "Here the imagery is utilized to express God's victory over evil when he triumphed over the waters in the exodus and brought his people through. . . . [He] conquered the chaos of evil once for all for his people at a certain time and in a certain place."[49]

While we might separate justice and the message of salvation, in the Old Testament these two elements are inseparable. God's justice is a saving, healing, and restorative justice. His plan of redemption, in which the story of the exodus is front and center, is that his creation, which is frustrated and distorted by the presence of sin and evil, will be restored and brought to glorious completion. Interwoven with the theme of God's justice in Isaiah is the figure of the Servant in chapters 40 through 55, who fulfills the promises originally made to Abraham and through whom YHWH's purpose of justice and salvation will be carried out. This picture of the Servant comes into sharp focus in Isaiah 53, which describes the suffering and death of the Servant himself who bears the sins of many. As N. T. Wright argues, the suffering Servant "embodies the covenant faithfulness, the restorative justice, of the sovereign God; and with his stripes 'we' (presumably the 'we' of the remnant, looking on in wonder and fear) are healed."[50] Central to God's justice and his ultimate victory over evil, then, "is the picture of God's faithfulness to unfaithful Israel." And central to that picture is the picture of YHWH's Servant.[51]

---

49. Ibid., 95–96.
50. Wright, *Evil and the Justice of God*, 64–65.
51. Ibid.

4

The Divine Bridegroom and the Song of Songs

It is not hard to find instances of the emphasis on self in our culture. On a recent reality TV show, a girl wants a major road blocked off so a marching band can precede her grand entrance on a red carpet for her sixteenth birthday party. It is now possible to hire fake paparazzi—videographers and photographers who follow you around filming and snapping your photograph when you go out on the town. In typical Hollywood fashion, the event is then featured in a faux celebrity magazine which you can take home to document the experience. A book called *My Beautiful Mommy* explains plastic surgery to pre-school children whose mothers are going under the knife for a "Mommy Makeover." The author, a plastic surgeon, explains: "You and your child will follow along as Mommy goes through her plastic surgery experience and learn how the entire family pitches in to help Mommy achieve her beautiful results."

These are actual cases cited by Jean Twenge and W. Keith Campbell in their book *The Narcissist Epidemic* as examples of the "relentless rise" of narcissism in our culture.[1] American culture, they argue, places an inordinate amount of emphasis on self-admiration and self-love under the false belief that it will improve our lives. Americans "love to love themselves."[2] But excessive self-love is destructive of both self and others. Like the mythical figure who sees his own reflection in the water and gazes at it until he dies, narcissists are so self-absorbed and frozen by self-admiration that they find it difficult to connect with anyone outside of themselves. Narcissism is

1. Twenge and Campbell, *The Narcissist Epidemic*, 1.
2. Ibid., 13.

associated with negative characteristics such as arrogance, conceit, grandiosity, and self-centeredness. Narcissists are limited in their ability to develop emotionally warm, caring, and loving relationships with others. They tend to manipulate and exploit people; they view others as tools to make themselves look and feel good.[3]

Narcissism is perpetuated in our culture by pop psychology, America's celebrity obsession, reality TV shows, the internet, and social media such as MySpace, Twitter, and Facebook. It has infected every aspect of our culture, including business (advertising), religion, and politics. So it is perhaps not surprising that we now even have a president who displays characteristics of the narcissistic personality.[4]

The Song of Songs might be viewed as providing a biblical response to narcissism in our culture. At its most basic level it is a celebration of healthy, passionate, and self-giving love. It describes love characterized by fidelity and mutuality. In this respect, it can be interpreted as a poem about human love. But it is important for us as modern readers to try to see this book through ancient Jewish eyes. In this chapter I will argue that when placed within its proper historical and theological context this love poem should also be viewed in terms of the ancient Jewish concept of the bridegroom God of Israel.[5]

The Song of Songs, Israel, and the Future Hope

The question has been raised, to whose love is the Song referring? Commentators have tended to take either of two approaches. Most modern interpreters view it as a secular, and often erotic, song that describes the love and sexual union between two humans. Their ancient and medieval counterparts, on the other hand, tended to interpret it as an illustration of God's love for his people. These two interpretations are not necessarily mutually exclusive, however. A better way of understanding this book of the Bible is that it presents a theology of love in which the realms of human love and the religious experience of divine love interpenetrate.[6] In the words of one commentator,

3. Ibid., 18–19.
4. Ibid., 53–54. Twenge and Campbell distinguish between the more outgoing, exhibitionist form of narcissism, or the "narcissistic personality" and Narcissistic Personality Disorder (NPD). Many psychologists have described President Trump as having a narcissistic personality, but are cautious about concluding that he has a "personality disorder."
5. See Pitre, *Jesus the Bridegroom*, 22.
6. See Davis, *Proverbs, Ecclesiastes, and Song of Songs*, 234.

> As wisdom literature, the Song is designed to show us an idealized picture of married love, in the context of a fallen and broken world. As it does so, it tends to convict each of us of how far short of this perfection we fall, both as humans and as lovers, and thus to drive us repeatedly into the arms of our true heavenly husband, Jesus Christ."[7]

Our broken human relationships point to our broken relationship with God (1 Jn 4:20). But the true remedy for our failed loves is found always and only in God's unfailing love, which is most fully demonstrated in the sending of his only Son into the world to die for us (1 Jn 4:10).[8]

We can go even further in describing the contemporary importance and value of this book. The Song is a depiction of redemption from the curse of the fall which occurred in the garden of Eden. In its description of an ideal marriage it implicitly "evokes desire for God, and it stirs up an eschatological hope for the final consummation of that hope and desire."[9] This reference to Eden in the Song cannot be fully understood without considering the connections of the Song with the Old Testament prophets. We need therefore to first look at the larger Old Testament context and the use of the marriage metaphor in some key prophetic passages.

The Significance of the Marriage Metaphor in the Old Testament

A number of Old Testament prophets (especially Isaiah, Jeremiah, and Hosea) characterize God's covenant with Israel following the exodus as a marriage or a divine wedding, with Israel as a bride and God as the divine bridegroom (Jer 2:1–2). These prophets retell the story of Israel's covenant with God on Mt. Sinai as a divine love story.[10] When the Israelites commit idolatry by worshipping foreign gods, they therefore portray Israel's behavior as the profound and destructive betrayal of a marriage relationship. This image of spiritual adultery and "promiscuity" is most graphically depicted by Hosea's marriage to a prostitute (Hos 1:2). But these prophets also look forward to a future age of salvation—a time when Israel's sins will be forgiven and there will be marital reconciliation between God and his estranged wife.[11] In other words, they use the metaphor of the marriage to *both* describe God's covenantal relationship with Israel *and* portray the

---

7. Duguid, *The Song of Songs*, 37.
8. Ibid.
9. See Clarke, "Canonical Interpretations of the Song of Songs," 307.
10. Pitre, *Jesus the Bridegroom*, 12.
11. Ibid., 17.

future age of salvation (or the eschatological age) as a *reuniting* of former marriage partners.¹²

We have seen that the Old Testament prophets frequently describe the coming days of salvation in terms of eating and drinking. In chapter three, for example, we saw that a key passage which describes this "eschatological banquet" is Isaiah 25:6-9; these verses give us a picture of people celebrating with excellent food and wine on Mount Zion. The language used to describe this joyous occasion to which "all people" are invited is often associated in the Old Testament with the celebration of a marriage covenant. It is also language that is used to depict enthronement and victory—in this case ultimate victory over the enemy of humanity (death).¹³

In Isaiah 40-66 the prophet likewise uses the imagery of a banquet to describe the restoration of Israel, but in this later section the focus is on the theme of a return from exile in the desert or wilderness. The well-known verse, "A voice of one calling: 'in the desert prepare the way for the Lord' . . ." (Isa 40:3) is an invitation to participate in the return from exile. It is "an invitation for Israel to re-unite with her husband of old and to travel once again through the wilderness to the land given to her."¹⁴ These are the words later preached by John the Baptist in the desert of Judea to call the people of Israel to repentance and prepare them for the coming of the kingdom through Jesus' ministry (Matt 3:1-3). Isaiah characterizes the marital reunion between God and Israel in terms of a renewal of Israel's land which has been devastated (Isa 62:4-5). As we have seen, the prophet associates this renewal of the land with the new heaven and new earth (Isa 65:17-19) in which all participate in an ongoing feast (Isa 55:1-5).

In both Hosea and Jeremiah the marriage metaphor is employed to describe the past (the sins of Israel), the present (Israel as estranged from God), and the future (the restoration of Israel to its former relationship with God).¹⁵ Jeremiah 2-3 describes the Lord as "brokenhearted and bitter, angry and ashamed," but still faithful despite the unfaithfulness of his wife, Israel.¹⁶ Of particular importance for our purposes is Jeremiah 31, since it is recited directly by Jesus during his final meal with his disciples (Lk 12:20; 1 Cor 11:25). Here, the breaking of the old covenant by the Israelites is described in terms of the breaking of a marriage vow: "I was like a husband to them" (31:32). But God's love for his people is enduring; it is an "everlasting

12. See Long, *Jesus the Bridegroom*, 8-9.
13. Ibid., 43-67.
14. Ibid., 81-83.
15. Ibid., 121.
16. Ibid., 129.

love" (31:2). A new covenant (or "fresh betrothal") will be enacted which will result in the restoration of the people of Israel to the position of God's people. The phrase "I will be their God and they will be my people" (31:33) is reminiscent of the language that Hosea uses to describe the restoration of the marriage between God and his people (Hos 2:23).[17]

The Image of Eden and Marital Union in the Song

The prophets therefore fuel the hope for the future wedding of God.[18] This marital reunion is directly tied to the forgiveness of sins which God will remember no more (Jer 31:34). But, and this is of utmost importance, in each of the prophecies I have discussed, salvation is not limited to the forgiveness of sins. It is also about *union with God in a spiritual marriage* which is totally the result of his love and grace. "From this point of view, all of human history is a story of divine love—given, betrayed, forgiven, and renewed because of the mercy and compassion of God."[19] And it is this prophetic celebration of God's enduring passion for "the bride" that provides the larger context for understanding the Song of Songs.

To see this more clearly it is necessary to return briefly to the description of the fall of Adam and Eve in Genesis 3. In that account, we read that as a result of sin there is a three-fold rupture in the original harmony or order of creation. First, there is a disruption in human relationships. Sin results in shame (Gen 3:7), distrust (Gen 3:12), male power over women (Gen 3:16), and violence (Gen 4:8). Secondly, there is alienation of humans from nature as represented by the cursing of the ground and painful toil (Gen 3:17–19) and the pain of childbirth (Gen 3:16). Finally, and most fundamentally, there is alienation from God. Following their sin, Adam and Eve hide from God (Gen 3:8); and they are banished from the garden where they had experienced the uninterrupted presence of God (Gen 3:23–24).

The theology of love that is poetically described in the Song "represents a reversal of that primeval exile from Eden."[20] It is a symbolic description of the healing of relationships at all three levels. At the level of human relationships it depicts the ecstatic union of husband and wife based on total fidelity and mutuality. The physical consummation of their love is likened to the blossoming of a garden, with all of nature rejoicing with the couple. Most importantly, this lover's garden represents a return to the idyllic garden of

---

17. Ibid., 132.
18. Pitre, *Jesus the Bridegroom*, 19
19. Ibid., 19
20. Davis, *Proverbs, Ecclesiastes, and Song of Songs*, 232.

Eden where life might be lived fully in the presence of God.[21] In this sense, the Song is a symbolic portrayal of the future wedding between God the bridegroom and his chosen people.[22] As we will see in later chapters, in the Last Supper Jesus is pictured as the divine bridegroom. From this perspective, the Song of Songs points to the eternal marriage between Christ the bridegroom and his bride (the church) which is anticipated in the Eucharist (Rev 21:2; 1 Cor 11:26).

The Song and Israel as the Bride (4:1–5:1)

These three levels of ecstatic union (physical union between husband and wife; spiritual union with God; and the future wedding between God the bridegroom and his chosen people) are depicted most clearly in 4:1–5:1, which comprise the midpoint in the Song and in a number of respects serve as the "center of gravity" for the entire book.[23]

This central section of the Song focuses on the consummation of the marriage, which the couple has looked forward to since the beginning of the poem.[24] This consummation is described in conjunction with a transition from the wilderness or desert (3:6) to the garden (4:12–15). It therefore "resembles a return to the blessings of Eden from the chaotic and broken wilderness of our normal experience."[25]

There are several characteristics of this passage that are worth noting. The first concerns the appearance of the beloved. What is striking is the imagery used to describe various features of the bride—eyes like doves and hair like a flock of goats (41); teeth like a flock of sheep (4:2); temples like halves of a pomegranate (4:3); a neck like the Tower of David (4:4); and two breasts like two fawns (4:5). To modern ears this sounds like a strange way to describe a wife-to-be! But to the Jew familiar with the Hebrew Scriptures it would have been clear that the language used here to describe the beloved is used elsewhere to describe the temple and the city of Jerusalem (2 Chron 3:15–16; Lev 2:2; cf. Song, 4:14).[26]

---

21. Ibid. Note: one point where my interpretation of this passage differs from that of Davis is that in her view the poem never really describes a physical consummation of the marriage.
22. Pitre, *Jesus the Bridegroom*, 20.
23. Davis, *Proverbs, Ecclesiastes, and Song of Songs*, 266.
24. Duguid, *Song of Songs*, 104.
25. Ibid., 105.
26. Pitre, *Jesus the Bridegroom*, 24.

This interpretation is supported by other symbolism in this passage. In the section describing the consummation of the marriage (4:8–5:1) there are three stanzas (verses 8–11, 12–15, and 4:16–5:1). The first stanza begins and ends with the word "Lebanon;" the same word also concludes the second stanza.[27] It is used a total of seven times in the Song (3:9; 4:8, 11, 15; 5:15; 7:4). The cedars of Lebanon were used in the construction of Solomon's Temple (I Kgs 5:6). In the Old Testament Lebanon is viewed as a desirable place (Deut 3:25); and the word is used by the prophets in connection with healing (Hos 14:4–5; Isa 35:2; 60:13).

We have seen that in the Old Testament the tabernacle and later the temple is the place of God's presence among his people (e.g., Lev 26:11, "I will put my dwelling place among you"). This theme of God's presence is inaugurated in the opening chapter of Genesis, which describes God as "resting" on the seventh day—that is, he takes up his rule in his sacred space, which is centered in Eden. The garden functions like a temple. That is why—as I have argued—the tabernacle and the temple were designed like a garden.[28] Verses 4:10–5:1 of the Song are rich with imagery which both has strong sexual connotations and takes the reader back to the original innocence of the garden of Eden. The picture of the bride as a "garden locked" (vs 12) reminds the reader of the story of Adam and Eve, who are "locked out" of the garden of Eden because of their sin (Gen 3:23–24). Other imagery used to describe the bride (i.e., "garden fountain" and "well of flowing water" in verse 15) depicts not only a human love scene but also the renewal of special intimacy between God and Israel, which reaches its high point in temple worship.[29] The prophet Zechariah uses the same language in describing the day of a transformed relationship between God and Israel: "On that day *a fountain* will be opened to . . . the inhabitants of Jerusalem. . . . On that day *living water* will flow from Jerusalem. . . ." (Zech 13:1; 14:8). The Song therefore reflects ancient Jewish tradition, which views the wedding of God and Israel as consummated through sacrifice and worship. It highlights the Jewish expectation of the coming of the bridegroom God of Israel, who will forgive their sins and reunite himself to them in an everlasting marriage covenant.[30]

---

27. Duguid, *Song of Songs*, 114.
28. Walton, *The Lost World of Adam and Eve*, 49–51.
29. Davis, *Proverbs, Ecclesiastes, and the Song of Songs*, 269.
30. Pitre, *Jesus the Bridegroom*, 27.

The Significance of the Song for Us Today

I have suggested that at one level the Song is a beautiful description of romantic love between humans. At another level, however, this love poem is a metaphor for the deeper and more passionate love of God for his people. In the New Testament, this picture of God's "spousal love" is dramatized in the incarnation of Christ, who left the glories of heaven to dwell among us as a servant and sacrifice his life for us on a Roman cross. The middle section in the Song concludes on a joyous note of marital celebration: "Eat, O friends, and drink, drink your fill, O lovers" (5:1). That too, is how we should remember or participate in Christ's death in the Eucharist. As a reenactment of his incredible love for us, it ought to be celebrated with joy and thanksgiving.

In Ephesians 5, Paul further describes the "great mystery" of the marriage of Christ and the church (5:32). In this passage he says that the Christian marriage between a man and a woman should be patterned after the supernatural love of Christ for the church. To quote Brant Pitre: "Christian marriage is a living icon of the sacrificial love between Christ and the Church. It is (or ought to be) an outward sign of the invisible mystery of Jesus' love for his bride and the bride's love for him."[31]

I can think of no better example of this biblical teaching than my parent's marriage of 73 years. After months of battling a terminal illness, my father went to be with the Lord on May 21, 2018 at the age of 94. My mother suffered from Alzheimer's and passed away into glory about nine months later, on February 4, 2019 at the age of 99. As I reflect on their long and productive lives, I am deeply impressed by their sacrificial love for each other and their family, and their devotion to Christ and the church. My parents were missionaries in Japan for almost eleven years. After returning from the mission field, my father accepted a position as professor of missions at Trinity Evangelical Divinity School (Deerfield, IL), where he served for twenty-five years. On various occasions, he was offered opportunities in the business world that would have been significantly more lucrative, financially speaking. But he turned them down to follow a different calling. My mother was a homemaker who was devoted to her family and well-known for her hospitality. Though I grieve my parents' passing, I rejoice in their lives of dedication to the gospel of God's love through Jesus Christ. Though not wealthy by any means, they were generous beyond measure, both to me and my two siblings; and to the work of the church and missions. They were

---

31. Ibid., 151

both prime examples of what it means to "lay up for yourselves treasures in heaven, where moth and rust do not corrupt."

In the last chapter of the Song we are given the following profound description of the incorruptibility, endurance, and incomparable worth of divine love:

> Place me like a seal over your heart,
> like the seal on your arm;
> for love is as strong as death,
> its jealousy unyielding as the grave . . .
> Many waters cannot quench love;
> rivers cannot wash it away.
> If one were to give
> all the wealth of his house for love,
> it would be utterly scorned.
> (8:6–7)

In the Old Testament tradition there was the belief that YHWH's love for his people and faithfulness to his promises would eventually result in a return from exile. The writer of the Song expresses the profound insight that God's love is "as strong as death." Reflected in these words is the passionate hope that death itself would not, in the end, thwart God's purposes.[32] The value and importance of the Old Testament for us is the instruction it gives concerning God's plans and purposes in the world. The specifics of that plan are now taking place under the new covenant as described in the New Testament. As God's representatives of the new covenant, we are given the awesome privilege and responsibility to participate by his Spirit in his work of redemption.[33]

---

32. Middleton, *A New Heaven and a New Earth*, 151–52.
33. Walton, *Old Testament Theology for Christians*, 274.

Part Two

New Exodus and New Creation

5

The Exodus Motif in the Gospels and Pauline Epistles

THE battle of Dunkirk has been described as one of the most miraculous events of the Second World War. In early May of 1940 the German Army had invaded northwestern Europe and captured many of the ports along the English Channel. Hundreds of thousands of soldiers of the British and French armies were trapped by the advancing German Army on the beaches around Dunkirk. They were a sitting target for the Germans. Winston Churchill, who had just been elected as prime minister of Britain, was faced with leading the nation in its darkest hour and against fearsome odds.[1] While Churchill was desperately trying to rally the nation and coordinate an evacuation of Allied forces, a few of his government's senior members were pressing hard to negotiate peace terms with Hitler. At the risk of isolating himself in his new administration, Churchill vowed to fight on. Through a combination of extraordinary factors the British Navy managed to rescue a large percentage of the trapped forces (about 330,000). Had Churchill yielded to the appeasers, there can be little doubt that it would have resulted in Hitler's complete triumph in Europe. He understood this. As the British leader warned in his own recollection of these events, if Hitler wins "then the whole world including the United States, including all that we have known and cared for, will sink into the abyss of a new Dark Age . . ."[2] Although the final liberation of Western Europe was not achieved until the Allied invasion of Normandy in June of 1944, Dunkirk was a decisive battle that marked the beginning of the end of the Third Reich.

1. Humes, *Churchill, the Prophetic Statesman*, 1.
2. Ibid., 4.

In the Gospels and Pauline Epistles, Jesus' death and resurrection are similarly portrayed as acts of divine rescue or liberation. Chris Wright observes that the New Testament often presents the redeeming death of Jesus through the lens of the exodus. "Jesus as redeemer is the champion who will do whatever it takes to achieve rescue for his people."[3] Jesus dramatically portrays this liberation in the Last Supper when he asks his disciples in ingesting the bread and wine to participate in his death by faith.[4] But what specifically did Jesus mean by this?

Jesus' story needs to be read, at least in part, through the lens of Israel's story. This is particularly true of the Last Supper, which Jesus intentionally identifies with the Passover and exodus. When he says that his death (and our identification with it) establishes a covenant (Mk 14:24; Matt 26:28; Lk 22:20; 1 Cor 11:25), he is, in effect, saying that the meal becomes for Christians what the covenant ceremony was for Israel following the exodus.[5] For the Israelites, the Passover was a remembrance of God's faithful, gracious, and mighty act of deliverance from bondage in Egypt. This act of liberation created a covenantal community. Likewise, the Lord's Supper is a celebration of divine rescue, or "new exodus"/"new creation" that involves three things: 1) the defeat of sin and evil; 2) ransom from sin to new life; and 3) liberation from oppression to life in a new community of love and justice. Let's explore each of these themes in a little more detail as they are presented in the New Testament.

Defeat of Sin and Evil

When we read the gospel accounts of Jesus' ministry, we see the assault by the forces of darkness and evil.[6] Matthew opens his Gospel with the scheme by Herod to kill Jesus, who has just been born. Warned by an angel, Joseph and Mary flee to Egypt (Matt 2:7–15). Mark relates how the Pharisees plot with the Herodians to kill Jesus early on, following his healings on the Sabbath (Mk 3:4–6). Luke tells of how the citizens of Nazareth attempt to throw Jesus off a cliff after his inaugural sermon (Lk 4:28–29). John describes how concern over Jesus' popularity and the loss of their own privileged status within the Roman Empire leads the chief priests and Pharisees to conspire to kill Jesus (Jn 11:45–53).

---

3. Wright, *The Mission of God's People*, 103.
4. McKnight, *A Community Called Atonement*, 84.
5. Ibid.,
6. On this, see Wright, *The Day the Revolution Began*, 203.

This conflict with forces of evil reaches a feverish pitch on the week of the Passover and culminates in Jesus' ignominious death on a Roman cross. But what appeared to be certain defeat is turned into victory. Through Jesus' death there is forgiveness of sins and a divine rescue of individuals from the powers of evil, death, and darkness. Jesus' death and resurrection mark a revolution—a dramatic reversal in the course of human history characterized by victory over the powers of evil, the inauguration of God's kingdom, and the "beginning of the end" of Satan's rule.

This story of evil drawing itself together and then being overthrown is repeated time and time again throughout the New Testament.[7] Often, parallels are drawn with the defeat of the mighty Pharaoh and God's rescue of the Israelites from their captivity in Egypt. We can see this, for example, is in the Apostle Paul's description of our liberation from captivity to sin in chapters 7 and 8 of Romans. Using language reminiscent of the Israelites' captivity in Egypt, Paul describes every person in their natural state as "sold as a slave to sin" (7:14). He then continues to describe this bondage to sin: "When I want to do good, evil is right there with me. . . What a wretched man I am! Who will rescue me from this body of death?" (7:21, 24)[8]

In the next chapter Paul gives the solution to this dilemma when he declares that those who are in Christ and have his Spirit are "set free" from the law of sin and death. (Rom 8:1–2; cf. 6:1–14). It is crucial to keep in mind, again, that throughout chapters 6–8 of Romans (and elsewhere) Paul uses language of the Passover.[9] Just as God released the Israelites from their captivity under Pharaoh in Egypt, so Christ has defeated and freed us from the powers of the "present evil age" and effected a "new exodus" through his representative and substitutionary death (cf. Gal 1:4).

The exodus imagery is particularly strong in the book of Colossians, which describes believers as delivered by God from the domain of darkness and transferred to the kingdom of his beloved son (Col 1:13). Just as the exodus was God's great defeat of the mighty Pharaoh, so through the cross he has disarmed the powers and authorities and made a public spectacle of them (2:15). In both the Old and New Testaments, redemption is the act of God whereby he pays the full cost of rescuing his people from all that opposes and oppresses them. "It involves the defeat of all oppressive power and the reversal of all dimensions of bondage that afflict people."[10]

---

7. Ibid., 206.

8. Wright points out that the Greek word that Paul uses describe the individual's captivity to the law of sin in 6:7 is the same word that it often used in the OT to describe Israel's exile and captivity as the result of sin (Ibid., 277–81).

9. Wright, *The Day the Revolution Began*, 276–94.

10. Wright, *The Mission of God's People*, 104.

Ransomed from Sin to New Life

In Mark's Gospel, Jesus describes his death in terms of giving his life "a ransom for many" (Mk 10:45). These words, again, are best understood in the context of the Passover sacrifice during which the Israelite fathers sacrificed a lamb and then smeared its blood on the door frames. The slain lambs were, in effect, a "ransom" price that enabled the Israelites to escape both God's judgment on Egypt and the clutches of the Pharaoh.[11] In the Greek, the word for ransom (*lutron*) means "to buy the freedom of a slave or prisoner." In order to procure his freedom, the ransomer would make a huge sacrificial payment that matched the value, or paid the debt of the slave or the prisoner.[12] With these words, then, Jesus is describing his own death as a "ransom price" to release his followers from God's judgment on sin and their captivity.[13]

But in what sense are we "set free" by Jesus' death on the cross? Timothy Keller puts it well when he states that "since the slavery he is dealing with is of a cosmic kind—that is, cosmic evil—it required a cosmic payment."[14] In "proclaiming the Lord's death" through the taking of the elements (1 Cor 11:26) we acknowledge that Jesus payed a ransom that none of us could possibly pay. To again quote Keller: "Jesus didn't have to die despite God's love; he had to die *because* of God's love. And it had to be this way because *all life-changing love is substitutionary sacrifice.*" The debt had to be paid; but is was *God who came and paid it himself.*[15] So we can rejoice in forgiveness of sins through Jesus' substitutionary death on the cross.[16]

But Jesus' death is not *only* a "legal transaction" in which Jesus pays the penalty for my sin. Stopping there separates the cross from the kingdom and misses the scope and breadth of God's salvation or deliverance. This is made clear in Romans 8, where Paul expands the story of Israel and the exodus to include the entire world. All of creation groans, he says, waiting for liberation from this bondage to futility and decay (8:19–22). Even those who have tasted of this liberation through faith, groan within themselves, as they too wait for the final cosmic exodus from slavery to sin and death (8:23–25).

---

11. McKnight, *A Community Called Atonement*, 86.
12. Keller, *King's Cross*, 140.
13. McKnight, *A Community Called Atonement.*, 87.
14. Keller, *King's Cross*, 140.
15. Ibid., 141–44.
16. The concept of "penal substitution" is expressed in Galatians 3:13: "Christ redeemed us from the curse of the law by becoming a curse for us, for it is written: 'Cursed is everyone who is hung on a tree.'"

In her brilliant book, *Joy Unspeakable*, Barbara Holmes describes the language of the "moan." It is the language generated by slavery from ancient to modern times. Just as the Israelites groaned under the burden of slavery in Egypt (Exod 6:5) so the men, women, and children from Africa and West Indies who were kidnapped, chained together, and forced to lie side by side in the bowels of slave ships moaned their horrific transition from personhood to property and non-identity.[17] Holmes describes the "moan" as the vehicle for articulating what cannot be voiced, expressing unspeakable fears, and yet hoping for a joy yet unknown (cf. Rom 8:22–27).[18] Today, it is the language of girls enslaved in brothels, and of the victims of AIDS, hunger and malnutrition, and terrorism around the world.

Sin (and evil) violate *shalom*, or God's intention for the way things ought to be, whether spiritually, morally, physically, or otherwise.[19] Stated in another way, sin is an idolatrous attachment to alien forces that enslave us and thwart God's purposes for his creation. But in Christ's atoning death and resurrection there is the promise of the final kingdom when the Creator will make all things new (Rom 8:38–39). Even in this life, Paul says, those who are united with Christ in his death and resurrection are raised to new life (Rom 6:8–10). Certainly, then, one of the central messages of the New Testament is that "in the midst of a powerless death emerges a divine saving power to forgive, redeem, and renew . . . In the apex of death, life rises with healing in its wing."[20]

Liberation from Oppression to Life in a Community of Love and Justice

The Israelites' liberation from slavery was only one part of the meaning of the Passover. In response to God's loving and gracious act of deliverance the Israelites were called to a "covenant vocation," meaning that they were to both love and worship God and represent his character to the nations around them. There were thus two inseparable categories of the covenant—the vertical (God-oriented) and horizontal (human-oriented)—as expressed in the two tables of the Law given to Moses (Exod 31:18).[21] This symbiosis of vertical and horizontal love is best summarized in Micah 6:8:

---

17. Holmes, *Joy Unspeakable*, 69–70.
18. Ibid., 70–75.
19. See Plantiga, *Not the Way It's Supposed to Be*, 7–18.
20. Bird, *Evangelical Theology*, 394.
21. Gorman, *The Death of the Messiah*, 29.

> He has showed you, O man, what is good,
> And what does the Lord require of you?
> To act justly and to love mercy
> and to walk humbly with your God.

The Israelites, of course, failed miserably. Instead of worshiping God and representing him and his purposes for his creation, they turned their covenant vocation upside down by idolatrously giving worship and allegiance to forces and powers within creation itself.

When Jesus speaks of the covenant (or new covenant), then, he is speaking of the creation of a new covenant community. By partaking of the bread and wine, Jesus' disciples indicate that they are part of a new ecclesial community which is established by his death.[22] In Mark 10:35–45, Jesus contrasts the Roman practice of power and the disciples' quest for power and control with the life of service which should characterize the new community. In effect, he is proclaiming liberation *from* sin and oppression *to* life in a new community of love and justice where people can be restored to a right relationship with God, others, self, and the world.[23] Keller describes what Mark is saying in this way:

> If [Jesus] is indeed our substitutionary sacrifice, and if he has paid for our sins, if he has proved to our insecure, skittish little hearts that we are worth everything to him, then we have everything we need in him. It's all a gift to us by his grace. We don't need to do good things to connect to God or feel better about ourselves. . . . Now you don't *need* to help people, but you *want* to help them, to resemble the One who did so much for you, to bring him delight. . . . Only the gospel gives you a motivation for unselfish living that doesn't rob you of the benefits of unselfishness even as you enact it.[24]

The Apostle Paul says essentially the same thing in Ephesians, where he indicates that the church contributes to the cosmic task of reconciliation in three ways: 1) By overcoming hostility between Jew and Gentile and creation of "one new man" through Christ (2:11–22). 2) Through growth in the knowledge and love of Christ (3:19; 4:13). And 3) with deeds of goodness, justice, and truth, as well as exposure of the works of darkness (2:10; 5:8–11).[25]

---

22. McKnight, *A Community Called Atonement*, 84.
23. Ibid., 88, 126.
24. Keller, *King's Cross*, 151.
25. Mott, *Biblical Ethics and Social Change*, 103.

Conclusion: the Exodus and New Creation

The entrance of Jesus into the world through the incarnation can be viewed in two ways—his coming to earth from heaven was both "from above" and "from the end."[26] It will become more apparent as we proceed that "heaven" is another way of speaking about the "age to come," the time when the evil of this age will be totally defeated and the hope of final restoration will be fully realized. When Jesus "came down from heaven," he brought some of heaven with him. "The kingdom of God is in the midst of you," he said to his disciples (Lk 17:21 RSV). Through his words and acts of healing he was beginning to bring the heaven of the "end of time" (eschatology) into the middle (history).[27] The apostle Paul therefore describes the church as the community of believers "on whom the fulfillment of the ages has come" (1 Cor 10:11).

Jesus' incarnation, followed by his ministry, death and resurrection, collectively comprise the great climatic entrance and saving act of God on the stage of human history. But the New Testament presents this ultimate story of redemption through the lens of the other great saving action of God—the exodus of the Israelites out of Egypt. The clearest reference to the exodus in the Gospels is found in the account of Jesus' encounter with Moses and Elijah on the Mount of Transfiguration. Here, Jesus' impending death, or hour of fulfillment, is described as a "departure" (lit. *exodus*). As Luke describes this event:

> And behold, two men were talking with him, Moses and Elijah, who appeared in glory and spoke of his departure, which he was about to accomplish at Jerusalem (9:30–31 ESV).

Unfortunately, the significance of this passage is lost in English versions, which translate the Greek word *exodus* as "his departure."[28] In this passage the "exodus," which was achieved for the nation of Israel under Moses, is compared to the death of Jesus on the cross. To repeat what was said earlier, there is a "gospel" in exodus and an "exodus" in the gospel.[29] The exodus was not just a saving event or "divine rescue" from bondage; it was a "saving relationship," a means by which Israel was to become for God a "treasured possession" and a "holy people." But it turns out that Israel's exodus out of Egypt is simply a preview of a far greater saving event: the cross.[30]

26. Vanhoozer, *Faith Speaking Understanding*, 93.
27. Ibid.
28. Wright, *The Mission of God's People*, 103.
29. Vanhoozer, *Faith Speaking Understanding*, 93
30. Ibid.

Israel's deliverance from bondage looks forward to Jesus' "exodus," by which there would be deliverance from a far worse bondage, the bondage of sin.

To take the above analogy even further, just as the exodus foreshadows the cross, so those who are made to be "in Christ" through his death and resurrection in *this age* are called to be a "sneak preview" of the final defeat of sin, evil, and death in the *age to come*. In his letter to the church in Corinth the Apostle Paul describes the death and resurrection of Christ as the great apocalyptic event which signals the end of the old age and portends the beginning of the new.[31] Those who have died and risen "in him" are, he says, "a new creation" (2 Cor 5:14–17). Richard Hays describes the church as a "new creation" in this way:

> *The church embodies the power of the resurrection in the midst of a not–yet redeemed world.* . . . In the present time, the new creation already appears, but only proleptically; consequently, we hang in suspension between Jesus' resurrection and Parousia. . . . In Christ we know that the powers of the old age are doomed, and the new creation is already appearing. Yet at the same time, all attempts to assert the unqualified presence of the kingdom of God stand under judgment of the eschatological reservation: not before the time, not yet.[32]

All of this, of course, has deep relevance for how we approach the Lord's Supper. In chapter one, I noted that the Bible speaks of this ordinance as being not just a recollection of Jesus' death. It is also the "real presence" of Jesus. It celebrates the "in-breaking" of God's kingdom into the world, and especially into the lives of believers and the life of the church. It is, as Vanhoozer argues, a "theater of the gospel" inasmuch as it communicates what being in "communion with" Christ means, at both the spiritual level (our union with Christ) and at the social level (our community with one another in Christ).[33] At the same time, the fact that we are to proclaim Christ's death *until he comes* is a reminder that we stand in the juncture of the "now and not yet." This creates a critical framework which opposes presumptuous triumphalism as well as complacency and despair.[34]

In the next three chapters we will explore these themes in greater detail. We will see how the "new exodus"/"new creation" motifs are developed in three New Testament passages that either directly or indirectly refer to the Last Supper. My purpose will also be to draw out some practical

---

31. Hays, *The Moral Vision of the New Testament*, 19.
32. Ibid., 198.
33. Vanhoozer, *Faith Speaking Understanding*, 160–65.
34. Hays, *The Moral Framework of the New Testament*, 198.

applications for the church as a community of faith. I will first look at two passages from the Gospel of John—the feeding of the multitude (Jn 6:1–50) and Jesus' washing of his disciples feet (Jn 13:1–17). Then, I will survey Paul's instructions to the church in Corinth, particularly as they relate to the church's practice of the Lord's Supper (1 Cor 11:17–34).

6

Feeding of the Multitude and Manna in the Wilderness

CHARLES Dickens' novel *Oliver Twist* portrays the degrading effects of poverty in nineteenth century English society. With poverty came desperate hunger. The story revolves around Oliver Twist who was born in a workhouse in the 1830s. His mother, whose name no one knew, was found on the street and died just after Oliver's birth. At the age of nine, he was transferred to a workhouse for young children, where he was the victim of slow starvation. His diet consisted of three small bowls of oatmeal gruel a day, with an onion twice a week, and a roll on Sunday. Under this regimen, Oliver and the other boys were reduced to living skeletons. Their voracious hunger caused them to take desperate measures. In a council meeting, they resolved to pick by lottery one of their number who would ask the overseer for more gruel. Oliver was the unlucky one who was chosen. That evening the boys took their places around the tables. The gruel was served and grace was said over the scant food. After the gruel had disappeared, the boys whispered among themselves and winked at Oliver. His neighbors nudged him. Desperate with hunger and reckless with misery, Oliver rose from his table and advanced to the master. "Please sir," he said, "I want some more." The master, a fat and healthy man, gazed at the boy in astonishment. "What?" he said in a faint voice. "I want some more," replied Oliver. At this, the master aimed a blow at the boy's head with the ladle and grasped him in his arm. Oliver was sent into instant confinement. The next morning, a sign was posted outside the gate offering a reward of five pounds to anyone who would take Oliver Twist off of the hands of the parish.

John 6 tells the story of another feeding, but with strikingly different results. In this account, the large crowd which follows Jesus is provided with as much food as they want. In fact, there is so much food that the disciples gather twelve baskets of leftovers (6:11–13).

The Symbolic Significance of the Feeding of the Multitude

Jesus uses this miraculous feeding of the multitude to teach deeper spiritual truths. He employs the core symbol of bread to convey transcendent realities.[1] But we should bear in mind that the image of "bread" contains *multiple* meanings. In other words, the multiplication of bread signifies several things simultaneously.[2]

The Feeding of the Multitude, the Passover, and the Last Supper

In both the Synoptic Gospels and John, the juxtaposition of Jesus' water crossing with the feeding of the multitude recalls the crossing of the Red Sea and Moses' provision of manna for Israel in the wilderness at the exodus. All of the Gospels therefore intentionally present Jesus' miraculous feeding as a new exodus.[3] John makes this connection with the exodus even more explicit by describing Jesus' miracle as taking place near the time of the Jewish Passover (6:3).[4] Furthermore, the image of Jesus taking the bread, giving thanks, and distributing it to the people (6:11; cf. Matt 14:19) foreshadows the Last Supper with his disciples.[5]

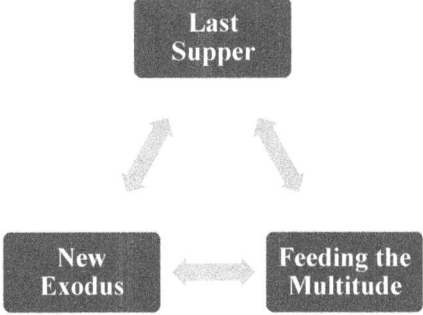

Figure 4: Feeding of the Multitude, New Exodus, and Last Supper

1. Koester, *Symbolism in the Fourth Gospel*, 4–5.
2. Ibid., 25.
3. See Pennington, "The Lord's Last Supper," 49.
4. Kostenberger, *A Theology of John's Gospel and Letters*, 211.
5. Ibid.

This connection of the feeding of the multitude with the new exodus and the Last Supper comes into even greater focus in Jesus' "bread of life" discourse, where he describes himself as the *"bread of God" who comes down from heaven and gives eternal (or everlasting) life* (6:26, 33, 47–50). Later in this discourse Jesus more explicitly associates the true bread with his crucifixion (6:53–58). So Jesus is basically echoing his earlier well-known statement to Nicodemus: "For God so loved the world that he gave his one and only Son, that whoever believes in him should not perish but have eternal life" (3:16). These words express the ultimate paradox that the death of Christ is both the ultimate expression of God's love and the source of true life in God.[6]

The Meaning of Eternal Life

We humans naturally order our desires and affections (even if unconsciously) in such a way as to achieve a vision of human flourishing and the "good life." But it is worth asking ourselves whether our affections and desires are correctly oriented toward that which truly gives life.[7] As someone once wisely asserted: "It would be a tragedy to climb the ladder of success only to find it leaning against the wrong wall!" Various studies of contemporary society have found that increased technology, bureaucracy, individualism, mobility, and consumerism have created a deep sense of social isolation and rootlessness, or homelessness.[8] Increased technological capacities, the tendency to find one's identity in work, and the lack of stable roots have contributed to fewer friendships and less meaningful relationships.[9]

It is critical, then, that we have a correct understanding of Jesus' description of himself as the "bread of life." Often, our assumption is that in referring to himself as the source of "life" or "eternal life" Jesus is referring to longevity of life—that our souls will live forever in postmortem bliss. But this common spiritualized and individualistic interpretation does not adequately express the real meaning of the concept. Although the idea of duration is not absent from the word "eternal" (*aiones*) that John uses, the primary emphasis is on the *quality* of life that Jesus brings.[10] In Jewish

---

6. Koester states: "It is by dying that Jesus reveals the love of God, and when this love evokes faith, it brings people into the relationship with God that is true life (3:16)" (*Word of Life* 123). See also Gorman, *The Death of the Messiah*, 47.

7. Jipp, *Saved by Faith and Hospitality*, 77–8.

8. See Berger, Berger, and Kellner, *The Homeless Mind*.

9. Jipp, *Saved by Faith and Hospitality*, 78.

10. See Tasker, *The Gospel According to St. John*, 71–72.

thinking, "eternal" literally means "life of the age." It refers to the "new age" when God's good, loving, just, and life-giving purpose will be realized in a new heaven and new earth.[11]

Imagine, for a moment, what heaven (lit. the "new heaven and new earth") will be like. What will be the greatest "reward" of heaven? Most assuredly it will be close intimacy with the One who spoke the entire universe into existence and the One to whom we owe our own existence. At the very heart of the "life of the age" that John is referring to is the saving presence of the God who is the source of all other beauty, joy, and pleasure (Jn 17:3). So, while the idea of "quantity of life" is not absent in John's thinking, what he stresses is a new and different "quality of life"—or having life more abundantly through Christ (Jn 10:10).[12] Furthermore, this intimacy with God isn't experienced in isolation. Humans are joined in fellowship with one another. There will be a joyous reunification with loved ones, friends, and fellow believers—all joining in worship of our Creator. In short, eternity will be a "worshiping fellowship" in which we celebrate our redemption and liberation.[13]

The biblical writers describe this new life in the final age of salvation as a great banquet. *The feeding of the multitude is a prefiguring of this future banquet.* But—and this is a crucial point—while this "new life" is most fully experienced in the "age to come;" John presents it something that can be experienced to a significant degree in the here and now (Jn 3:36; 5:24). The promise of "eternal life" is thus not of some future "pie in the sky." It has immediate and fundamental bearing on present everyday life.[14]

The "New Creation" in John's Gospel

Before looking at Jesus' bread of life discourse in greater detail, it is important that we consider another theme which runs like a red thread throughout John's Gospel. That is the idea of the "new creation." This is foundational to John's message; and it provides the broader theological context for understanding Jesus' description of himself as the "bread of life." The relationship between Jesus' statement, "I am the bread of life" (6:48) and the theme of "new creation" can be shown as follows:

---

11. Carter, *John and Empire*, 209–210.
12. Tasker, *The Gospel According to St. John*, 71–72. See also, Turner, "Soteriology in the Gospel of John," 276.
13. McKnight, *A Community Called Atonement*, 25–26.
14. Cook, "Eschatology in John's Gospel," 88, 99.

"I Am the Bread of Life" (Jn 6:48)		
Prologue (1:1–18)	The Book of Signs (1:19–12:50)	Passion Narrative (18:1–21:25)
God the Creator dwelling among us	God's glory displayed in Jesus	Jesus as the "new Adam"

Table 2. Jesus as the Bread of Life and the New Creation in John's Gospel

The Prologue (1:1–18)

John begins his Gospel with the affirmation: "In the beginning was the Word, and the Word was with God, and the Word was God . . . Through him all things were made . . . In him was life, and that life was the light of men" (Jn 1:1–4). John's words are clearly intended to point the reader back to the original creation story (Gen 1:1) and tie Jesus with creation.[15] The themes of "life" and "light," which are found throughout John's Gospel, are intertwined and constitute creation terminology. These creation motifs indicate that John is espousing a "new creation" theology that presents Jesus' coming and mission as God's eschatological renewal of his original creation.[16]

John's prologue reaches its climax in 1:14 where he states: "The Word became flesh and made his dwelling among us. We have seen his glory, the glory of the One and Only, who came from the Father, full of grace and truth " The word that John uses for "dwelt" or "dwelling" can also be translated "tabernacled" or "pitched his tent."[17] It is an obvious reference to the original tabernacle of the exodus, which, as we have seen, was a "microcosmos" or picture of the entire creation. Just as the divine glory was located in the tabernacle (and later temple), John says, so now it has come to dwell in the incarnate Son of God. The rest of this Gospel makes clear that "grace" points to God's love as manifested through Jesus' actions while "truth" is a reference to his words.[18] With this imagery, John is placing his "Christodrama" squarely within the context of Israel's story.[19] He is describing the "ultimate exodus" through which God's glory is revealed and creation itself is rescued and renewed to be a new creation.[20]

15. Emerson, *Christ and the New Creation*, 57.
16. Kostenberger, *A Theology of John's Gospel and Letters*, 337.
17. Ibid., 406.
18. Tasker, *The Gospel According to St. John*, 48.
19. Kostenberger, *A Theology of John's Gospel and Letters*, 412.
20. Wright, "The Royal Revolution," 7.

The Book of Signs (1:19—12:50)

The theme of new creation can also be seen in the "signs" which John emphasizes in the first half of his Gospel. These signs point to God's glory displayed in Jesus. Their purpose is to elicit faith (Jn 20:30–31). The first of the signs that Jesus performs is the changing of water into wine at the wedding of Cana, which John describes as beginning on "the third day" (2:1). As I will discuss in greater detail in chapter fourteen, this miracle points forward to Jesus' death and resurrection. It also foreshadows the future wedding supper of the Lamb (Rev 19:6–9; cf. Jn 1:29) and final "marriage" of heaven and earth (Rev 21). John concludes this account by describing it as the first of Jesus' miraculous signs which "revealed his glory" (2:11), thereby connecting the signs with the prologue and pointing us forward to a sequence of signs.[21]

In this section there are a total of six signs: 1) the changing of water into wine (1:1–11); 2) the healing of the nobleman's son (4:46–54); 3) the healing of the lame man (5:1–15); 4) the feeding of the multitude (6:1–15); 5) the healing of a blind man (9:1–41); and 6) the raising of Lazarus (11:1–57). What is unmistakable is that each of these signs is concerned with the redemptive transformation of the old creation and the ushering in of the new.[22] Even the multiplication of loaves and fishes is a "new creation" story in that it points us to God's provision for the new people of God, just as he provided for the Israelites in the wilderness following the exodus.[23]

But John doesn't stop there. Numbers are significant in the Bible. And the number 6 carries little significance compared to the number 7. This is true also of John's Gospel. As he indicates in chapter 12 and in the Passion Narrative, the seventh and greatest sign—that which all of the other signs point to—is the cross, Jesus' death and resurrection. The cross is where God's glory is supremely revealed.[24]

At the end of this section, where the first half of the Gospel comes together, John describes Jesus' triumphal entry as fulfillment of the messianic prophecies of Isaiah (12:12–19). Then, following Jesus' prediction of his death, comes a crucial passage: "Now is the judgment of the world, now the prince of this world will be driven out. But I, when I am lifted up from the earth, will draw all people to myself" (12:31–32). These words of Jesus are an echo of the time when the Israelites were healed by looking at the bronze

---

21. Wright, *Following Jesus*, 34.
22. Emerson, *Christ and the New Creation*, 58.
23. Ibid., 59.
24. Wright, *Following Jesus*, 35.

serpent that Moses put on a pole in the desert (Num 24; cf. Jn 3:14–16). Similarly, the whole world would find healing and new life through Jesus' dying love. "Jesus' death will be the means by which the power that has gripped the world of Greek and Jew alike will be overthrown by a greater power," the revolutionary power of royal love.[25]

The Passion Narrative (18:1—21:25)

The Book of Signs is followed by the Farewell Discourse (13:1—17:26) and the Passion Narrative (18:1—21:25). The Passion Narrative at the end of the Gospel builds on all of the previous references that we have alluded to and sets Jesus' crucifixion and resurrection within the context of a new creation.[26] There are a number of features unique to John's Gospel which indicate this. First, unlike the other gospels, John sets the Passion Narrative in a garden (18:1, 26; 19:41). This may be an allusion to the original garden of Eden. Secondly, Pilate's reference to Jesus as "the man" (19:5) may be understood as a "double entendre" which identifies Jesus as the "new Adam." Third, Jesus' breathing on his disciples and giving of the Spirit in the final scene (20:22) invokes the image of God breathing into Adam the breath of life (Gen 2:7).[27]

We can conclude that John's entire Passion Narrative "reverberates with 'new creation' theology, harking back to the opening references to the original creation in the introduction to the Gospel."[28] So John's Gospel is the gospel equivalent to the book of Revelation, which ends with the New Jerusalem as an eschatological consummation of what began in the garden of Eden.[29]

Responding to Jesus as the Bread of Life

One of the central questions that John raises in his account of the feeding of the multitude is, what kind of Messiah is Jesus? A related question is this: How should we respond to Jesus? Throughout this episode, the unbelief of the crowd is contrasted with the belief of the disciples. The crowd, which

---

25. Wright, "The Royal Revolution," 10.

26. Kostenberger, *A Theology of John's Gospel and Letters*, 352.

27. Ibid. See also Emerson, *Christ and the New Creation*, 59–60; and Wright, *Following Jesus*, 39.

28. Kostenberger, *A Theology of John's Gospel and Letters*, 352.

29. Ibid.

misunderstands the miraculous feeding by Jesus on the mountain, tries to make him king to suit their own liking. Their demand that Jesus act on their terms is a form of unbelief.[30] In response to this unbelief, Jesus gives the bread-of-life-discourse, after which Peter confesses: "You have the words of eternal life" (6:68). My purpose in what follows will be to highlight some key points in this episode.

The Response of the Crowd (6:14–15)

In the Roman Empire during Jesus' time, life for most people was a constant struggle for survival. While famine was rare, food shortages were frequent. Food production, distribution, and consumption were controlled by an elitist, hierarchical, and oppressive political and economic system. The imperial system was characterized by abundance for a few and deprivation for many.[31] For the most part, the elite were not involved in efforts to alleviate poverty and hunger. To the extent that there was any philanthropy, those in power often used feeding as a tool of reward and punishment to consolidate their own power and control the masses. This is probably the reason why Jesus makes the sobering statement, "You will always have the poor among you" (Jn 12:8).[32] Given this historical situation, it is not surprising that there was a revolutionary messianism among the Jews which sought to overthrow Roman rule. There was also a common Jewish expectation that a prophet—a new Moses—would come and restore the gift of manna.

In John's account of the feeding of the multitude, the people who are fed (like the typical crowd in a Greco–Roman city) have little interest in anything but bread. As Craig Koester remarks, the mob's readiness to make Jesus king on the basis of bread distribution (6:15) would have been consistent with popular expectations among the Jews in the Greco–Roman world. Most could not move beyond the material level. Jesus recognizes this, so he says to those who have followed him, "You are looking for me, not because you saw miraculous signs but because you ate the loaves and had your fill" (6:26). But this is an orientation which he rejects.[33]

The popular response to Jesus contains an important lesson for us. Like the crowd, the image we have of Jesus can become a projection of our physical and materialistic desires. Don't get me wrong. There are many stories in the Bible of God's material provision. The entire context of this

---

30. Koester, *Symbolism in the Fourth Gospel*, 99.
31. Carter, *John and Empire*, 221.
32. Longenecker, *Remember the Poor*, 107.
33. Koester, *Symbolism in the Fourth Gospel*, 54–59.

episode indicates that Jesus himself cared about the physical needs of people (Jn 6:2; cf. Matt 14:14). I further agree with those who argue that asceticism, or the denial of pleasure, is just as unscriptural as materialism. But in our affluent society, the "gospel" of the American dream is easily confused with the gospel of the kingdom. The subtle attraction of the prosperity gospel is indicated by the popularity of television preachers like Joyce Meyer, who is reported in *Time* magazine to have said: "Who would want to get in on something where you're miserable, poor, broke and ugly and you have to muddle through until you get to heaven? I believe God wants to give us nice things."[34] Skye Jethani aptly comments, "She has a point. Who would want an uncontrollable, mysterious, and holy God when you could have a genie in a Bible?"[35]

Kathi and I are part of a multicultural church called Christian Neighbor's Church (CNC), which is located in a poorer section of the city of Waukegan, IL. Many members of the congregation live in substandard housing; some can't even afford a car. We have often wondered how the tendency of Christians in American society to use material comfort as a barometer of God's blessing affects those who barely scrape by from day to day. Almost half of the world's 6 billion people live on less than $2 a day. About 1.5 billion live on less than $1 a day.[36] Many of the world's poor are Christians. Is God less faithful or good to these poor fellow believers? Are they lacking in material possessions because they have less faith than the rest of us? It is true that the allure of "health and wealth" promised by the prosperity gospel is often most strongly felt among the poor. For rich and poor alike, too much of an emphasis on the checkout line puts our loves out of order. By contrast, Jesus' teaching on the kingdom of God relativizes and puts into proper perspective what the gospel of the checkout line says is essential. Most importantly, it places a highest priority on love for God and others.[37]

The Response of Faith (6:26–71)

When Jesus says to the crowd that they are seeking him because they ate their fill and not because they "saw the signs" (Jn 6:26), he is indicating

---

34. Biema and Chu, "Does God Want You to Be Rich?"
35. Jethani, *The Divine Commodity*, 35
36. Blim, *Equality and Economy*, 1
37. See Lawson, "The Gospel According to Safeway" 78. For a theological evaluation of the prosperity gospel in Africa, see Ehioghae, "A Theological Evaluation of the Utopian Image of Prosperity Gospel," 69–75.

that those whose lives are shaped by his words rather than by their own limited frame of reference are able to discern the meaning of the signs.[38] We have seen that in John's Gospel the signs of Jesus are meant to elicit faith (Jn 20:30–31). They point to God's glory displayed in Jesus and convey the new creation which becomes a reality for those who believe in him. They express an entirely different order of things.[39] Therefore, in the first part of the sermon (26–34) Jesus deliberately contrasts: 1) the bread that perishes and the bread that endures to eternal life (vs 27); and 2) the physical manna that Moses provided for the Israelites in the wilderness and the bread of God which comes down from heaven *and gives life to the world* (32–34). As N. T. Wright states, the people are looking for "a king like other kings, a strong this-worldly figure who would lead them in their strong this-worldly agendas."[40] Jesus is indeed a king, but his kingship is very different from what the crowd expects or wants. Jesus' feeding is a sign that points to the true food provided by the "Son of Man" (v 27). In the Old Testament, the expression "Son of Man" is a reference to the Messiah's divine sonship. Both the psalmist and Daniel picture the Messiah as enthroned beside God (Ps 110:1 Dan 7:13–14). So, what truly matters is who Jesus is. Only if we are prepared to be confronted in a new way by the nature of Jesus' kingship can we begin to understand what he does for us.[41]

In the rest of his sermon Jesus weaves together a number of themes, which I can only briefly summarize here. Clearly, the most important phrase is the expression: "I am the bread of life," or "I am the living bread." The words "I am" are repeated by Jesus at three critical junctures in this sermon (35, 48, 51), and they anticipate other "I am" sayings in John's Gospel (e.g., 8:12, "I am the light of the world"). In this context, the expression connects several key ideas. First, as I have already suggested, Jesus is intimating that the God who confronted Moses with his identity ("I Am who I Am," Exod 3:14) and was at work in the exodus is the same God who is at work in his own life and ministry. In fact, in describing himself as the "bread that came down from heaven" (vs 38), he is identifying his own person with the God of the exodus story.[42]

Secondly, Jesus connects his description of himself as the "bread of life" with the promise that whoever believes in him will be raised up by him in the last day (vss 39–40, 44). This seems to be a clear reference to

38. Koester, *Symbolism in the Fourth Gospel*, 99.
39. Ibid.100.
40. Wright, *John for Everyone*, 78.
41. Ibid., 79.
42. Ibid., 80.

the resurrection life which he had previously described to his disciples (5:25–29). Jesus further describes the "last day" as the time when all people "will be taught by God" (vs 45). This is a clear reference to Isaiah's prophecy of a great renewal, when Israel will be brought out of exile (Isa 54:13). Isaiah goes on to invite everyone who thirsts to "come to the waters" (55:1)—an image which is repeated by Jesus in his sermon ("whoever believes in me shall never thirst," vs 35). Jesus probably has this entire passage from Isaiah in mind.[43] The "eternal life" that he offers is, as we have seen, not simply "life after death;" it is a quality of life of the "age to come." It is the resurrection life which is God's plan for the world in the future, but which begins (however partially) in the present when someone believes in Jesus.[44]

The final connection Jesus makes is between his identity as the "living bread" and eating his flesh and drinking his blood (6:51–59). Much has been written about this passage. It is commonly recognized by New Testament scholars that the words by Jesus foreshadow the eucharistic food and drink, which he will give his disciples in the Last Supper. As one commentator has noted, the most notable feature of the last part of this discourse is how the miraculous feeding of the multitude, Jesus' death, and teaching relevant to the sacrament of communion are all blended together.[45] But in what sense do believers ingest the flesh and blood of Jesus? Some spiritualize this passage, so that it refers to the inward, non-physical event of meditation on the meaning of Jesus' death. However, the word that Jesus uses for "eat" in verses 54–58 has physical connotations. In the Greek it often has the meaning of "munch" or "chew." Jesus is therefore saying that in some mysterious way his body and blood are offered to believers to be eaten and drunk.[46] In chapter one I gave scriptural support for the Reformed view of the "real presence" of Jesus in the Eucharist. John Calvin, for example, argued that in the ingesting of the elements in the Eucharist (an act which is intimated in John 6) there is a real communication of and communion with the risen Christ through the Holy Spirit.[47] This seems to be the meaning of Jesus' words that whoever feeds on his flesh and drinks his blood "abides in me, and I in him" (6:56). This union with Christ takes place through the Spirit, who gives life to those who believe (6:63).

---

43. Ibid., 83.

44. Ibid., 84.

45. Tasker, *The Gospel According to St. John*, 95–96. See also Bird, *Evangelical Theology*, 788; and Pitre, *Jesus and the Jewish Roots of the Eucharist*, 101.

46. Wright, *John for Everyone*, 86.

47. Bird, *Evangelical Theology*, 788–90.

John indicates that at the end of this teaching many would-be disciples turn away and no longer walk with Jesus. Only Peter and his other closest disciples believe that he is "the Holy One of God" (6:68–9).

John 6 and the Church's Mission

Ben Witherington observes that the Fourth Gospel is the "only canonical Gospel that gives us something like the whole plot or arc of the Christian narrative, from his pre-existent work in creation (Jn 1:1–18) to his Parousia (Jn 21:20–23)."[48] Furthermore, Witherington continues, the "V-pattern" strongly affects John's portrayal of Jesus as the One who came down from heaven and must return to heaven. Jesus is the Wisdom come in flesh who is "both the means and the end of understanding if one wants to know the 'way, the truth, and the life.'"[49] He, in other words, is the key to the meaning of human existence, the source of life and human flourishing which all people seek. In John's portrayal of Jesus' words in the bread-of-life discourse, the bread and wine of the Eucharist are a foretaste of the day when the earth will be flooded with God's presence (6:53–58). We have to bear in mind that in this passage Jesus is not just talking *about* God's new age. Peter's confession, "You have the words of eternal life" (6:68) is an acknowledgement that by his words Jesus is *already* bringing into existence the life of the age to come.[50] The pre-existent One who spoke the world into existence is also the "Word made Flesh" (Jn 1:14) who brings a new creation through his death and resurrection.

It is on this basis that we should understand the church's mission. Again, what must be emphasized is that salvation is basically wholeness, the restoration of God's original intention for creation. We must therefore speak of the whole gospel—a gospel which is individual and corporate, vertical and horizontal, and spiritual and physical.[51] The mission of the church is to participate in God's work of redemption whereby he brings life, wholeness, and healing to those who are alienated from him and each other. In his insightful book *Saved by Faith and Hospitality*, Joshua Jipp shows that hospitality is another fundamental theme in the Fourth Gospel. As the episode of the feeding of the multitude demonstrates, the hospitality that Jesus offers consists of the very physical and tangible elements of human life. No one has life apart from food, drink, and friendship. But at a deeper level, the

---

48. Witherington, *New Testament Theology and Ethics, Vol. One*, 547.
49. Ibid.
50. Wright, *John for Everyone*, 88–92.
51. See Guder, *Be My Witnesses*, 175.

hospitality that Jesus gives satisfies our spiritual craving for transcendence and ultimate meaning—for life with God and the freedom it brings. The church should be the community where the life-giving and transformative presence of Christ is most clearly manifested and through which his promise of eternal life is made known to the world.[52] In Christian Neighbors Church there are stories of release from bondage to drugs and alcohol; of freedom from homelessness, sexual slavery (trafficking), and incarceration to new life in Christ; and of reconciliation, both with God and with others across racial and cultural boundaries.

In the city of Waukegan there is a homeless shelter called PADS (Providing Advocacy, Dignity, and Shelter), which is confronted with the attitude of nimbyism (not in my backyard). Hostile neighbors have accused the homeless of littering, although it is abundantly clear that this is a community-wide problem. The city council prevented the shelter from providing showers for the homeless on the grounds that it violated local zoning ordinances. And it denied a permit for expansion and renovation of its facilities. There has been obvious pressure from the city for PADS to relocate to another community. In response, various churches, including our own, have banded together to support PADS. Volunteers have been organized to pick up trash that accumulates in the areas surrounding the shelter. Bethel Lutheran Church, which is located in a neighboring community of Gurnee, has further assisted the homeless by providing showers in its building and transporting them to and from the shelter. At one point during this controversy, Rev. Ben Squires, the pastor of this particular congregation, was out in the neighborhood around PADS with other volunteers picking up trash. What caught his eye was the juxtaposition of flowers and trash. So he took a "prayer walk" from Gurnee to Waukegan, during which he took a series of pictures, a number of which showed trash intermixed with the beauty of flowers—or what he called "beautified trash." Part of pastor Squires' purpose was to show that the "trash problem" is not limited to areas surrounding the shelter. But he also hoped that the photographs would inspire a more coordinated effort to address the problem. This photo exhibit was displayed in our church. Residents, pastors, and city officials were invited to a reception as part of the exhibit for the purpose of creating a healthy dialogue around the issue of homelessness in our communities.[53]

In some respects, the above story serves as a modern-day parable of how God through Christ can transform the "trash" in our lives individually

---

52. Jipp, *Saved by Faith and Hospitality*, 92–3.

53. Coleman, "Controversy Over PADS." At the present time, these issues surrounding PADS and the homeless population in Waukegan have not been resolved.

and corporately to create something beautiful, to his glory. Jesus used parables to subvert conventional wisdom and point people to the in-breaking reality of God's kingdom. The church is similarly called to perform parables of the kingdom inaugurated in Christ—to exemplify the truth, goodness, and beauty of the gospel by "speaking the truth in love, calling for justice, forgiving rather than judging, and creating a place for undistorted communication by lifting up every voice."[54] Certainly, like every other church, our congregation and other congregations in Waukegan and the neighboring communities are far from perfect. All of us, both individually and collectively, live in the tension between the "now" and "not yet" of the gospel. Jesus' bread-of-life sermon challenges us in our brokenness to grow in our understanding of the Lord's Supper, as both a preview and an anticipation of the future heavenly banquet when eternal life will be experienced in its fullness.

---

54. Vanhoozer, *Faith Speaking Understanding*, 181–82.

7

The Meaning of Servanthood and the Last Supper

THERE are churches today which go to great lengths to make the Lord's Supper culturally relevant for modern-day churchgoers. To accommodate the hectic pace of life, one drive-in church in Florida mimics fast-food restaurants like McDonalds and Burger King by giving communion bread and juice in sealed plastic containers as people drive in and then listen to the service from their cars.[1] Even more extreme is the view of some proponents of "virtual churches," which use on–line networks like Facebook, that individuals can "participate" in the sacraments of baptism and the Lord's Supper by meditating on the image of the sacrament on the computer screen.[2]

Ben Witherington describes the innovative approach to the Lord's Supper of one seeker-friendly church in a large northern city. Everyone present would be invited to participate. And, to reflect the casualness of the attire and proceedings, they made up a large batch of Kool–Aid and brought an assortment of tasty crackers. In the middle of the service, "Communion" was served. At the end of the service, a first-time visitor came up to the pastor and remarked, "You know what I liked best about the service?" "No," replied the pastor, "do tell me." She then said, "I liked that you stopped what you were doing and we all had snacks in the middle. That was very nice." A bit taken back, the pastor described an unacceptable image which flashed through his mind—"This is my snack, given for you."[3] Referring to our

---

1. Anderson, "The Business of Busyness," 156.
2. See Estes, *SimChurch*, 115–29.
3. Witherington, *Making a Meal of It*, x–xi.

need to rethink the meaning and practice of Lord's Supper in our culture, Witherington remarks, "We need to relearn how to make a meal of it rather than a mess of it, as we so often do."[4]

Granted, the above cases are extreme examples. But, they illustrate a general tendency to diminish what is arguably the most significant ordinance of the church. Why is this the case? In part, I would suggest, it is because we have tended to reduce the gospel to abstract theories about the atonement which do not directly impact the way we live our daily lives. N. T. Wright highlights this problem when he states that we need "a larger vision of the biblical narrative if we are to understand, preach and live out the message and meaning of the cross."[5] This is *not* to minimize the importance of doctrinal correctness. But, as Wright argues, theories about the atonement are "signposts" that point toward a larger reality.[6] It is significant that when Jesus wants to impress on his followers what his death would mean, he doesn't just give them a "doctrine" or creed. He also gives them a meal along with a dramatic "in flesh" demonstration of sacrificial service—he washes their feet (Jn 13:1–20). In this most humble act and the lengthy sermon which follows, he focuses on the creation of a new countercultural community characterized by mutual love, service, unity, and solidarity which is rooted in his own supreme act of sacrificial love on the cross.

The Historical Setting

For us to gain a clearer picture of what Jesus is saying in this crucial passage we need to be aware of the historical setting, both of the Fourth Gospel and the readers to which the Gospel is written and of Jesus' own actions in the days leading up to his death. Fortunately, modern scholarship has given us significant insight into this historical context and the pastoral issues facing the Christian community that are addressed by John's Gospel (as well as his three epistles).[7]

The Johannine Community

The community to which the Fourth Gospel is written is predominately made up of Jewish Christians. While their exact location is unknown, it

---

4. Ibid., 141–42.
5. Wright, "The Royal Revolution," 16.
6. Ibid., 5.
7. Hays, *The Moral Vision of the New Testament*, 146.

is likely that they lived in major urban centers such as Ephesus and in surrounding towns. Initially, they maintained membership in the local synagogue and participated in the Jewish festivals. But their efforts to convince other Jews that Jesus was the Messiah often brought them into conflict with the majority who rejected their claims about Jesus.[8]

Sometime after the destruction of Jerusalem in 70 A.D. the Jewish Christians were expelled from participation in the synagogue. The trauma experienced by this small group of Johannine Christians of being declared *aposynagogos* ("put out of the synagogue") has been described by one author in this way:

> The Christians who were expelled would have been cut off from much that had given identity and structure to their lives. Expulsion would have meant social ostracism and thus the loss of relationship with family and friends, and perhaps economic dislocation as well. It would certainly have meant religious dislocation. The synagogue meetings, the public liturgy, the festivals and observances were all now denied them, and the authoritative interpretation of sacred scripture itself was in the hands of their opponents. What was threatened was thus the entire universe of shared perceptions, assumptions, beliefs, ideals, and hopes that had given meaning to their world within Judaism.[9]

It is probably no coincidence that the only New Testament books that explicitly refer to this expulsion are the Fourth Gospel (see Jn 9:22; 12:42; 16:2) and Revelation. The community of believers to which John is writing is under duress and faces persecution. Some of the believers have even been martyred. Under these circumstances, John's readers are in need of teaching that will offer hope and encouragement and help them stand unified again false teachings and rejection in the synagogues and elsewhere.[10]

Bur the Johannine message is not simply a call for individual conversion or the acceptance of a set of beliefs. It is also a call for this group of believers to enter into a new type of community—a step which entails both a "dangerous social relocation" and a "public transfer of allegiance" to Jesus.[11] In the words of one biblical scholar, "We should not underestimate the risk [John] is asking them to take. . . . The group they are being asked to join has no status, no power, no place in the world. They are being asked to

---

8. Ibid.
9. Quoted in Ibid.
10. Witherington, *New Testament Theology and Ethics*, 550.
11. Hays, *The Moral Vision of the New Testament*, 147.

dislocate and displace themselves socially, to undertake an act of deliberate downward mobility. Quite possibly they are being asked to risk their lives."[12]

Jesus, the Temple, and the Roman Empire

It is crucial that we keep this experience of the Johannine community in mind as we read John's account of the events leading up to Jesus' passion. The Fourth Gospel is replete with references to Jesus as the new temple. In the prologue, John describes Jesus, the Word made flesh, as the "tabernacle" of God's presence (Jn 1:14). As we noted in the previous chapter, this description of Jesus also has strong "new exodus" and "new creation" overtones. Just as the glory of God filled the old tabernacle (Ex 40:34–35) so now God's glory has begun to burst forth in the person of Jesus, the incarnate God.[13]

We have further seen that, for the Jews, the temple was the place where heaven and earth are joined together. At the very beginning of his ministry, Jesus reveals to Nathan that "you will see heaven opened, and the angels of God ascending and descending on the Son of Man" (1:51). This statement is an allusion to God's appearance to Jacob at Bethel (Gen 28:12) which resulted in the building of a temporary altar/sanctuary as a precursor to the larger temple to be built in Jerusalem. In this Old Testament story the sanctuary at Bethel is pictured in a dream as a ladder to heaven with angels ascending and descending from God's presence (28:12–23). So, in effect, Jesus is identifying himself, and not the Jerusalem temple, as the primary link between heaven and earth.[14] In the very next chapter Jesus cleanses the temple and describes himself as the temple that will be destroyed and raised up in three days (2:18). Jesus' identification of himself as the "living water" (e.g., 4:14; 7:37–39) is also an allusion to the waters flowing from the temple.[15] Because the temple was a depiction of God's original creation, Jesus is also giving a creation image (Gen 2:10–14; cf. Ezek 47:1–12).

This description throughout John's Gospel of Jesus as a replacement for the temple culminates in his high priestly prayer before his crucifixion (chapter 17), where he speaks of himself as the high priest who consecrates himself so that his people may be sanctified and joined to God and to one another in an intimate, loving family relationship.[16] All of this provides the

12. Ibid., 147–48.
13. Beale and Kim, *God Dwells Among Us*, 82.
14. Ibid., 85.
15. Ibid., 85.
16. Wright, *Following Jesus*, 38.

necessary context for a proper understanding of the foot-washing story, in which Jesus removes his outer garments and takes on the role of a slave to cleanse the disciples. N. T. Wright clearly articulates the force of this scene in describing it as an "acted parable of what Jesus is about to accomplish through his incarnation and death. He has laid aside the garments of heaven to reveal his glory on the cross, cleansing his followers so that they can be part of God's new Temple, the microcosm of God's new creation."[17]

As we read through John's account of Jesus' washing of his disciples' feet, we are further impressed by the danger and intrigue surrounding this entire event. Jesus has just performed his sixth and most astounding miracle—the raising of Lazarus from the dead (11:38–44). Yet, even after having performed his miraculous signs, many Jews refuse to believe (12:37) and the chief priests and Pharisees plot to kill him (11:45). Even one of his disciples is conspiring against him. But, as is the case with the Johannine community, Jesus' conflict is not just with the religious establishment. His announcement of the coming of God's kingdom in his person also sets him at odds with the power and authority of the Roman government—a conflict of kingdoms which is most clearly evident in Jesus' trial before Pontius Pilate (19:1–11). Again, Jesus' statement that the ruler of this world is about to be cast out (12:31) by his death is not just a religious statement. It is a political affirmation that the powers of this world are defeated by an entirely different kind of power—the power of radical, transformative love.[18] This is why, with all the controversy and hostility surrounding him, Jesus chooses the Passover as the time to go to Jerusalem, where in the Upper Room with his disciples he couples the eating of a supper (13:2) with a powerful and moving demonstration of sacrificial service (13:3–5).[19]

---

17. Wright, *The Day the Revolution Began*, 412.

18. Wright, "The Royal Revolution," 11.

19. There is some question as to the nature of the "farewell dinner" referred to in 13:2. Witherington argues that this meal (or series of meals) occurred sometime during the week of the Unleavened Bread/Passover celebration but not necessarily on the eve of Passover. Consequently, the Fourth Evangelist does not portray the dinner as a Passover meal or make any connection to the Last Supper. "Instead of a Passover meal, we have a portrayal of a Greco-Roman banquet complete with closing symposium and the religious rites associated with such a meal" (*Making a Meal of It*, 64-65). McKnight argues, however, that the exact day of the meal is really unimportant. "Passover was an eight-day event and not simply a one-night meal. Every meal during Passover would be Passover-like." What matters is that "Jesus 'storifies' his death by setting that death in the context of *Passover and exodus*" (*A Community Called Atonement*, 83–84)

Cruciformity: Spirituality of the Cross

The section of John generally referred to as the "Farewell Discourse" (chaps 13–17), which looks forward to the crucifixion, is basically an extended commentary on the claim that Jesus' death creates a community of people who are forgiven by God and restored to a new covenantal relationship with him.[20] This new covenant community is empowered by his Spirit to live a life of cruciform or cross-shaped love for God and one another. Jesus' washing of his disciples' feet is therefore a paradigmatic act of self-giving love which enjoins his disciples to *participate* in his death, *both* as beneficiaries and as imitators. *Jesus' death is both a gift and a demand.*[21] What Jesus models, in other words, is *cruciformity* or a spirituality of the cross.

The Foot Washing as a Demonstration of Jesus' Love (13:1–5)

Jesus' act of washing his disciples' feet is set within the context of his own impending death on the cross, which is the ultimate display of his love for his disciples. Knowing that the hour has come to leave this world to be with the Father and "having loved his own who were in the world," Jesus, John says, "showed them the fullest extent of his love" (13:1). In this scene, then, we see the meaning of "God so loved the world that he gave his one and only Son" (3:16). At the supper, Jesus "lays aside" his outer garments and "takes up" a towel to tie it around his waist (13:4 ESV). This language of *laying aside* and *taking up* is reminiscent of language that he had used earlier to describe his death and resurrection: "For this reason my Father loves me, because I lay down my life that I may take it up again" (Jn 10:17 ESV). Jesus' washing of his disciples' feet is "thus an extension of his action as the Good Shepherd, who lays down his life for the sheep (10:17–18) and ties in with the love command he will offer shortly."[22]

In Jesus' day, foot washing was a common practice, as dust and other refuse on the streets would rapidly accumulate on feet. People often washed their feet when returning home. Proper hospitality included providing guests with water to wash their feet or providing a slave or a servant to wash their feet. But for a person of status, particularly a patron host, to wash his guest's feet was unthinkable. Jesus' adoption of what is considered to be the

---

20. Gorman, *The Death of the Messiah*, 45. In repeating Jesus' words concerning the "new covenant" (1 Cor 11:25) Paul is making the fundamental claim that Jesus' death is the inauguration of the new covenant (Ibid., 53).
21. Ibid., 43–7.
22. See Jipp, *Saved by Faith and Hospitality*," 88.

most menial task befitting only a servant or slave is an act "unrivaled in antiquity."[23] It is, as one author describes it, an act of "eschatological hospitality" that symbolizes the love that Jesus will display for his disciples at the cross.[24]

Community and Atonement (13:6-16)

Jesus' loving act as servant-host is too much for Peter who sees it as an "astonishing breach of social convention."[25] So he says, "You shall never wash my feet" (13:8). Jesus' response, "If I do not wash you, you have no part with me" (13:8) is another way of saying, "If I do not die for you, you have no part with me."[26] In other words, Jesus is asserting the utter necessity of being totally forgiven and cleansed of sins through his death on the cross. His washing of the disciples' feet is a sign of the forgiveness of sins through Jesus' supreme demonstration of love on the cross, which brings us into a saving relationship with him (13:7–10). But Jesus' act of sacrificial love is not just a soteriological act; it is also something that his disciples are to replicate in their own lives. So, he goes on to encourage his disciples: "I have given you an example, that you should do just as I have done to you" (13:15 ESV).

Another way of describing what Jesus is saying is that when we are forgiven and our sins are atoned for through Jesus' work on the cross, we are to become *reciprocal performers* of the same act of forgiveness, love, and reconciliation. Atonement is something that we *both* experience as individuals and participate in as a community of believers in the here and now.[27] When God provides atonement he also creates a fellowship of persons who love God and others, who find healing for themselves in their relationship to God, others, and the world.[28] We are a community created *by* Jesus' atonement. And through our union with Christ and by his Spirit we are a community *of* atonement.[29] As Michael Gorman emphasizes, Jesus' parabolic act of foot washing is more than a symbol; it is more like a sacrament, an invitation to *participate* in Jesus' death *both* as beneficiaries and as imitators. These two aspects of Jesus' death are inseparable. "*There is no cleansing*

---

23. See Keener, *The Gospel of John, Vol. Two*, 903–7.
24. Jipp, *Saved by Faith and Hospitality*, 89.
25. Koester, *Symbolism in the Fourth Gospel*, 130.
26. Ibid., 132.
27. See McKnight, *A Community Called Atonement*, 30–31.
28. Ibid., 121.
29. Ibid., 29; Gorman, *The Death of the Messiah*, 45–49.

without discipleship, no vertical relationships without horizontal relationships, no atonement without ethics."[30]

For the Jews, the celebration of the Passover was an important family and national event. It was a time when they would gather together to emphasize their common bond as a covenantal community, which was originally created following the exodus. In this entire passage, then, Jesus is emphasizing the "re-formation" of the people in their relationship to God and one another. Jesus' sacrificial death forms God's people into a new community or family and reorients their identity around him.[31] Over the years, I have talked with other Christians who, for various reasons, have left the church. When I have asked why they are no longer part of a local church body, often the response is something like, "I don't feel comfortable in church. I prefer to stay at home. I can worship God better by watching a church service on TV." In some respects, this type of response is understandable. Unfortunately, instead of exhibiting mutual love and service, relationships in some church cultures can become toxic and unhealthy. When we are hurt by other people in the church, our natural response is to withdraw into our own personal cocoons. But, in many cases, the rationale that Christians give for leaving the church reflects a Western view of spirituality which is decidedly private, individualistic, and narrowly focused on "me and Jesus." In this approach to spirituality the church is optional. Salvation is a private, "spiritual" matter. Jesus' example of cruciform love and service, however, teaches us that while true Christian spirituality is deeply personal, it is not private. Service which is rooted in the experience of "co-crucifixion" with Christ requires community. By definition, it is a communal spirituality.[32]

Jesus, Servanthood, and Politics

While it is not possible in this book (nor is it my purpose) to engage in a detailed discussion of the thorny issue of the proper relationship between the church and American politics, we also cannot neglect some further lessons in this area which are implicit in Jesus' teaching and modeling of servanthood. The Jews of Jesus' day often opted for one of two responses to Roman rule. The first option, promoted by the Essenes, was the quietist one of withdrawal or retreat into separatist enclaves. The second option, espoused by the Zealots, was a revolutionary uprising. Jesus rejects both

---

30. Ibid., 46.

31. Ibid., 45; Pennington, "The Lord's Last Supper in the Fourfold Witness of the Gospels," 53–4.

32. Gorman, *Cruciformity*, 384.

96   PART TWO—NEW EXODUS AND NEW CREATION

of these options. Yet, throughout the history of the church, Christians have lurched between both of these strategies of the "privatistic church" and the "crusading church."[33] They remain temptations for the church today, particularly when we feel that the church and our "religious freedoms" are under attack by forces of liberalism and secularism.

The Temptation of Withdrawal

As I have mentioned, there are numerous indications in John's Gospel that his readers were experiencing persecution (15:18–21; 16:33; 17:11–16). In response, John emphasizes the importance of love *within* the Christian community. In times of persecution and difficulty it is critical that there be an ethos of unity, mutual love, and support.[34] But is John calling for separation or withdrawal from the world?

There are times when the church has adopted the general approach that the Christian ethic is a community ethic which is directed primarily, if not exclusively, to relationships within the Christian community. The church has therefore withdrawn into the private sphere, and has thought of the Christian life as a matter of the individual's relationship to God and other believers, with little or nothing to say to the rest of the world.[35] Some have further objected to the church's involvement in the public sphere on the grounds that the church's sole mission in the world is to preach the gospel. Neither Jesus nor the New Testament church actively participated in "worldly politics." So, they argue, neither should we.[36]

The value of this approach it that it seeks to protect the purity of Christian witness from the messiness of public social and political engagement. However, in John's Gospel the emphasis on love and service is placed within the context of an equally strong emphasis on *mission*. First, Jesus states unequivocally that mutual love between believers will be a witness to the world of God's love and mercy as revealed in Jesus. It will bring glory to God and his Son (13:31–35). Secondly, Jesus prays specifically that Christians will *not* be taken out of the world, even as they are protected from the evil one (17:15). And he goes on to pray to the Father, "As you have sent me into the world, I have sent them into the world" (17:18). Here, Jesus is saying that his own love for the world serves as a pattern for his disciples' mission in

33. See N.T. Wright, *Following Jesus*, 43–51.
34. Gorman, *The Death of the Messiah*, 47–48.
35. Wright, *Following Jesus*, 49.
36. For a further description of this approach, see Gushee, *The Future of Faith in American Politics*, 7–8.

the world. The disciples will share in Jesus' mission, which is, in fact, God's mission.[37] The Fourth Gospel is therefore not calling for withdrawal from the world.

Furthermore, as David Gushee argues, what matters most is the *nature* of Christian public involvement. That is, public engagement should focus on the declaration and embodiment of core moral or ethical values rather than, say, overly partisan alignment with either political party. Rightly understood, the church's public witness can be situated within the broader context of Christian mission. As Gushee states: "To confine the church's mission to a message and a ministry that entirely excludes political engagement is to risk truncating the gospel proclamation quite profoundly. And yet, of course, we are also at risk of placing so much emphasis on the political dimension of the Christian mission as to neglect or truncate the gospel in an entirely different way."[38]

The Temptation to Power

In the case of the second temptation, Mark reports that it was John and his brother James who came to Jesus and asked that they might sit, one at his right side and the other at his left, when he comes into his kingdom (Mk 10:37). Throughout Mark's Gospel it is James and John who are eager for Jesus to mount a Jewish revolution. Like the other holy revolutionaries of the day, they want to resort to military force to defeat Rome, cleanse the land of paganism, and restore Israel's glory and might.[39] But Jesus rebukes them for embracing a wrong vision of God's kingdom and he gives his followers an entirely different picture of discipleship:

> You know that those who are regarded as rulers of the Gentiles lord it over them, and their high officials exercise authority over them. Not so with you. Instead, whoever wants to become great among you must be your servant, and whoever wants to be first must be slave of all. For even the Son of Man did not come to be served, but to serve, and to give his life as a ransom for many. (Mk 10:42–45)

---

37. Gorman, *The Death of the Messiah*, 48.
38. Gushee, *The Future of Faith in American Politics*, 8–9.
39. Wright, *Following Jesus*, 44.

The fact that John places so much emphasis on service in his own Gospel indicates that he learned this lesson from Jesus well.[40] God's kingdom involves an entirely different sort of power.

It is possible, and indeed obligatory, for Christians to employ "intervening power"—that is, to engage in sacrificial acts of service and public witness on behalf of the victimized and oppressed. This includes acting on behalf of the unborn, those who are tortured or wrongly imprisoned, sex slaves, those suffering in war, and so on.[41] This sort of intervening power, however, needs to be distinguished from efforts to use political power to restore a form of Christendom. Unfortunately, throughout its history, the church has often succumbed to the "Constantinian Temptation" to blend church and state and use political power to enforce Christian beliefs. In our day, the idea of America as a "Christian nation" has become a sort of "master signifier" of evangelicalism.[42] This notion of a Christian America, which is advanced through right-wing causes such as the *Patriot's Bible* and the *Conservative Bible Project*, blends free-market capitalism and a conservative political ideology with a belief in "American exceptionalism," or the view that the United States is a unique nation, created by God to play a special role of carrying out his will in human history.

It would be wrong to paint all of those on the "religious right" with the same brush.[43] There are many Christians on the political right who have sought to create maximum room for the free exercise of religion in the public square. Christians can legitimately espouse a constrained, critical

---

40. I am assuming, here, that the author of the Fourth Gospel is also the disciple referred to as John, the son of Zebedee (Mk 3:17; 10:35). This is the traditional view.

41. Gushee, *The Future of Faith in American Politics*, 10, 16. See also Mott, *A Christian Perspective on Political Thought*, 21.

42. See Fitch, *The End of Evangelicalism?*, 27, 100–22.

43. It should be pointed out that not all who espouse the idea of a "Christian America" believe that America is a "chosen nation" in the sense that it was chosen by God to be a "New Israel." In *One Nation Under God?* Wilsey identifies a number of versions of the idea of a "Christian America." Indeed, one of the problems with the concept of a "Christian nation" is that it is inherently ambiguous (122–23). Nonetheless, the idea of American exceptionalism, particularly the belief that American was uniquely chosen and blessed to fulfill God's purposes in history, has been very influential among conservative Christians (71–78; 161–62). Undoubtedly, Christianity and Christian ideals have played a central role in American history. Christian theology has significantly contributed to notions of individual rights under God, human dignity, and religious freedom. But, as Wiley rightly argues, "the central constitutional tenet of religious liberty is at the heart of the creation of the American republic." In fact, the assertion that America is a "Christian nation" does not account for the high value the Founders placed on religious liberty. "In sum, the United States was founded as a nation with religious liberty, not with a Christian identity (Ibid., 187).

patriotism that recognizes the uniqueness of the American experiment.[44] However, there are a number of problems with the idea of America as a Christian nation, not the least of which is that: 1) it easily confuses America's story with Israel's story and the unique covenant that God made with his people; and 2) it can contribute to national hubris and the lust for political power on the part of those who espouse it.[45] Unfortunately, Christians who promote the idea of America as a chosen nation too often exhibit the chest-thumping tribalism of patriotic nationalism instead of the suffering servanthood of a savior who died for the whole world.[46] When church leaders such as Robert Jeffress claim that we should not treat all religions equally and that non-Christian religions are imposters, they conflate the church and the state in a way that degrades individual freedom and ultimately corrupts the church.[47] The human quest to monopolize power which shows up in Constantinianism is, in the words of Mark Griffin and Theron Walker, a "Tower of Babel instinct." "It is the instinct to build the earthly city as if it were the heavenly one."[48]

The Politics of Jesus' Kingdom

We need to bear in mind that the quest for a "Christian nation" is not unique to religious conservatives. It is characteristic of many Christians on the "political left" as well. The error of both extremes is that they view "kingdom work" as *primarily* a *political* process and fail to see that the cross of Jesus Christ is the paradigm, the resurrection is the power, the Holy Spirit is the transforming agent, and the church is the primary place where God is at work.[49] David Crump rightly states that "God's one and only covenant peo-

---

44. Gushee, *The Future of Faith in American Politics*, 44–45, 89.

45. For a discussion of the errors and dangers of American exceptionalism, see Crump, *I Pledge Allegiance*, 115–33; Wilsey, *One Nation Under God?*, 163–70; and Gregory Boyd, *The Myth of a Christian Nation*, 87–115.

46. Crump, *I Pledge Allegiance*. 117.

47. See Fea, *Believe Me*, 164–65.

48. Griffin and Walker, *Living on the Borders*, 180.

49. McKnight, *Kingdom Conspiracy*, 220. Gushee rightly points out that the main failing of both the evangelical right and evangelical left is that they have aligned themselves so tightly with either the Republican or Democratic Party that they tend to sacrifice their fundamental allegiance to Jesus Christ and abandon any pretense of political neutrality or grounding in a transcendent Christian moral vision. Politics often involves shady deal making, moral compromises, and temptations to misuse of money and power. "One reason why Christians must retain their political independence—because they are totally dependent on Jesus Christ as Lord—is so that they can retain their moral compass when they do venture into the political arena." It is not possible to be

ple are now gathered together in the universal church of Jesus Christ, a community of faith spread throughout the world, made up of internationally dispersed 'strangers and aliens,' a countercultural people not of this world, citizens of God's heavenly kingdom on earth."[50] The participation of Christians in worship generally and specifically in the Eucharist is the church's alternative to the world's liturgy of domination and power. The church is the transnational community of the new covenant which transcends all political divisions and all other political and national allegiances.[51]

Toward the end of John's Gospel, before Jesus is sentenced to be crucified, Pilot asks Jesus the final rhetorical question: "Don't you realize I have the power either to free you or to crucify you?" (19:10). This is the language of a worldly kingdom, power, and glory. Jesus responds by reminding Pilot that that all power comes from on high, thereby conveying the truth of a different kind of kingdom, one that is not of this world (19:11). In this age, these two empires collide—one which operates according to the quest for status, power, influence, and control and the other which follows the example of Jesus who "did not come to be served, but to serve, and to give his life as a ransom for many" (Mk 10:45). Unfortunately, as Crump points out, there are many in the church who want the resurrection without the cross; who, in other words, are looking for an easy detour around the road of Jesus' sacrificial suffering and death so that they can quickly arrive at a state of power, glory, victory, and success. But Christ's kingdom does not work that way. The unavoidable sequence of events is that believers will share in Christ's glory *if and only if* they have first shared in his suffering.[52] In fact, when we seek to maintain positions of privilege and status through the use of political power, we divorce ourselves from the very suffering Servant whom we claim to serve.

In C. S. Lewis's famous and influential *The Screwtape Letters*, the senior devil, Screwtape, instructs his junior devil, Wormwood, in the art of temptation. The letters are a parody from the perspective of the devil on

---

both a party strategist and a Christian prophet (*The Future of Faith in American Politics*, 49). Gushee is among a group of evangelicals who, in May of 2008, released "An Evangelical Manifesto: A Declaration of Evangelical Identity and Public Commitment." The Manifesto decries the politicization of evangelicalism in recent years. While it affirms that freedom, justice, peace, and well-being are at the heart of the kingdom of God and that Christians should seek to bring these gifts into the public life for the common good, it also maintains that the City of God should never be completely equated with "any party, partisan ideology, economic system, class, tribe, or national identity" (14).

50. Crump, *I Pledge Allegiance*, 126.

51. Gorman, *The Death of the Messiah*, 235.

52. Crump, *I Pledge Allegiance*, 178–9.

how to outwit the Enemy (God) by manipulating his followers. Concerning the temptation to political power, he writes:

> Certainly we do not want men to allow their Christianity to flow over into their political life, for the establishment of anything like a just society would be a major disaster. On the other hand we do want, and want very much, to make men treat Christianity . . . as a means to their own advancement. . . . Men or nations who think they can revive the Faith in order to make a good society might just as well think they can use the stairs of heaven as a short cut to the nearest chemist's shop. Fortunately, it is quite easy to coax humans around this little corner."[53]

C. S. Lewis came from a nation where a state church was closely aligned with the power of political institutions. He was well aware of how attempts to use the power of the state to "Christianize" a nation—regardless of the merits of the particular political agenda—inevitably make the Faith into a tool or instrument of a political ideology and sacrifice Christian witness on the altar of politics.

Of course, arguments on behalf of gospel truth are important and we should continue making them. Christians should also act on behalf of victims of injustice and engage in a prophetic denunciations of evil. But the world will regard as hypocritical any Christian political involvement that is divorced from evidence of love and justice *within* Christian communities. In a time of political turmoil, when politics increasingly shapes one's version of "truth," and we're pretty sure it's the other person, not us, who is being taken in by partisan propaganda and "fake news," it will be the cross-shaped and Spirit-driven witness of Christian lives which has the greatest impact on hearts and minds. George Weigel rightly argues that this is especially true when Christians live nobly, courageously, and compassionately in service of those who have been most deeply wounded by the tsunami of social division and conflict. Because of that type of witness "those who have been touched by Christian compassion or Christian nobility or Christian courage may be moved to ask, 'How can you live this way?' And at that point, the door to the offer of friendship with Christ has been opened."[54]

---

53. Lewis, *The Screwtape Letters*, 87.
54. Weigel, *The Fragility of Order*, 196.

8

Eating Unworthily

It has been said that "you are what you eat." Nutritionists commonly recommend the correct amounts for the daily intake of each of the "four food types" (vegetable, grains, dairy products, and meats). Eating healthy "organic" foods has become the new slogan, for both retailers and consumers in America.

Nevertheless, our tastes and eating habits are rarely governed solely by nutrition. We are also, to use a geographical version of the above adage, *where* we eat. The Japanese eat sushi and raw fish, and drink tea. The French eat white bread and drink wine. And the Irish eat potatoes and drink beer. Ethnic foods become identity markers. In America, the concept of the "melting pot" is quite literally celebrated in the diversity of foods that are found in the local grocery store. We have Greek yogurt, Italian pasta, Chinese chow mein, Polish kielbasa, German sausage and sauerkraut, Belgian waffles, English muffins, Swiss cheese, Mexican enchiladas, Japanese teriyaki . . . the list could go on and on.[1]

But we should not stop there. For we are, thirdly, *how* we eat. How we eat and drink together contains coded messages about ourselves, social status, shared values, and expectations for behavior. Consider, for example, the three main forms of shared meals in our society—the dinner party, the potluck, and the barbecue. Each of these group meals symbolically conveys differing expectations about roles and how one ought to behave in the social gathering. One does not show up at a barbecue wearing a party dress or a tuxedo!

---

1. Fox, "Food and Eating," 1–2.

The physical setting is also important in getting the message across.² Why, for example, don't we eat all of our meals in the dining room? The description of this part of the house as a "dining" room rather than the "eating" room gives us the answer. The dining room is usually reserved for special occasions—for larger family gatherings or for entertaining special guests. Originally, the whole idea of separating the dining room from the kitchen was a way of mimicking the upper class, who wished to keep the dirty, noisy, and smelly kitchen area separate from the large banqueting hall. In the years following the Second World War, the fledgling middle class imitated this practice, though on a smaller scale. Servants were relegated to the kitchen and entered the dining area only as menials.³ The book (and movie) *The Help* dramatically portrays this practice of segregation—which involved the relegation of colored people not only to separate eating areas but also to separate water fountains, bathrooms, and seating (or non-seating) on buses and other forms of public transportation. We have as a society attempted to put this overt practice of racial segregation behind us. Some have suggested that a more egalitarian ideology may at least partly be reflected in more open housing designs.⁴

But, as we all know, our society is still deeply divided by racial and cultural differences. This was recently dramatized by an incident at a Starbucks in Philadelphia involving two black men who were arrested on suspicion of trespassing for sitting in the restaurant without buying anything. According to the men, they were waiting for a third man to discuss a potential real estate opportunity. When they refused to leave, they were led out of the restaurant in handcuffs. The incident sparked national outrage and was a major embarrassment for Starbucks which has striven to project an image of hospitality and corporate responsibility. In response, it launched a "race together" campaign designed to encourage discussions of race in the United States.

Divisions of various types—racial, ethnic, social, religious, and political—continue to be a major issue facing our society and the church. Both social research and experience tell us that people like to associate with those who are most like themselves. This is especially true of American churches, which, despite the fact that our society is becoming more and more diverse, are increasing in racial, cultural, and theological homogeneity. As sociologists Michael Emerson and Christian Smith point out, over 90 percent of our churches are made up of congregations that are at least 90 percent racially

2. Ibid., 5.
3. Ibid, 5–6.
4. Ibid.

homogeneous. Furthermore, the same processes that contribute to racial/ethnic sameness also contribute to ideological and theological homogeneity. The American church, is, on the whole, "divided by faith."[5]

From an emotional standpoint, this preference to spend time with and worship with those who are familiar to us and most like us is understandable. According to Christena Cleveland, research indicates that "our need for personal affirmation creates a greater desire to surround ourselves with those who subscribe to our culturally distinct ways of life and an aversion to those whose mere difference threatens our unstable identities."[6] Furthermore, there is "the power of the familiar." The more we interact with a person, the greater the perception that he or she is safe, likeable, and trustworthy. But the reverse is also true. As the Starbucks incident illustrates, persons who are unfamiliar and less like us are more likely to be perceived as less likable, unsafe, and untrustworthy. "Our homogeneity is like a cage surrounding our group, preventing us from becoming familiar with culturally different others."[7] Certainly, most of us do not see our churches as contributing to prejudice or intolerance. But various studies indicate that "group separation and prejudice have a bidirectional relationship—that is, prejudice tends to result in division between groups and division between groups tends to result in prejudice."[8] Cleveland concludes: "Until we relativize our smaller cultural identities and adopt a common in-group identity, our diversity initiatives are doomed to failure because we will never fully appreciate our diverse brothers and sisters and they will not feel appreciated."[9]

It has been said that if Romans is the letter where Paul most systematically explains the meaning of the gospel, 1 Corinthians might be the one that most directly applies the gospel to Christian life in a church.[10] The Corinthian church is beset by various types of divisions and conflicts. In

---

5. See Emerson and Smith, *Divided by Faith*, 135–51; and Cleveland, *Disunity in Christ*, 28.

6. Ibid., 87.

7. Ibid., 29.

8. Ibid., 33.

9. Ibid., 184–85. It should be noted that cross-cultural contact by itself does not necessarily improve attitudes and eliminate prejudice. Cleveland argues that four elements are needed for positive cross-cultural interaction: 1) working toward a larger goal; 2) creating equal status; 3) engaging in authentic personal interaction; and 4) providing positive leadership (152–76). Emerson and Smith argue that while factors such as repentance, forgiveness, and interpersonal interaction are necessary components in responding to the racial divide they cannot be divorced from the need to address structural issues, such as inequality in health care, economic inequality, police mistreatment, and job and housing discrimination (*Divided by Faith*, 127–32).

10. Hamilton, "The Lord's Supper in Paul," 69.

his letter, Paul appeals to their primary identity in Christ as the foundation for overcoming conflict and finding a unity that transcends their social and cultural differences. In 1 Corinthians 11:17–34, in particular, he corrects abuses of the Lord's Supper by the Corinthian church and calls for a practice of the meal that comports with the equality that exists in the body of Christ, without regard for social distinctions or social status.[11] In order to more clearly understand what Paul is saying in this passage, we need to first look at how meals functioned in the first-century Greco-Roman world. We also have to observe how the abuses that Paul addresses with respect to the Lord's Supper are bound up with other problems in the church that he addresses in the previous chapters.

Wining and Dining in Corinth

Corinth in Paul's day was significantly Roman in its character and life. As a Roman colony, it became the capital city of the whole province of Achaia. The city had been destroyed by the Romans in 146 BC, but was then recolonized by Julius Caesar in 44 BC, largely because of its strategic commercial benefits. After its recolonization, it became like a modern boomtown in the American West during the days of the Gold Rush. It was the San Francisco of ancient Greece.[12] As the crossroads of Europe and Asia, it was a thriving commercial city. Many of its residents had acquired considerable wealth. And the society as a whole was highly status conscious. Even Freedmen (former slaves) could raise their status by achieving wealth or participating in religious practices. Corinth was similar to our own postmodern culture in its emphasis on success, self-promotion, competitive pragmatism, and radical pluralism.[13]

Corinth was home to temples or sanctuaries that were devoted to an abundance of gods; there were also edifices devoted to the mystery religions and to the Roman imperial cult worship. During the Roman era, huge dining rooms were built in the temple precincts. Meat that was not taken by the priests for sacrifices to the deities was made available for dinners in these temple restaurants or special rooms. Some of the meat might also be sold in the marketplace.[14] In addition, to boost their prestige, city officials would offer a community sacrifice during which large quantities of meat would be

---

11. Witherington, *Making a Meal of It*, 49.
12. Johnson, *1 Corinthians*, 14.
13. Ibid., 18
14. Ibid, 132–33.

consumed. On some special occasions or festivals, the general public would be invited to the cookout (or eat in) at the temple precincts.[15]

Another form of "dining" in Corinth was the "group meal" or "symposium" (from the Greek *symposion*, which literally refers to a group sharing a meal). In New Testament times, these group meals were generally by invitation only and took place in the home's *triclinium*, or dining room, complete with tables and couches. When it comes to dining, the Romans were the original "couch potatoes."[16] During the Roman era, these dinners (*deipna*) became more and more like drinking parties. To increase their social status, members of the social elite would invite friends and clients to a feast *(cena)* which was followed (usually after the wife and children were dismissed) by a drinking party *(convivia)*. To spice things up, the drinking party usually involved some form of after-dinner entertainment. Rowdiness, vulgarity, excess, and sexual immorality (including prostitutes) were not uncommon at such affairs.[17] Basically, behavior at these meals reflected the group's character. In other words, the meals revealed and were *supposed* to mirror the values that the particular group upheld. As we will see, this cultural context largely explains why Paul was so upset with the behavior of the wealthier members of the Corinthian church during the Lord's Supper.[18]

An Overview of Paul's Message to the Corinthian Church

While there was a Jewish community in Corinth, it is most likely that most members of this fledgling Christian community were Gentiles rather than persons of Jewish ancestry. In addition, it was composed of a range of social and economic classes—from prosperous households to slaves. Undoubtedly, this combination of factors contributed to a laundry list of problems, from divisive cliques and factionalism (chaps 1:10—4:21) and abuses of the Lord's Supper (11:17–34) to sexual immorality (5:1–8; 6:12–20) and legal disputes (6:1–11). The behavior of the Corinthian converts was thus simply a reflection of the surrounding pagan culture.

---

15. Witherington, *Making a Meal of It*, 34.
16. Ibid.
17. Ibid., 35.
18. Ibid., 35–36.

Paul's Call to Embody the Gospel

The various problems facing the Corinthian church are symptomatic of a deeper problem, namely a failure to understand the real-life implications of *knowing* Jesus Christ, and him crucified (2:2).[19] In fact, we might say that this is our problem as well. Anyone who is involved in some way in the economic and social life of the world (which is all of us) is confronted with the temptation to compromise the demands of the gospel. Paul's purpose is to convince the Corinthians (and us) to embody the cross in daily life. The goal of all Christians is to become for others what Christ is for us. This is what Paul means when he says, "For our sake he made him to be sin who knew no sin, *so that in him we might become the righteousness of God*" (2 Cor 5:21 ESV). In other words, the divine character traits that are revealed through Christ's self-gift on the cross—God's love, peace, justice, righteousness, and hope—are to be manifested both individually and corporately by those who are *in* Christ to the world.[20]

In response to the existence of factions and conflict based on identification with specific teachers (1:12; 3:3–4; 4:6), Paul therefore teaches a theology of the cross. The gospel message declares that all are totally bankrupt before God and come to him solely on the basis of his grace. The gospel levels and nullifies all the things that divide people from one another and are the source of prideful distinctions. Since Christ is the sole source of wisdom, power, righteousness, and redemption, those who truly embrace the gospel and identify with Christ will boast only in him (1:28–31; 3:21; 4:6–7, 18–20) and not in human wisdom, eloquence, or power (1:20–29; 2:6–10). It is critical that we understand what Paul is saying here, for it informs his entire letter.[21] First, God is in the business of subverting the status quo by making somebodies out of nobodies—and vice versa (1:28). God has chosen the weak of the world to demonstrate his power to bring healing, wholeness, and justice. Secondly, the truly spiritual person is the one who sees the connection between the cross and the Spirit; such a person has the "mind of Christ" (2:16; cf. Phil 2:5). Third, to know Christ crucified (2:2) means that we experience what Christ himself experienced—ridicule, abuse, and even physical suffering (4:8–16; cf. Matt 5:44; Lk 6:28). This is a far cry from what we hear from many preachers of the "health and wealth gospel" today!

---

19. Gorman, *Apostle of the Crucified Lord*, 227.
20. Gorman, *Becoming the Gospel*, 6–7.
21. See Gorman, *Apostle of the Crucified Lord*, 240–45.

Conversion of the Imagination

Paul also calls these Gentile converts to a "conversion of the imagination." He wants them to reshape their moral imagination and identity by projecting their lives into the larger narrative of God's dealing with Israel.[22] As we have seen, Paul repeatedly reconfigures the story of Israel and the exodus in terms of the cross and the resurrection. At one point in his letter to the Corinthians, then, he makes reference to the Passover celebration and to Christ as the "Passover lamb" (5:6–8) as a basis for expelling an incestuous believer from the church. His description of Christ as the Passover lamb who has been sacrificed reinforces the analogy between the lamb of the exodus and the death of Jesus, which delivers God's people, the church, from sin and the evil of the world.[23] Through the death and resurrection of Christ, the Passover lamb, the Corinthian converts have experienced a new exodus. They ought therefore to identify themselves as those who have been rescued from sin and are empowered by Christ's Spirit to live a new life in him.

Paul also uses the example of Israel when he addresses the issue of eating meat sacrificed to idols (8:1–3). He first treats the issue of eating sacrificial idol food in temple restaurants or precincts (10:14–22); and then turns to such food which is sold in the market and eaten in homes (10:23–11:1). While there is some disagreement among commentators on the interpretation of these passages, Paul *seems* to be *prohibiting knowingly* eating of *any* food that has been sacrificed to idols–demons.[24] He gives two reasons for such a prohibition. To begin with, such behavior violates the conscience of "weaker" Christians. Paul contrasts what we might refer to as "just love" or cruciform justice with justice in the sense of entitlement. As Michael Gorman states. "in Paul's exhortation about the treatment of the weak, he calls the Corinthians to practice a counterintuitive justice/love that is rooted in the cross and involves the renunciation of rights, for the benefit of the other, as the practical demonstration of just love."[25]

Second, knowingly eating food offered to idols is also idolatry. Here Paul warns the Corinthian converts not to be like the Israelites in the wilderness, who were given the provision of spiritual food and drink but turned away from God by eating idolatrous meals and practicing sexual immorality as part of the worship of pagan deities (10:1–15).[26] He then

---

22. Hays, *The Conversion of the Imagination.*, 5, 10.
23. Johnson, *1 Corinthians.*, 90–91.
24. Ibid., 135–77.
25. Gorman, *Becoming the Gospel*, 241.
26. Jipp, *Saved by Faith and Hospitality*, 57

states categorically: "You cannot drink the cup of the Lord and the cup of demons too; you cannot have a part in both the Lord's Table and the table of demons" (10:21). The Corinthian believers apparently thought that they were protected from divine judgment by baptism and participation in the Lord's Supper. They employed the freedom slogan "everything is permissible" to justify eating meat offered to idols and anything else they desired. Paul gives the example of the Israelites to disabuse them of this false sense of security. Just as God judged the Israelites in the desert for their idolatry, even though they were baptized into Moses and partook of the "type" of the Lord's Supper, so God will judge the Corinthian Christians for their idolatry and immorality, even though they have been baptized and take part in the Lord's Supper (10:1–13).[27]

Finally, Paul places his ethical admonitions within the larger context of the final resurrection, when everything will be made new and those who are united with Christ will participate in the final victory over sin and death (15:50–57). In sum, as Richard Hays notes, "Paul sees the community of faith being caught up into the story of God's remaking of the world through Christ."[28] The death and resurrection of Christ is the pivot point in history through which the future righteousness and justice of God has broken into the present. This is to be manifested most fully in his people, the church, who are being conformed into the image of Christ. The new life through Christ is not just personal virtue; it also involves the unity and harmony of the community in Christ. Paul emphasizes the positive aspects of this unity in his discussion of spiritual gifts (12:1–31) and his great chapter on love (13:1–13).

Abuse of the Lord's Supper (11:17–34)

This passage is well known and of particular importance, since it is the only time when Paul (in conjunction with some verses in chapter 10) directly refers to the practice of "the Lord's Supper." Thus, it is frequently the main text that is used in our observance of Communion or the Eucharist. Paul's explicit reference to Jesus' words concerning the "new covenant" (1 Cor 11:25) indicates that he derives the meaning of the Lord's Supper from the tradition about Jesus' "Last Supper." In this context, the Lord's Supper has a number of meanings. It is: 1) an experience of solidarity or fellowship (*koinonia*); 2) an "event of memory," or appropriation of and participation in Christ's death; 3) an act of proclamation or "parabolic sermon;" and 4) a

27. Hamilton, "The Lord's Supper in Paul," 75.
28. Hays, *The Moral Vision of the New Testament*, 45.

"foretaste of the future messianic banquet." But, in addition to these meanings, the Lord's Supper is also a model of cruciform love—or what Gorman describes as "a microcosm of the new covenant life affected by the cross."[29] In the words of another commentator: "The ritual of the Lord's Supper calls the participants to behavior based on values such as equality, rather than hierarchy; mutual servitude, rather than competition; and humility rather than the upward mobility enshrined in the power structures of the Greco-Roman world."[30] It is seldom recognized, however, that one of Paul's main concerns in this passage is the gulf between the rich and the poor within the church body.[31]

The Problem

Part of the reason we miss much of what Paul is saying is because we often have little sense of the social and historical context of his words. To begin with, the Corinthians are gathering together as a "whole church" (11:18; cf. Rom 16:23)—or in larger gatherings as opposed to smaller gatherings in apartments. This explains the presence of persons representing a variety of socioeconomic groups.[32] Unlike our usual practice of celebrating communion as a liturgical ritual within a separate church building, the first-century church most likely celebrated the Lord's Supper as part of a group meal, or "love feast." This meal took place in the private home of a wealthier believer. As we have previously noted, these homes typically contained a larger dining area for entertaining guests, which was separated from the outer courts.

The essential problem that Paul is concerned about is summarized in verses 20–22: Again, we need to imagine the social and cultural context of his readers as we try to reconstruct the scenario that he describes:

> When you come together, it is not the Lord's Supper that you eat, for as you eat, each of you goes ahead without waiting for anybody else. One remains hungry, another gets drunk. Don't you have homes to eat and drink in? Or do you despise the church of God and humiliate those who have nothing? What shall I say to you? Shall I praise you for this? Certainly not!

---

29. Gorman, *Apostle of the Crucified Lord*, 268–69 and *The Death of the Messiah*, 54.
30. Quoted in Ibid., 110.
31. See Blomberg, *I Corinthians*, 228–33.
32. Johnson, *1 Corinthians*, 204. Johnson states; "Individual church groups in the city may have developed different social habits in their gatherings. When they came together, these differences were incompatible with their unity and equality as the body of Christ, and thus the Lord's Supper was being nullified."

While the meaning of Paul's word is not entirely clear, recent archeological investigations help us to reconstruct the sequence of events. The typical dining room (*triclinium*) in Corinth could accommodate only nine persons; other guests would have to sit or stand in the larger space outside. It is likely, then, that the host's higher-status friends and associates have been invited to dine earlier in the *triclinium*, while the lower classes and slaves who arrive later are relegated to the outer court. Essentially, the wealthier believers are treating the meal like a regular symposium or dinner party, with its emphasis on status, drinking, and entertainment. Typically, the better food and service are provided for guests of higher status while those with lower social status are served in the atrium or outside area with scraps of food. Thus, the wealthier converts indulge in alcohol and get drunk, while the poorer latecomers are ostracized and have to scrounge for leftovers.[33] Archeological evidence further indicates that there was a famine in the Corinthian area during the period that Paul was writing this epistle. If this is indeed the case, the failure to include and provide food for all to share is doubly shameful and insulting.[34]

Paul's Response

It is further possible that the Corinthians have completely abandoned the religious or ritual aspect of the Lord's Supper, which is, of course, the heart of the meal. At the very least, their behavior nullifies "the Lord's meal."[35] Thus Paul's strong rebuke in verse 20: "It is not the Lord's Supper that you eat" (Lit. "When you come together, it is not in order to eat the Lord's Supper."[36]). In the verses that follow (11:23–26) he then reminds them of the meaning and significance of the bread and special cup. The expressions "the table of the Lord" (10:21) and the "Lord's Supper" (11:20) indicate that Jesus himself (as opposed to the wealthy members of the church) is the real host of the meal which the Corinthian church is supposed to celebrate. The meal expresses an exclusive relationship between Christ and his people, which (as we have seen) is why the Corinthians cannot participate in both the Lord's table and the table of demons (10:21).[37]

---

33. See Hays, *First Corinthians*, 195–96; and Gorman, *Apostle of the Crucified Lord*, 268.
34. Johnson, *1 Corinthians*, 206.
35. Ibid., 205.
36. Das, "1 Corinthians 11:17–34 Revisited," 202
37. Jipp, *Saved by Faith and Hospitality*, 58–9.

But Paul is clear that the treatment of the poor believers is inconsistent with and, in fact, contradicts the fellowship and union with Christ which is expressed in the Lord's Supper. In other words, communion with the Lord is necessarily connected with communion with other Christian brothers and sisters. The "one loaf" in which all believers participate (10:17) is itself symbolic of the unity and fellowship of believers. This is why the Lord's Supper is celebrated in conjunction with an "agape meal." In the words of Richard Hays, "the church's common meal should symbolize the unity of the community through equitable sharing of food at the meal."[38] By using the Lord's Supper as the occasion for reaffirming social privilege, hierarchy and division within the Christian community, Paul says, the "haves" are expressing utter contempt for the church and humiliating the "have nots" within the community (11:22).[39]

In addition, the Corinthians have failed to fully comprehend the meaning and significance of Christ's death. As we have seen, elsewhere in 1 Corinthians, "proclaiming Christ's death" (11:26) does not just mean proclaiming salvation through his death on the cross. It also means reflecting the cruciform love of God. Those who fail to embody this love within their own lives make a mockery of Jesus' death.[40] Since Jesus died for all persons equally, his death on the cross is the great equalizer. All persons are equally loved by God. The ultimate irony is that "the weak" for whom Christ died (1:18–31) are the very ones who are being treated unjustly. Whereas Christ chose the weak of the world to shame the strong (1:27), it is the strong in the Corinthian church who are shaming the weak. By showing contempt for those who have nothing, they are "profaning the body and blood of the Lord" (11:27).[41] As David Downs describes what Paul is saying, "unless the [Corinthian] community embodies concern for others, particularly the poor, modeled on the self-giving love of Jesus Christ, it cannot rightly proclaim the Lord's death."[42] Paul is basically reiterating what he has already said in 8:12—that in sinning against their "weaker" brothers and sisters and "wounding" them, the more well-to-do believers are sinning against Christ himself!

There is a further sense in which the Corinthians are sinning against Christ's body. As we have seen, the Last Supper of Jesus takes place in the context of the Passover. It is essentially a Passover meal. Paul himself places

---

38. Hays, *First Corinthians*, 107.
39. Jipp, *Saved by Faith and Hospitality*, 60.
40. Gorman, *Cruciformity*, 234.
41. Gorman, *Becoming the Gospel*, 244.
42. Quoted in Longenecker, *Remember the Poor*, 154.

the Lord's Supper within this Old Testament tradition by twice instructing the Corinthians to "do this in remembrance of me" (11:24–25). In the Old Testament, the Israelites are told that the feast of the Passover is to be repeated as a "memorial day" (Exod 12:14), a day when they "remember" God's deliverance of his people from bondage. It is not clear whether the Corinthian Christians are actually celebrating a Jewish Passover meal. However, it seems clear that Paul *intends* the Jewish Passover meal to be the *context* for properly understanding the Lord's Supper.[43] It is to be an occasion for the people of God to *remember* God's action of deliverance from sin through Christ's death. We must keep in mind that for the Jews "remembering" was never merely recollecting; it meant fully responding to and "living out" God's saving actions. Just as the exodus event brought the Israelites into a covenantal relationship with God and one another, so the "new covenant" through Christ's death binds believers to Christ and to each another. This is what it means to "discern" the body of Christ (11:29). Alan Johnson rightly points out that while Paul's first concern is the proclamation of the cross (1:18–25), his second concern is with the social transformation that comes through participation in and identification with the cruciform Christ.[44] By mistreating those who have nothing, the Corinthian believers are acting as though Christ's death has not decisively changed the nature of their relationship to Christ or to one another as his "body."[45]

In sum, the Corinthian believers are acting in ways that obscure and distort the meaning of the Supper so thoroughly that it no longer points to Christ's death and resurrection as the decisive event in history through which all things are made new (2 Cor 5:17).[46] For Paul, this is such a serious matter that to avoid God's discipline (11:29), the Corinthians must do two things: 1) They must carefully examine themselves (11:28); and 2) there must be an actual change in behavior which reflects their unity and equality in Christ (11:33). Paul is not calling for sinless perfection; the Lord's Table is always a reminder that there is forgiveness at the cross. But he is calling for honest self-examination and confession that lead to new life, both individually and collectively.

---

43. Johnson, *1 Corinthians*, 206; Hamilton, "The Lord's Supper in Paul," 84–92.
44. Johnson, *1 Corinthians*, 211.
45. Hays, *First Corinthians*, 199.
46. Ibid., 200.

Some Implications for Today's Church

Like the Corinthian church, today's church is plagued by various divisions—including walls between congregations and denominations over what are ultimately trivial differences in theology or worship styles; divisions rooted in varying personality preferences, differences of race, culture and class; and conflicting political and social agendas. But, as I suggested at the beginning of this chapter, perhaps the biggest challenge facing the contemporary church is the racial divide, which is intertwined with social inequality and the separation of congregations along ethnic, cultural, and geographical lines. Let me begin by placing the issue of race in our society within the larger historical context.

The Gospel Torn in Two

In *Reconstructing the Gospel*, Jonathan Wilson-Hartgrove recounts his experience of visiting Saint Matthew's Episcopal Church, a quaint chapel in Hillsborough, North Carolina.[47] The chapel was built by North Carolina's elite in 1824. One prominent member of the church was Paul Cameron, who by the end of the Civil War was the wealthiest man in North Carolina, owning most of the land in what is now Durham County and nearly 1,000 slaves. The priest of the chapel showed Wilson-Hartgrove and the other visitors the balcony which was added to the church in the mid-nineteenth century to segregate its enslaved members from the landed gentry below. These southern gentlemen considered themselves to be the great fathers, and they frequently wrote in their personal letters about "our family, black and white." But they and every enslaved person knew that the entire plantation economy rested on a common understanding of the difference between being slave and free.[48]

While the visitors were standing at the front of the chapel, looking up at the balcony in the back, one of them turned to the Communion rail behind him and asked, "Were masters and slaves segregated when they came forward for Communion?" "Oh, no," the priest responded. "They had very good sacramental theology. 'One Lord, one faith, one baptism, one God and Father of all.'" According to the priest, one of his predecessors waxed eloquent on how during one Easter service a master and slave knelt together at

---

47. Wilson-Hartgrove, *Reconstructing the Gospel*, 12–15.
48. Ibid.

the altar, receiving the body and blood of Christ. This was to him a notable image of the reconciliation that Christ makes possible.[49]

The cruel irony is that the Christian slave owners who referred to their slaves with whom they shared Communion as "family" also treated them as property and assessed their value and worth based on their age, health, and market demands. In the slave markets, the slaves were carefully examined, as horses are, by those who intended to buy them.[50] Through every phase of their lives and even at death, enslaved people were given an economic value as human commodities. Children were routinely separated from their parents and siblings.[51] And when the slaves died, some of their bodies were sold to medical schools for human anatomy courses at major institutions throughout the north and south.[52] Like the Corinthian believers, the Christian slaveholders were blind to the fact that their treatment of slaves and their zealous support for an institution from which they profited financially contradicted the very meaning of the Lord's Supper, which they so faithfully observed.

Separate But Equal?

We recoil in horror at such stories. We like to think that we have come a long way from this dark chapter in the history of our nation and the church. But today, instead of white and black Christians sitting in separate pews in the same church, the vast majority of us attend different churches entirely. As we have seen, the Corinthians were doubtless preserving this type of homogeneous grouping, and it is precisely this which Paul condemns![53] James similarly rejects any practice of partiality and physical segregation of believers within the church (Jas 2:1–4).

Most white evangelicals today consider racism and racial segregation to be a thing of the past. But according to recent studies, our churches are ten times less diverse than the neighborhoods in which they are located and twenty times less diverse than the public schools of their neighborhoods. In our country, the average wealth among whites is eighteen times that of Hispanics and twenty times that of blacks—a statistic which has doubled since the 1980s.[54] As Wilson-Hartgrove states, "To be white and Christian

49. Ibid., 13–14.
50. Berry *The Price for Their Pound of Flesh*, 71.
51. Ibid., 33–57.
52. Ibid., 3, 148–93.
53. Blomberg, *1 Corinthians*, 239.
54. These statistics are from a presentation, "Racialization and its Impact on the

in America is to be, on average, more segregated than your unchurched neighbors, whatever the color of their skin. How could this be?"[55]

Uniracial congregations (particularly all-white congregations) are often justified on the grounds that this is the most effective approach for multiplying churches through evangelism and growing healthy, vibrant congregations. In addition, many minorities (African-Americans, Latinos, and Asian-Americans) favor uniracial congregations as a way of protecting themselves from what they perceive to be white domination and racism and preserving their own culture.[56] But, as we have noted, racial separation itself breeds misunderstanding, mistrust, and prejudice. In *Divided by Faith: Evangelical Religion and the Problem of Race in America*, Emerson and Smith maintain that we live in a racialized society in which "race matters profoundly for differences in life experiences, life opportunities, and social relationships."[57] They further argue that racial divisions perpetuate inequalities of power that disadvantage racial and cultural minorities.

Racial practices that produce racial divisions in our society are increasingly covert and invisible to most whites. When confronted with the issue of race in our churches, most white Christians today will say that they are "colorblind." The present reality of all-white or predominantly white congregations in the United States is rarely justified by using the racist rhetoric of the past. In that sense, we are far removed from the days of Jim Crow. But racism or racial prejudice does not have to be overt or even intentional. We can be blinded by our own cultural values and practices. Despite our good intentions to promote racial reconciliation we can unwittingly perpetuate racial divisions by not recognizing the structural and institutional sources of inequality; failing to promote patterns of leadership that are racially diverse; and promoting principles of "church growth" such as the "homogeneous unit principle" that, "People like to become Christians without crossing racial, linguistic, cultural, or class boundaries." Tony Evans, the African–American senior pastor of Oak Cliff Bible Fellowship in Dallas, Texas, maintains that "the racial division of its members and the resulting classism is the greatest problem facing the kingdom of God."[58] Wilson-Hartgrove is right when he states:

Church." (2018) given by Michael Emerson at Trinity Evangelical Divinity School, Deerfield, IL.

55. Wilson-Hartgrove, *Reconstructing the Gospel*, 79.

56. DeYoung et al., *United by Faith*, 113–27.

57. Emerson and Smith, *Divided by Faith*, 7.

58. Quoted in Gushee, *The Future of Faith in American Politics*, 109.

> The systemic nature of racial inequality is complex. . . . But long before we get to public policy, the bald face of inequality exposes how white supremacy is ultimately about who we love and who we listen to, who we long to be with and how we interact with the so-called other. It's about the pattern of our daily life and the desires that are tied up with them. . . . For any Bible-believing American who is heartbroken by racial strife and offended by the crude bigotry of the alt-right, [the pattern of segregation in our churches] is a serious reality to grapple with. Everything we know to be true suggests that Jesus is the answer. But the gospel of white evangelicals hasn't interrupted our racial habits; it has reinforced them.[59]

Christians are often reticent to talk about the issue of race. But when the topic does come up, one of the most common errors that occurs in the church is the tendency to frame the conversation almost exclusively in terms of individual morality and personal responsibility. Granted, these are factors that need to be considered. But when the problem of racial conflict is reduced to individualistic explanations and "personal sin," what goes unaddressed is the social context—the structures of society and social sins which perpetuate patterns of racial segregation. Study after study has shown the close connection between inequities in housing, education, and transportation and what amounts to "racial apartheid" in our nation. In countless ways, those of us who are white have benefited from this segregation. Despite our good intentions, many of us in the church have passively accepted and participated in patterns of inequality and exclusion which characterize the communities where we live.[60]

David Leong's thought-provoking book, *Race and Place: How Urban Geography Shapes the Journey to Reconciliation*, describes the "theology of geography." Patterns of exclusion are perpetuated by walls, fences, boarders, and boundaries—both literal and symbolic—which divide us. When it comes to the issue of race, our preaching of the gospel often does not have the effect of tearing down the "walls of hostility" between Christians (Eph 2:14–16). Kids, both white and minority, learn early on that there are certain boundaries or geographic markers that one just doesn't cross. The "social logic of homogeneity" becomes imbedded in our collective psyche. We find comfort and safety in settings where people are familiar to us. Clustering

---

59. Wilson-Hartgrove, *Reconstructing the Gospel*, 78–9.

60. See Leong, *Race and Place*, 63–67; 101–103. Leong gives a helpful summary of how the construction of our highway system and "white flight" to suburbs, redlining, an unequal educational system, gentrification, and public housing have contributed to segregation and the problem of race in our country.

into groups of similarity affirms our own sense of identity and belonging. The unfortunate result of these patterns of social homogeneity, which are masked by platitudes like "separate but equal," is the perpetuation of privileges for many (a home mortgage, home equity, and upward mobility) and dead-end cycles for others (public housing, generational poverty, and institutional dependence). Geography accomplishes what Jim Crow laws enforced in the past. "After decades of an uneven playing field and the ongoing entrenchment of racially biased policies," says Leong, "is it any wonder that today's suggestions of colorblindness reek of hypocrisy and ignorance?"[61]

There are multiple ways of breaking down the barriers of race, social class, and status that involve sharing resources and promoting unity within the body of Christ. Churches should think creatively about how they can apply the principle of cruciform love which Paul enjoins in 1 Corinthians. More affluent churches are to be commended, for example, when they seek to help poorer communities, particularly when these efforts involve real cooperation between churches in ways that transcend racial, class, and cultural differences. But, a movement of multiracial congregations is the best answer to the racial and cultural divide in the United States.[62] For the most part, the congregations of the early church included people from across lines of race, economics, gender, and culture which divided first-century society. In 1 Corinthians Paul urges the Corinthian church to be *authentically inclusive*. When possible, then, local church bodies in the United States should strive to become multiethnic or multiracial congregations. Granted, this goal is not easily achieved. And it may not always be possible in the present age of the "now" and "not yet." But it should be the ideal.

The problem of race, ethnic, and class conflict is, of course, not limited to the U.S. It can also be seen in places like India where the lowest class—the "Dalit," or "untouchables"—are shunned by the upper classes; and Europe, where the Roma people (often pejoratively referred to as "Gypsies") are systematically excluded from the larger society. Wherever prejudice and discrimination rears its ugly head the church is called to exhibit the "Magna Carta" of humanity that, "There is neither Jew nor Greek, slave nor free, male nor female, for you are all one in Christ Jesus" (Gal 3:28). In one form or another, we have heard these words preached from the pulpit numerous times. But it is one thing to preach these words, and quite another to practice them. This oneness in Christ is not merely spiritual; it is to be an objective social reality that is evident in a whole new set of attitudes, reactions,

---

61. Ibid., 179.

62. See DeYoung et al., *United by Faith*, 181–86. They define an "integrated multiracial" congregation as one in which minority groups reach at least 20 percent (169).

and behaviors. A story that is often heard in the church comes from John 4, which describes Jesus and the Samaritan woman. As one wise advocate of true racial reconciliation reminds us, "One can talk about Samaria, theologize about Samaria, preach about Samaria, liturgize about Samaria, sing about Samaria . . . but one can do all these things and still not walk through Samaria."[63] The road through Samaria is a rocky and difficult one. But it is a journey that Jesus calls us to take. The church exists not only for the conversion of individuals, but also as a "prototype" of a new order that has been called into being through Christ.[64] The celebration of God's reconciling grace at the Communion Table rings hollow when it is not accompanied by the fellowship and friendship of equals, regardless of class, culture, or racial background. Race is an issue that continues to conquer and divide, both in the church and in our society. My hope and prayer is that God will give us the grace, courage, and imagination to follow a different roadmap and practice a different story.[65]

---

63. McNeil, *Roadmap to Reconciliation*, 9.

64. See Longenecker, *New Testament Social Ethics Today*, 30–31; 96

65. Hays concludes on the basis of his detailed examination of key Pauline texts that: "Individual prejudices and cultural–societal structures that divide Christians into groups based on skin color or other ethnic distinctions are contrary to the teaching of the New Testament" (*From Every People and Nation*, 200).

Part Three

Eucharistic Hospitality

9

Connecting Hospitality to the Lord's Supper

A NUMBER of years ago, I had a brief conversation with an elderly member of a church I was visiting regarding the importance of ethical conduct in the church. "Yes," she said, "young people in our church often lack proper etiquette. They need to learn better manners." This person's equating of "ethics" with "etiquette" (along the lines of Emily Post's guidelines for proper "social etiquette") was revealing. Basically, what this church member had in mind was similar to what most Christians mean by the term "hospitality." As one theologian has observed, for most of us, hospitality conjures up images of "tea parties, bland conversation, and a general atmosphere of coziness."[1]

Today, most people connect hospitality with having family, friends, and business associates over to their homes for a meal. We also associate the term with courtesy and politeness in social interactions; exchanging pleasantries at a woman's luncheon; and taking on specific roles in the local church such as greeting people at the door or serving on the hospitality committee. Or we may think of the "hospitality industry." The word suggests getting away from the rat race and grind of everyday life and enjoying a cruise to the Bahamas, a nice dinner at a fancy restaurant, or a weekend at a four-star hotel. For the most part, the term has lost its moral or ethical dimension.[2]

To be sure, given the heated political rhetoric and demonstrations and counter-demonstrations of our day, we could benefit from more "etiquette"

---

1. Pohl, *Making Room*, 3.
2. Ibid., 4.

and civility in our public discourse. With our society torn by a growing "culture war" and deep political, racial, and social divisions, we desperately need to become more "hospitable" toward one another. But even this does not fully explain the rich meaning of the term or its importance within the Christian tradition.

In part three of this book I argue for the need to connect (or, better, reconnect) hospitality with the celebration of the Lord's Supper. This is what is meant by the term "eucharistic hospitality." In this initial overview my purpose is to briefly: 1) explain the biblical meaning of hospitality and its significance for Christians; 2) discuss its Old Testament roots and their connection to the New Testament, particularly as this connection pertains to the meaning of the Eucharist; and 3) show how the communal "agape meals" of the New Testament (which in the early Christian tradition included the Lord's Supper) were a continuation of the table fellowship that Jesus practiced during his earthly ministry. I will conclude with some further observations on the practical implications of an ethic of hospitality for Christians today.

Christians and the Meaning of Hospitality

In the ancient Near East, hospitality was regarded as one of the pillars of morality. It signified a sacred bond between guests and hosts.[3] In addition to the normal network of relationships within one's community, the practice of hospitality also revolved around the ancient custom of welcoming strangers and travelers into one's home, and providing necessary provisions and protection.[4] Travel in the ancient world was risky business. Not only was there the harsh environment that had to be navigated. As the story of the Good Samaritan illustrates, travelers were also easy prey for thieves and robbers who roamed the highways in sparsely populated areas. Of course, mysterious strangers also posed a potential threat to self and community. The relationship between guest and host therefore involved reciprocal responsibilities and obligations, the violation of which would undermine the social bonds between individuals and families and shake the moral foundations of their social world.[5]

---

3. Koenig, *New Testament Hospitality*, 2
4. Arterbury, "Entertaining Angels," 20.
5. Ibid., 21; Koenig, *New Testament Hospitality*, 2.

Christians Enjoined to Hospitality

In the New Testament and early Christian tradition, hospitality means "extending to strangers a quality of kindness usually reserved for friends and family."[6] This meaning is suggested in the term itself. One of the key Greek words for hospitality (*philoxenia*) combines the general word for love or affection for people who are connected by kinship or faith (*phileo*) and the word for stranger (*xenos*). But emphasis is placed on strangers in need, the weakest and "lowly and abject" who have little to offer in return.[7]

The New Testament regards hospitality as central to the authenticity of the gospel and a distinguishing feature of the Christian faith. It is listed as a requirement for church eldership (1 Tim 3:2; Titus 1:8). But it is not optional for *any* Christian, nor is it limited to those who are specially gifted in this area (Rom 12:13; Heb 13:2; 1 Pet 4:9).[8] Jesus regards it as so important, that he equates ministering to the needs of strangers with ministering to him (Matt 25:34–36). It is most likely that the "least of these" that he is referring to in this passage are fellow believers (25:40). But in the parable of the Good Samaritan (Lk 10:29–37) he expands the obligation of hospitality to the stranger to include anyone in need, *even* someone considered to be a sworn enemy.[9]

Christine Pohl notes that hospitality in these New Testament passages is a concrete expression of love—love for fellow brothers and sisters; love extended outwardly to strangers, prisoners, and exiles; love that not only ministers to physical and social needs but also recognizes and values the stranger or guest.[10] In the practice of hospitality there is a reconnecting of righteousness and justice. We tend to think of righteousness as avoiding temptation, particularly in matters pertaining to sexual morality. We also associate it with spiritual activities, such as prayer and Bible reading. But in both the Old and New Testaments, righteousness and justice are often used together or interchangeably. Job, for example, eloquently describes the righteous person as one who helps orphaned children, rescues the poor, makes the "widow's heart sing," and takes up "the cause of the stranger" (Job 29: 12–13, 16). James describes religion that is pure and faultless before God as "looking after widows and orphans in their distress" and "keeping oneself from being polluted by the world" (Jas 1:27). These, and many other

---

6. Pohl, *Making Room*, 19.
7. Ibid., 17–19, 31
8. Ibid., 31.
9. Ibid., 75.
10. Ibid., 31.

passages in the Bible, challenge our tendency to bifurcate personal and social concerns.

Recovering the Practice of Hospitality in the Church

The reader might naturally ask, what does this have to do with our practice of the Lord's Supper? I'll come to that shortly. But, first, it is important for us to see how a limited and truncated understanding of righteousness and faith often enables us to distance ourselves from issues of social justice. Consider, for example, the impact that our lifestyle choices and patterns of consumption can have on others. Christopher Heuertz and Christine Pohl observe that we rarely think about how the things we buy, the activities we enjoy, and the food we eat have anything to do with other people's pain and suffering. They relate the life-changing experience of John Wesley. One day, a young woman came to his door asking for help for herself and her baby. They were cold and hungry. Though sympathetic to their plight, Wesley was unable to give much assistance because he had just spent almost all of his available money to decorate his house. The beautiful pictures on the wall that he had purchased earlier in the day were a painful reminder of the choices he had made.[11]

This experience when he was a young university student was one of a number of other experiences which led the eighteenth-century reformer to adopt a strong stance on possessions and the use of money. Every penny spent on expensive clothing is, in his view, essentially money stolen from God and the poor. The issues are complex. But, for Wesley, spiritual apathy, social heartlessness, and greed are intertwined. In response to the excuse made by those with resources that they were not aware of anyone in need of help, Wesley responded: "One great reason why the rich, in general, have so little sympathy for the poor is that they so seldom visit them. Hence it is that . . . one part of the world does not know what the other suffers. Many of them do not know, because they do not care to know . . ." Voluntary ignorance, in other words, does not make us blameless.[12]

None of this is meant to imply that there are not ambiguities and tensions in this area. While we can and should be more conscious about what we buy and how we use our resources, none of us can entirely withdraw from the economy. Kevin DeYoung and Greg Gilbert make the valid point that when it comes to helping the poor in the world "let's not turn every possibility into a responsibility and every opportunity into an ought." In

---

11. Heurtz and Pohl, *Friendship at the Margins*, 53–55.
12. Ibid., 56–8.

our practice of hospitality, we are on safer ground when grace and not guilt is our operating principle.[13] We will look in greater depth at the issue of sharing possessions in chapter twelve.

Perhaps even more contentious and messy are the issues of immigration and treatment of refugees. Here, many Christians harbor strong reservations about helping the "strangers" in our midst. A recent poll conducted by the Pew Research Center reveals increasing polarization among Christian religious groups on attitudes to refugees. Of those questioned, 43 percent of white mainline Protestants, 50 percent of Catholics, and 63 percent of black Protestants believe that America has a responsibility to house refugees. However, just 25 percent of white evangelical Protestants believe this, while 68 percent believe it "does not" have this responsibility.[14] Seventy-six percent of white evangelical Protestants also approved of President Trump's temporary travel ban on refugees from Muslim countries.[15] Evangelical organizations such as the National Association of Evangelicals (NAE) have advocated a balanced approach to the issue of immigration. While acknowledging the right of nation states to protect their borders, the NAE has urged tolerance and a humane treatment of immigrants who cross the border illegally.[16] Yet, almost half (48 percent) of white evangelicals favor policies that enforce laws against undocumented immigrants rather than those that create a path to citizenship.[17] Polls have consistently found that white evangelical Protestants are more likely than any other religious group to support hardline immigrations policies. A recent survey indicates that 70 percent of white evangelicals are in favor of expanding the boarder wall between the U.S. and Mexico—a level of support for this policy of the Trump administration which is much higher than that of white mainline Protestants (50 percent), white Catholics (51 percent), black Protestants (26 percent), and Hispanic Catholics (20 percent).[18]

None of these issues is easily resolved. Pohl reminds us that offering hospitality to strangers in a world characterized by injustice, sin, and brokenness will be rarely easy.[19] What is noteworthy, however, is the lack of attention that many Christians give to what the Bible says on this topic.

---

13. DeYoung and Gilbert, *What is the Mission of the Church?*, 176–77.

14. Burton, "68% of White Evangelicals Think America Shouldn't House Refugees."

15. Bruinius, "Why Evangelicals are Trump's Strongest Travel-ban Supporters."

16. See Anderson et al., "Open Letter on Immigration Reform."

17. Dallas, "Faithfully Engaging the Immigration Debate in the Age of Trump."

18. Thomson-DeVeaux, "Why Rank-And-File Evangelicals Aren't Likely to Turn on Trump."

19. Pohl, *Making Room*, 149.

While Scripture does not provide specific policy guidance, it does offer important principles and perspectives that help guide thought and action on immigration and other policy issues.[20] Yet, according to another recent poll by the Pew Research Center, only 7 percent of Catholics, 3 percent of white mainline Protestants, and 12 percent of white evangelicals say that religion is the biggest influence on their immigration policy views. By contrast, among white evangelicals, 62 percent say that religious beliefs have the greatest influence on their views regarding homosexuality and 53 percent say their views on abortion are mostly influenced by religion.[21]

The phenomenon of partisan cherry-picking of Bible verses is evident when we look at Leviticus 18–20. Religious conservatives appeal to Leviticus 18:22 and 20:13, two of the five passages in Scripture which expressly condemn homosexual behavior.[22] Because of these and other verses in the Bible that clearly express "God's will," marriage amendments have been passed and conservative cake makers refuse to make wedding cakes for gay couples on the grounds that it violates their conscience.[23] In the heated debate over immigration, however, many conservative Christians conveniently gloss over Leviticus 19, particularly verses 33–34, which read:

> When an alien lives with you in your land, do not mistreat him. The alien living with you must be treated as one of your native-born. Love him as yourself, for you were aliens in Egypt. I am the Lord your God.

By the same token, there are evangelical leaders on the political left who emphasize biblical passages which talk about justice for the alien, but downplay, or reinterpret, those passages specifically having to do with same-sex relationships.[24]

20. Amstutz *Just Immigration*, 14.

21. Pew Research Center, "Few Say Religion Shapes Immigration, Environment Views."

22. The other three passages are Romans 1:26–28,1 Corinthians 6:9–11, and 1 Timothy 1:10. Some also cite the story of Sodom and Gomorrah in Genesis 18–19, which refers to homosexual behavior as among the sins which brought God's judgment upon these two cities.

23. Hilton, *A House United*, 132–33.

24. See, for example, Wallis, *On God's Side*. Wallis argues on the basis of Scripture that: "How God's people treat both strangers and the poor . . . will be a sign of how they will be judged—either blessed or cursed (111) In Scripture "God is always telling his people to welcome the strangers, the foreigners, the poor—the outsiders" (127). God's inclusion, however, pertains to gays and lesbians as well as undocumented immigrants and American Muslims (165). Wallis maintains that most biblical passages mentioning homosexuality are "not really about" committed same-sex relationships (269). He has recently endorsed same-sex marriage.

Ronald Sider points out that, while the plight of undocumented immigrants is one of the thorniest issues in the American landscape today, many of those who cross the southern border of the United States, with or without proper documentation, are fellow believers. Surely, the faith of immigrants and the faith of Christians in the host country should be decisive in the way churches, communities, and individual believers think about and respond to the current immigration crisis. "The Bible," he continues, "is the most important place to look for guidance. . . . Christians—both immigrants and those in the majority culture-must look at the issue through biblical lenses."[25] As Christians, we are driven, not by political or economic expediencies or partisan rhetoric, but by a whole new set of values, a way of life defined by God's kingdom.[26]

Old Testament Roots and the New Testament

To fully understand the emphasis that the Bible places on hospitality toward the stranger, we need to turn to the Old Testament roots. Worship among the ancient Israelites was not a docile or passive affair. Rather, it involved "a life-or-death verbal interaction with YHWH in which [their] future was profoundly at stake."[27] These utterances, often articulated in the psalms, took many different forms. They might be declarations of remembrance and of praise for God's past goodness to Israel; or lament and petition in the face of trouble; or an acknowledgement of guilt and failure to honor their covenant with God. But underlying all of these expressions of worship is "a *bodily, verbal, public* declaration that life is a gift and that all of life, in Israel and in all creation, is gladly dependent upon and derived from YHWH's extravagant, generous, reliable self-giving."[28]

Abraham: Faith, and Hospitality to Strangers

Embedded within this acknowledgement that the life of the entire community is a gift of God who rescues and blesses is Israel's very identity as an alien people or sojourners. When God forms a covenant with Abraham and gives him a promise of blessing, he calls him away from family and what was familiar to be a stranger within a foreign land (Gen 12:1–3). But, as Joshua

---

25. See the afterward to Carroll, *Christians at the Border*, 138.
26. Ibid., 139.
27. Brueggemann, *Worship in Ancient Israel*, 39.
28. Ibid., 58.

Jipp points out, what is striking in this story is that God's covenantal promise to Abraham that he would be the father of many nations (Gen 15:1–6; 17:1–14) is confirmed in Genesis 18 *after he has demonstrated his faith and piety through offering hospitality to three strangers* (18:1–5).[29] In this formative story on hospitality, Abraham graciously welcomes these strangers and then gives them water to wash their feet, a lavish meal, and a place to rest. Subsequently, he and Sarah receive divine confirmation through these three guests that they would have a son in their old age. The story therefore connects hospitality with God's presence, promise, and blessing.[30] Referring to this account, the author of Hebrews also emphasizes the connection between hospitality and the divine presence when, following the great chapter on faith (11:1–40), he exhorts his readers: "Do not forget to entertain strangers, for by so doing some have entertained angels without knowing it" (13:2).

In the narrative that follows, Sodom and Gomorrah are destroyed for their deliberate acts of inhospitality and abuse of strangers; on the other hand, Lot and his family are rescued from God's judgment because of their hospitality to divine visitors (Gen 19:1–3). It is probably on the basis of his hospitality that Peter refers to Lot as "righteous" (2 Peter 2:7).[31] "Lot's treatment of strangers distinguished him from his social context, and for this he is commended in the later tradition (2 Pet 2:7–8, 1 Clement 11:1)."[32]

The Exodus, Land, and Hospitality

When the Israelites finally inherit the land after being rescued from their sojourn in Egypt, God reminds them that the land belongs to the Lord and that "you are strangers and sojourners with me" (Lev 25:23 ESV). It is this identity as sojourners within a covenant relationship with God which serves as the essential framework for Israel's response to the poor and aliens within their own midst. First, it provides an experiential basis for identifying with the needs of sojourners and those who were powerless. The primary motivation behind extended hospitality to the helpless and needy is their own collective experience of having been aliens in Egypt (Exod 22:21; Lev 19:33–34). "You are to love those who are aliens, for you yourselves were aliens in the land of Egypt" (Deut 10:19).

---

29. Jipp, *Saved by Faith and Hospitality*, 5.
30. Pohl, *Making Room*, 24.
31. Jipp, *Saved by Faith and Hospitality*, 5.
32. Pohl, *Making Room*, 25.

Secondly, God loves the foreigner, giving them food and clothing (Deut 10:18). Just as God has by his grace and mercy rescued the Israelites when they were strangers in Egypt, so they are to show the same acts of justice and compassion toward the poor and vulnerable strangers in their own land (Exod 23:9; Deut 10:16–19). God essentially says to the Israelites: "Israel, you were liberated by me. You did not accomplish it—I performed it *for* you, by my grace. Now do the same for others."[33] Acts of mercy toward the stranger are indicative of faith in God. This is exemplified in the story of Rahab, the prostitute. Her hospitality to the spies is taken as a sign of her faith in the God of Israel (Josh 2:18–13) and results in her being shown "kindness and mercy" when the Israelites enter the land that God had promised (Josh 2:14).[34]

Finally, the Israelites are reminded that their land is a gift from God. There is no land without God. Israel's land is covenanted land. The non-negotiable character of Israel's land is that it is received as a free gift. This awareness that Israel's existence is a gifted existence comes with the warning to avoid the temptations of self-reliance, oppression, idolatry, tightfistedness, and lack of concern for the poor and needy. There can be no ultimate claim upon the land, because "the land is mine. For you are strangers and sojourners with me" (Lev 25:23, ESV). All are equal before God because everything is from God. "Israel's response to the 'other' is also a response to God. Hospitality to the stranger symbolizes Israel's response to God."[35] Oppression of the stranger and the poor is therefore an act against the covenant with God. Luke Johnson states:

> When God called Israel into being as a people, he redeemed those who were themselves oppressed (Exod 2:23–25; 3:7–10). His power to "work justice" for the oppressed has not ceased. Those who oppress the poor will have to deal with God's avenging anger. If the poor, the widows, or the oppressed cry out to God, he will hear them and punish the oppressor (Exod 22:21–27; Deut 25:9).[36]

The Old Testament record is clear, however, that hospitality involves reciprocal obligations. While the people of God are to show justice toward the aliens in their midst, the aliens are required to submit to the laws of those with whom they have come to reside (Lev 18:26).

---

33. Keller, *Generous Justice*, 93.
34. Jipp, *Saved by Faith and Hospitality*, 5.
35. Richard, *Living the Hospitality of God*, 25–28.
36. Johnson, *Sharing Possessions*, 94.

The Identity of Christians as Recipients of God's Hospitality

The New Testament likewise uses the concept of hospitality to portray God's saving work. The book of Ephesians describes believers as no longer strangers and aliens but, rather, those who have been welcomed into God's household (Eph 2:19). The good news of the gospel, in other words, is that God's hospitality has transformed us from strangers and enemies into God's friends and family. Joshua Jipp perceptively notes that humans have two competing alternatives for how we construe our fundamental identity. One alternative is for us to define our identity in terms of something about ourselves—our religiosity, education, ethnicity, vocation, etc. Or, alternatively, "you see yourself in every facet of your life as one whose identity, the very core of who you are, has been determined by God's gracious and undeserved saving and reconciling welcome of all of us into his family."[37]

This identity-shaping good news of God's hospitality, is, of course, what we celebrate in the Lord's Supper or Eucharist. But, as the rest of Ephesians makes clear, the saving welcome of God, which makes us part of his family, is also foundational for our response to others. Those who are made part of the household of God are to be characterized by acts of kindness and forgiveness, *even as* they have received God's forgiveness through Christ (Eph 4:32). The Lord's Supper, which is the hallmark of Christian worship, is both an assertion of and an act of gratitude for the free gift of God, from whom all life comes.[38] "From his fullness we have all received, grace upon grace" (Jn 1:16 ESV). The Eucharistic community "gives thanks" (*eucharistia*) to God in response to his abundant grace. Through the work of the Holy Spirit, the joy of the thanksgiving community which flows toward God also naturally overflows in acts of hospitality and self-giving love to those who are unable to secure their own existence in the world.[39] Hospitality is a necessary part of the new covenant spirituality which is rooted in both the Last Supper and the Eucharist. As Gorman states, "new covenant politics [is] a politics of hospitality and solidarity rather than exclusion and rejection, especially with the vulnerable and the suffering."[40]

In both the Old and New Testaments, then, worship is never an end in itself. It also issues a "missional" summons to be actively engaged in compassion for the needy in society.[41] In the New Testament, the examples

---

37. Jipp, *Saved by Faith and Hospitality*, 35–36.
38. Brueggemann, *Worship in Ancient Israel*, 59–60.
39. Schults and Sandage, *The Faces of Forgiveness*, 218.
40. Gorman, *The Death of the Messiah*, 222.
41. Brueggemann, *Worship in Ancient Israel*, 13.

of Abraham and Rahab are given to show that true faith is demonstrated through hospitality. The author of Hebrews says that Rahab's faith was manifested in her "welcoming the spies in peace" (Heb 11:31). And James argues that judgment will be severe for those "who do not show mercy" (Jas 2:13). Then (referring to both Abraham and Rahab) he goes on to state that true saving faith is demonstrated in works—including acts of hospitality (2:14–26).[42]

Both Paul (Phil 3:20) and Peter (1 Pet 2:11) also describe Christians as spiritual sojourners in the world. As in the Old Testament, this picture of the God's people as aliens in a strange land is connected with exhortations to a life of faith characterized by love, compassion, and hospitality to both fellow believers and outsiders (Rom 12:13–14; 1 Pet 2:12; Heb 13:2–3). Believers who as resident aliens are without a home in society are part of a "household of faith" which is characterized by a new order of values.[43] Mark Griffin and Theron Walker remind us:

> As for the church . . . the difference between it and all other cultures is that its members know themselves to be sojourners in this earthly city, with hearts "restless till they rest in God." And St. Paul reminds us that Christians are spiritual descendants of Abraham. We would do well to reclaim an ancient prayer, offered by Israelites as they gave their tithe: "A wandering Aramean was my father: and he went down to Egypt and sojourned there" (Deut 26"5). St. Paul brings this pilgrim sensibility to the church when he calls us, not just to tithe, but to present our bodies "as a living sacrifice, holy and acceptable to God, which is [our] spiritual worship," and to be "not . . . conformed to this world" (Rom 12:1–2). To be people of faith is to become strangers and aliens, to remember we work here under permit, under the proverbial Green Card.
>
> And the church is called not just to be a resident alien group, but a place of welcome and care for the dispossessed. . . . By claiming its pilgrim heritage, and by practicing that most pilgrim of virtues (hospitality), the church will be neither a ghetto (a walled enclave) nor a domesticated resort (sentimental but devoid of life) but an *inn* for weary travelers of the borderlands/

---

42. Jipp, *Saved by Faith and Hospitality*, 5–6. Jipp and others point out that when James states that Abraham was justified by his works (plural), in addition to speaking of his willingness to sacrifice his son Isaac (Gen 22) he almost certainly is also referring to Abraham's hospitality to strangers (Gen 18:1–18). Jipp concludes that "though faith alone is constitutive of salvation and the Christian's appropriation of saving grace, *both faith and acts of mercy* are ultimately necessary for salvation" (5).

43. Richard, *Living the Hospitality of God*, 36–37.

frontiers, and an *outpost of hope* for exiles bound for the city of God.⁴⁴

Jesus' Table Fellowship, Agape Meals, and the Lord's Supper

How would you complete this sentence: "Jesus came into the world to . . ."? Most of us would say, "To die on the cross so that our sins could be forgiven." In support of this response, we could appeal to verses like Luke 19:10: "The Son of Man came to seek and to save what was lost." No one would quarrel with this answer. As one theologian has stated, "Outstanding among the blessings brought by Jesus to [people] is the forgiveness of sins."⁴⁵

Few of us, however, would say that Jesus came to eat and drink with people. Yet, this is precisely what Luke 7:34 says: "The Son of Man came eating and drinking . . ." In fact, as we read through Luke's Gospel we see that a big part of Jesus' "mission strategy" is a meal with some grilled fish, a loaf of bread, and a pitcher of wine (5:27–31; 7:36; 10:38–41; 11:37; 14:1–23; 19:1–10; 22:1–30; 24:13–32).⁴⁶

Why was "table fellowship" such an important part of Jesus' ministry? At the most fundamental level, a meal is an expression of hospitality. Especially in Jesus' day, table fellowship bound people to each other socially and to God.⁴⁷ In sharing table fellowship with the "unacceptable" people in society, Jesus demonstrates God's acceptance of sinners, the poor, and the marginalized. Shared meals embody the "Jesus creed" to love God and to love others.⁴⁸

But instead of eliminating boundaries, tables can also create boundaries between people and maintain divisions between social groupings. For the Pharisees, who viewed the table as a way of excluding those who were regarded as morally and ritually impure, Jesus' behavior was regarded as offensive and dangerous. The second half of Luke 7:34 expresses their attitude towards Jesus: "Here is a glutton and a drunkard." To our ears, this might sound like a rather harmless tweet. But the accusation is far more serious than it appears. In Jesus' day, the term "glutton and a drunkard" was used to describe stubborn and rebellious sons who by law were to be stoned to death in order to purge evil from the community!⁴⁹

---

44. Griffin and Walker, *Living on the Borders*, 181–82.
45. Marshall, *Luke: Historian and Theologian*, 138.
46. Chester, *A Meal with Jesus*, 13.
47. Lemons, "Communitas at the Tables," 163.
48. McKnight, *The Jesus Creed*, 35.
49. Ibid.

In our day, the worldview of the Pharisees finds expression in group stereotypes which paint those on the other side of the border (or the other side of the tracks) as "bad" or "evil," while those on our side are "good." It is also reflected in two of the great false narratives of our day—nationalism ("my nation is God's nation") and tribalism ("all that matters is what benefits my group"). As was demonstrated most graphically in the August 2017 demonstrations in Charlottesville, Virginia, it is a combination of these two "isms" which fuel the anti-black and anti-Semitic rhetoric of hate groups such as the white supremacists, the KKK, and neo-Nazis.

Imagine a religious leader in the American South at the height of segregation prior to the 1960s holding public integrated meals and then declaring: "This is an expression of God's kingdom." This picture gives us some sense of the radical and revolutionary nature of Jesus' meal practice. When people sit at the table with Jesus they are made part of a new society—a society of inclusion and justice in which all persons can be restored to fellowship with one another and with God the father.[50]

There are indications throughout the New Testament and early church documents that in the years following Jesus' resurrection and ascension into heaven, community meals which included the Lord's Supper or the Eucharist became a church-wide practice. These community meals are variously referred to as bread-breaking (Acts 2:42–46); the Lord's Supper (lit. "a Supper of the Lord," 1 Cor 11:20); Agape or love feast (Jude 12; cf. 2 Pet 2:13); and the Eucharist (*Didache* 9:15). While eventually different groups came to emphasize one part of the meal over another, originally all of these terms fundamentally referred to the same thing.[51] Ben Witherington observes that "the practice of offering hospitality including meals, which began with Jesus and his disciples and continues throughout the New Testament era, was an ongoing feature of the Christian community that really helped the Christian cause of evangelism right up to the end of the Roman Empire as a pagan entity."[52] It seems clear, then, that what we call the "Lord's Supper" was originally a continuation and extension of Jesus' meal practice. The

---

50. Ibid., 38.

51. See Finger, *Of Widows and Meals*, 61–70. Finger points out that the references to breaking bread and eating with joy in Acts 2:42, 46 indicate the practice of table fellowship or communal meals. However, bread-breaking also has a sacramental meaning. In two early Christian texts (*Didache* 14:1 and Ignatius Ephesians 20:1) the term clearly refers to the Eucharist. This in combination with other passages (1 Cor 11:17–34; Jude 12; 2 Pet 2:13) strongly suggests the early Christian tradition of agape meals, or communal love feasts that included the Eucharist. Witherington also concludes on the basis of Jude 12 and the *Didache* that the early church likely celebrated the Lord's Supper in the context of an agape feast or fellowship meal (*Making a Meal of It*, 99-03)

52. Ibid., 89.

common thread in all of these meals is the principle of hospitality, which extends back to the Old Testament and God's covenantal relationship with Israel, especially following the exodus.

Concluding Reflections: Taking Hospitality Seriously

Today, "Christian love" is often reduced to a "positive feeling" toward other people as expressed in a warm hug or handshake and to occasional acts of "charity" toward the needy. It may therefore be difficult for us to fully grasp the social as well as religious significance which the apostles and early church attached to the practice of the Lord's Supper. We should not be so naïve as to think that the communal practice of the first-century church can be simply imported into our modern and postmodern societies. Nonetheless, it forces us to examine ourselves. How consistent is our meal practice with that of our Lord, whom we claim to follow? Were he to return today, would he find us faithful in following his example of welcoming the stranger? Concerning the issue of lifestyle, Heuertz and Pohl ask some further challenging questions: *"Could I invite my friends who are poor into my home and lifestyle and have a good time with them? Would I be ashamed of my comforts and expenditures?"*[53] These questions are not to be taken lightly. For we will be effective in communicating the gospel of God's grace only to the extent that we are thoroughly converted ourselves.[54]

When it comes to public policy, it again needs to be emphasized that the biblical ethic of hospitality does not give us a detailed blueprint for addressing the contentious issues of immigration and treatment of refugees. As Mark Amstutz rightly argues, "since the Bible is not an international-relations manual, it does not provide ready-made answers to the difficult and complex tasks of determining the degree and the way sovereign states should regulate borders."[55] Christian denominations and clergy therefore err when they advocate specific public policies in the name of the church.[56] But an ethic of hospitality is an important part of developing a biblically-informed normative framework—a moral compass—that helps Christians respond wisely and faithfully to these issues.[57] Here we need to keep a proper

---

53. Heuertz and Pohl, *Friendship at the Margins*, 86.
54. McKnight, *The King Jesus Gospel*, 156.
55. Amstutz, *Just Immigration*, 227.
56. Ibid., 229.
57. Sider argues that careful political decision–making from a Christian perspective requires four interrelated components: 1) a normative framework, largely informed by biblical revelation; 2) a broad study of society and the world; 3) a political philosophy

balance between inclusion and exclusion. An ethic of hospitality does not require admitting every person seeking asylum in the United States. Order needs to serve justice; but there cannot be justice without order. Thus, a just immigration and refugee policy requires an orderly process of enforcing laws that protect the common good. On the other hand, structures of order always need to be kept under moral criticism. Since the gospel is concerned with the redemption of all of creation, not just personal salvation, the church should illuminate how biblical morality applies to the social and political domains of society; and it should denounce government actions which are inconsistent with divine will.[58] For Christians, borders should be viewed morally from the perspective of our obligation to persons who are no less sons and daughters of God. Enforcement of an order that stifles the cries of the poor and needy and tramples on basic human rights is a violation of the moral law of God, who shows no partiality, defends the cause of the fatherless and widow, and loves the foreigners residing among us (Deut 10:17–19).[59]

Unfortunately, many Christians tend to limit their treatment of these complex issues to a simplistic defense of the "rule of law." Joshua Jipp points out that "Pockets of evangelical Christianity in North America are guilty of supporting the most radically xenophobic, intolerant public policies and public servants."[60] An example is President Trump's family separation policy, which was implemented in April 2018. Almost 3,000 children were separated from their parents who were caught illegally crossing the border— many of them fleeing rampant violence and gang activity in their homeland. While many Christians rightly condemned Trump's zero-tolerance policy, some have sought to justify this and similar policies by misinterpreting and misapplying passages such as Romans 13.[61] Jipp is right when he argues on

---

that emerges from a normative biblical framework and painstaking, extensive socioeconomic and political analysis; and 4) detailed social analysis on specific issues (*just Politics*, 24–28). For further insights on the formation of a Christian political philosophy and theology of justice, see also two books by Mott: *Biblical Ethics and Social Change* and *A Christian Perspective on Political Thought*.

58. See Amstutz, *Just Immigration*, 218.

59. See Wilbanks, *Re-Creating America*, 140.

60. Jipp, *Saved by Faith and Hospitality*, 9.

61. There are a number of reasons why the use of Romans 13 to justify such a policy involves a misuse of Scripture. First, Paul says that government is the servant of God to protect society against those who do evil (13:1–4). There is no moral equivalence between the "evil persons" referred to in this passage and immigrants who are fleeing violence and seeking asylum in this country. Second, in describing government as a "servant of God for good" Paul is implying that there are limits to government authority and power. The authority of God over government provides the basis for judging

the basis of both Old and New Testament teaching that "Christians must reject anything that dehumanizes, stigmatizes, and perpetuates violence against the marginalized and vulnerable." Too few Christians today "understand that hospitality to strangers and to the marginalized is a constituent component of their faith."[62]

In the next three chapters we will examine a number of accounts in the New Testament which highlight the practice of hospitality. Chapter 10 looks at three stories in Luke that reflect Jesus' habit of dining with sinners: 1) the call of Levi the tax collector (5:27–32); 2) the parable of the Prodigal Son (15:1–2; 11–32); and 3) Jesus in the house of Zacchaeus (19:1–10). The following chapter discusses Jesus' parable of the great banquet, which is a picture of the eschatological feast to which everyone is invited (Lk 14:1–24). The final chapter of part three focuses on the practice of community sharing in Jerusalem (Acts 2:42–47; 4:32–37; 6:1–7) and its relationship to the Lord's Supper.

---

specific acts of government as unjust and not in conformity with God's moral law. Third (unlike Paul's situation) Christians living in a democracy have the ability to call for a change in unjust laws or policies through their elected representatives. For a further discussion of Romans 13 see Mott, *Biblical Ethics and Social Change*, 145–66.

62. Ibid.

10

Fellowship with Sinners at Festal Meals

WHEN I was a college student I attended a church in an affluent northern suburb of Chicago. One Sunday, three young adults came to our church wearing tattered jeans and old sweatshirts. Their hair was disheveled, and they were unshaven. These days, in many of our churches the appearance of these young adults would not be particularly out of place. But back in my college days, a suit or sport coat and tie was the expected attire for churchgoers. One of these young men introduced himself to me. While I don't remember the exact substance of our conversation, I do recall him to be quite obnoxious. Although he was not vulgar in any way, much of his conduct seemed inappropriate, particularly within our conservative and straight laced church environment. At one point, he sat down next to me in Sunday school class (which was held prior to the morning service) and peppered me with odd questions like, "Why do you make so many markings in your Bible?" While I tried to be accommodating and friendly toward this person, inwardly I felt very uncomfortable. The next Sunday, the same young men came back to church, this time wearing more "appropriate" attire. The young man who had been so obnoxious to me the week before, explained that they were actually students from the seminary in the area who had decided to conduct a social experiment. They wanted to see how we would react to visitors who violated regular behavioral "norms" of church culture. He never told me if I "passed" his test.

The question that the seminarians in the above story were trying to raise is this: "How receptive are we as Christians of "strangers" in our midst who may not conform to our particular norms of "acceptable" behavior?" In fact, were Jesus himself to walk into most of our churches, how warmly would he be received?

These questions jump out at us when we read Luke's narrative of Jesus' ministry, particularly his description of how much time and effort Jesus spent eating and drinking with all sorts of people in a variety of settings. As one commentator has stated, "In Luke's Gospel Jesus is either going to a meal, at a meal, or coming from a meal."[1] The most important meal that Luke records is, of course, the Last Supper that Jesus had with his disciples; but this meal is really the continuation and culmination of a series of other meals. So the story of the Last Supper is really a story of Jesus' journeys in which meals and hospitality played a major role for Jesus as well as his followers.[2]

As I mentioned previously, there are three stories of hospitality in Luke's Gospel which I will focus on in this chapter: 1) the call of Levi the tax collector (5:27–32); 2) the parable of the lost son (15:1–2, 11–32); and 3) the episode of Zacchaeus (19:1–10). The context for each of these stories is Jesus' relationship with tax collectors and sinners. In addition, all feature a meal or banquet in some way. While Luke does not specifically refer to a meal in the episode of Zacchaeus, it is clearly implicit.[3] All of these stories are part of Luke's "travel narrative" (9:51–19:47), which describes Jesus' long journey to Jerusalem. Each tells us a lot about the nature of "eucharistic hospitality." I will conclude this chapter with a discussion of some implications of biblical hospitality for the proper response of Christians to the contentious "culture war" in America today.

The Hospitality of God

Jesus' words at the end of the Zacchaeus episode—"For the Son of man came to seek and to save what was lost" (Lk 19:10)—reveals the basic theme of Luke's Gospel: that Jesus offers salvation to *all* people.[4] Jesus frames salvation in terms of the "gospel of the kingdom." As I have previously noted, in the ancient world the term *gospel* was a word used for declaring good news about something. So, when Jesus speaks of salvation, basically he is referring to the "good news" of the arrival of God's kingdom. The three stories before us therefore show the close connection between the themes of salvation, the kingdom, and hospitality in Luke's Gospel.

The theme of hospitality is so prominent in Luke that one commentator sees the phrase "the hospitality of God" as summarizing the basic

---

1. Chester, *A Meal with Jesus*, 13.
2. See LsVerdiere, *Dining in the Kingdom of God*, 9; 195.
3. Ibid., 107.
4. Marshall, *Luke: Historian and Theologian*, 116.

message of the entire Gospel. "Luke sees the whole life and ministry of Jesus as a '*visitation*' on God's part to Israel and the world. From the start this raises the question: how will this guest, this visitor be *received*?"[5]

The Lukan "Triangle"

In his descriptions of Jesus' meals, Luke does not just focus on the interaction between Jesus and the character (such as Zacchaeus or Levi) who is the main object of his concern. Luke also introduces a third party—those who observe and comment on the event. This third group invariably has difficulty with what they see and reject the exchange of hospitality.[6]

One scene in the episode of Jesus in the house of Zacchaeus speaks volumes. When the people mutter and complain that he has become a guest in the house of a sinner (v 7), Jesus astounds the crowd with a strong defense of Zacchaeus (v 9): "*Today* salvation has come to this house, because this man, too, is a son of Abraham" (that is, a full member of the community).[7] In effect, Jesus is indirectly saying to Zacchaeus, "You are accepted into God's kingdom, which is a reality here and now." But he is saying even more. He is identifying *himself* as the Messiah foretold by the prophets, the fulfillment of Israel's hopes and aspirations.

The episode of Zacchaeus and other stories of Jesus' acts of hospitality toward sinners, then, give us a window into the motivations of people or groups for responding either positively or negatively to Jesus and his message of salvation. Acceptance and rejection—both human and divine—is a key trajectory running through these episodes and Luke's entire narrative.[8]

The Scandal of Jesus' Hospitality

Jesus' message of the kingdom is made in the context of other competing versions of Israel's story. Understanding this helps explain why Jesus' response to tax collectors and sinners is so scandalous in eyes of his contemporaries. Tax collectors are considered social outcasts who cheat and defraud people. As a chief tax collector, Zacchaeus stands at the top of the collection pyramid, which means that he receives a commission from those who collect taxes for him. He is therefore a wealthy man whose wealth is considered by

5. Byrne, *The Hospitality of God*, 4.
6. Ibid., 9.
7. Ibid., 10.
8. Ibid.

many to be acquired fraudulently.[9] Furthermore, because tax collectors are part of an oppressive system of taxation, they are also viewed as collaborators with the Roman occupation of the Jewish land and people. Many of the Jews side with those who preach "holy warfare" against the Romans. They look forward to the day when God will defeat the Romans and re-establish his kingdom. In their eyes, the tax collectors are traitors, both to the nation and to God.[10]

But there is another reason why Jesus' meals with those considered to be the "riff raff" of Jewish society are so offensive to the onlookers. In that culture, accepting an invitation to eat food with another person was deeply symbolic of friendship, intimacy, and unity. And when persons were estranged, a meal invitation opened the door to reconciliation.[11] In the ancient world there were many statements by wise men of the kinds of people with whom one should and *should not* share meals. The Jewish sage Sirach, for example, counsels that instead of inviting just anyone into your home, "let the righteous be your dinner companions."[12] The Jewish heroes often separated themselves from impure people and food.[13] Jesus' acceptance of tax collectors and other sinners in his practice of open table fellowship is therefore a direct affront to another religious group which wields considerable influence in Jewish society—the Pharisees, for whom Jewish food laws are a critical factor in maintaining cultural, religious, and moral boundaries.

In some respects, the Pharisees have gotten a bum rap. As Scot McKnight notes, they are the "good guys in white hats," the leaders of the "home Bible study movement" in the land of Israel. Apart from their opposition to Jesus, they are in some ways like many of us.[14] They believe that Israel has to be pure before it can be restored. Their vision for Israel is that God's blessing, including the Messiah and the kingdom, will come through the teaching of the law and obedience to it. The Pharisees' emphasis on strict adherence to the law and concern for moral respectability leads them to dissociate themselves from sinners and non-Jews who do not measure up to their standards of purity. The difference between Jesus and the Pharisees can be summed up by saying that the Pharisees teach the love of the Law

---

9. Bock, *Luke*, 478.

10. Chester, *A Meal with Jesus*, 19

11. Bartchy, "Table Fellowship," 796.

12. Jipp, *Saved by Faith and Hospitality*, 22–23.

13. Ibid., 23. See, for example, Dan 1:10–12; Macc 1:43, 62–63; 6:4–7; Tob 1:5; 10–12.

14. McKnight, *Kingdom Conspiracy*, 51.

while Jesus teaches a law of love.[15] Jesus' meals with tax collectors and other sinners depict the radical nature of God's grace. They represent Jesus' offer of "a new world, a new kingdom, a new outlook."[16]

The stories of Levi and Zacchaeus invite us to reconsider our own utter dependence on Jesus' hospitality. They expose two false narratives which can control our lives. On the one hand, some of us who have been believers for some time may be tempted to think that, after years of Bible study and church attendance or leadership, we have achieved a certain level of spirituality and holiness. This allows us to avoid any sort of identification with Zacchaeus, Levi, and the other stigmatized social outcasts and sinners in Luke's Gospel. At the opposite extreme, we might see ourselves as defined by our failings—our addictions, our marital failures, our mental illnesses, and the like. These stories in Luke's Gospel call for a complete transformation of how we think of ourselves. They demand, as Joshua Jipp points out, a recognition that "all of us are desperately needy and dependent in every way upon the welcoming and reconciling presence of Jesus."[17]

God's Hospitality and Human Hospitality

Throughout his Gospel, Luke reveals the effect that God's hospitality has on people who either accept or reject it. Luke "shows how people appropriate salvation, how they resist it, and the effect that reception or rejection, as the case may be, has on human lives."[18] This pattern is particularly evident in each of our three passages.

Levi, Zacchaeus, and the Pharisees (5:27–32; 19:1–10)

Tax collectors and sinners who accept Jesus' invitation to fellowship are transformed by the extravagance of God's grace. When Levi the tax collector is called by Jesus to be one of his disciples (5:27–9), he gives up his vocation and financial security and throws a huge banquet to which he invites his large circle of notorious friends ("tax collectors and sinners").[19] Likewise, Zacchaeus expresses his deep gratitude for Jesus' acceptance of him by giving tangible evidence that he is a changed man. He becomes an example of

---

15. Ibid.
16. Chester, *A Meal with Jesus*, 14.
17. Jipp, *Saved by Faith and Hospitality*, 36.
18. Byrne, *The Hospitality of God*, 10.
19. Bock, *Luke*, 159.

"compassionate justice" by declaring his intent to give half of his possessions to the poor and make fourfold restitution to those he has defrauded—actions which exceed the highest standards set by the law.[20]

Luke contrasts the response of Levi and Zacchaeus to the response of the rich ruler who declines Jesus' invitation to sell his possessions, distribute the money to the poor, and follow him (Lk 18:18–30). For Luke, possessions function as a symbol of one's response to God. Levi's giving up of possessions to follow Jesus and Zacchaeus' voluntary generosity are signs of repentance and faith while the rich ruler's hesitant stinginess reveals a heart that is unrepentant and closed to God's grace.[21]

The episodes of Levi and Zacchaeus also show that divine hospitality must precede human hospitality. Human hospitality is a celebration of divine hospitality, or God's gracious invitation to find forgiveness and life in Christ.[22] It is notable that Jesus' hospitality also comes at a price. By associating with tax collectors and sinners, he lowers his own social status. The forgiveness and acceptance that he gives is not offered at a distance. He brings healing, wholeness, and restoration to the marginalized by himself becoming marginalized.

Luke further juxtaposes the cruciform nature of hospitality—both divine and human—with the attitude of the Pharisees and other unbelievers who grumble against Jesus. In the Septuagint (the Greek translation of the Old Testament) the word that Luke uses to describe their muttering (*diegongyzon*) almost exclusively refers to the Israelites when they complained about being in the desert following the exodus (Exod 16:7; 17:3; Num 11:1; 14:27–29; cf. Lk 15:2; 19:7).[23] The people and religious leaders of the dominant culture are therefore completely out of step with the gracious promise of God to deliver the marginalized, those who, in the Exodus account, were the people of Israel themselves.[24]

The Prodigal God (15:1–2, 11–32)

The parable that is generally referred to as the story of the "Prodigal Son" (Lk 15:11–32) could also be described as the story of the "Prodigal God." The word "prodigal" literally means "recklessly extravagant," or "to spend everything until there is nothing left." It is therefore appropriate for describing

---

20. Ibid., 479.
21. Hays, *The Moral Vision of the New Testament*, 125.
22. Boersma, *Violence, Hospitality, and the Cross*, 216.
23. Bock, *Luke*, 479.
24. See Lorenz, "Leading from the Margins," 19.

the father of the story as well as the younger son. For the father's joyous welcoming of his wayward son is literally reckless, because he refuses to "reckon" or count his sin against him or demand repayment. It is the "reckless extravagance" of the father's hospitality toward the younger son which offends the elder son.[25]

Readers often miss the full message of the parable, which is indicated by the context of the passage. In the first two verses of the chapter (15:1–2) Luke states that there are two groups of listeners. First, there are the tax collectors and sinners, who are represented by the younger brother in the parable. Like the younger brother, they engaged in "wild living." But there is a second group of listeners—the "Pharisees and teachers of the law." This group is represented by the older brother. So, to whom is the parable directed? While the parable is about both groups represented by the two brothers, the context indicates that Jesus tells this story specifically in response to the attitude of the *second group*. "The parable of the two sons takes an extended look at the soul of the elder brother, and climaxes with a powerful plea for him to change his heart."[26]

While I cannot give an extended discussion of this parable here, it is important to briefly note some of the main points in the development of this story. First, the parable highlights the nature and consequences of sin. It begins with a shocking request by the younger son to his father: "Give me my share of the estate (15:12)." Since the division of the estate normally occurs when the father is deceased, the son is basically saying, "I wish you were dead!" This death wish represents a radical break in his relationship with his father. "On the deepest level, sinners want God dead and out of their lives."[27] The younger son's journey to the far country widens the gap between him and the family. When the younger son wastes his money on profligate living, he hits rock bottom. The parable highlights the fact that he has literally nothing to eat. This precipitates his "return" to the father.

It is not commonly recognized, however, that the elder "obedient" son is *also* a sinner. When the father celebrates the return of the prodigal son with a lavish banquet, the elder son is jealous and angry. He bristles at the injustice of the father's grace. He says: "Look, you.[28] I've slaved for you all of these years and have never been disobedient; yet, I have not received so much as a young goat. But although this son of yours has wasted his money

25. Keller, *The Prodigal God*, xv.
26. Ibid., 9.
27. Bailey, *Jacob and the Prodigal,* 207.
28. This is the basic meaning in the Greek. In a culture where emphasis is placed on deference to elders, this in an outrageous expression of disrespect. See Keller, *The Prodigal God*, 27.

on prostitutes and deserves nothing but expulsion, you have killed the fatted calf for him. What justice is there in this?" (15:29–30). The elder brother's response is one of open rebellion. His pride and self-righteousness keep him from understanding the nature of the father's love and mercy. Thus, for both the lawbreakers (represented by the prodigal son) and the law-keepers (represented by the elder brother) the fundamental nature of the sin problem is the same—pride, rebellion, and a rupture in their relationships with God the Father. This severed relationship results in their exile from God.[29]

The difference between the two sons is that the prodigal son repents of his sin while the eldest son does not (or so it seems). Here, again, we tend to miss the point of the parable. When the father sees the prodigal son at a distance, he is filled with compassion and runs to reconcile his estranged son. This action on the part of the father not only goes against community standards, which require that any Jewish boy who loses his family inheritance to Gentiles be cut off from his people. In Middle Eastern culture it would be humiliating for the family patriarch wearing long robes to run in this fashion. The parable clearly indicates that the father runs and kisses the youngest son *before* he makes his confession (15:20–21). The son's repentance does not cause the father's love. *Rather, it is the father's costly grace which elicits the son's humble request for forgiveness*

The father also responds graciously to the elder son's outburst. He encourages the elder son to join in the celebration of the prodigal son's return (15:31–32). But here is the crux of the matter. If the oldest son accepts the father's love, he will be obliged to imitate the father's compassionate response to the prodigal son and take part in the banquet. The parable does not indicate whether the older son is willing to take this step. By ending the parable the way he does, Jesus, in effect, is saying to the religious leaders who are represented by the older brother, "How are you going to respond to the prodigal sons in your midst—and to me?"[30]

Hospitality and Redefining Hope

Before making some further practical applications, one final point needs to be made. At the heart of the various stories of hospitality in Luke's Gospel is the paradigm of "exile and return." The three stories we have looked at in this chapter are not just accounts of individual salvation. They are also stories of the "new exodus" and the promise of hope for Israel in particular and the world in general, which is mired in selfishness, pride, and sin.

29. Bailey, *Jacob and the Prodigal*. 207.
30. Ibid., 115

The banquets and Jesus' meals of hospitality with sinners in these accounts, are the celebration of a return from exile through the forgiveness of sins. As I have indicated, they look forward to Jesus' final meal with his disciples in which he proclaims the forgiveness of sins through his impending death on the cross. But they are even more than that. They also foreshadow the final banquet which celebrates Jesus final victory over sin, evil, and death in the world. In this sense, Jesus' meals of hospitality with sinners announce the in-breaking of God's kingdom and the arrival of a completely new type of community—one marked by justice, holiness, peace, and love. All of this is what characterizes the "good news" of the gospel.[31] I will describe Jesus' depiction of this banquet of the kingdom in greater detail in the next chapter.

The Church and the Culture War

In *Vanishing Grace: What Ever Happened to the Good News?* Philip Yancey expresses deep concern about how we represent our faith to others. "We are called to proclaim good news of forgiveness and hope," he writes, "yet I keep coming across evidence that many people do not hear our message as good news."[32] Many millennials, in particular, are turned off by what they perceive to be the intolerance of the church. A constant refrain is, "I like Jesus, but not the church." How should Christians respond?

The current social and political climate is characterized by a bitter "culture war," which many in the church regard as a battle over the "soul of America." While we should not over-simplify the nature of this cultural conflict, basically it boils down to a "war" between two camps, both of which seriously distort the meaning of grace and hospitality as defined by Jesus.

Cultural Tolerance vs Intolerance

On the one side of this conflict, most often characterized as the "liberal left," there are those who equate hospitality with tolerance, diversity, and inclusiveness. The mantra of those in this camp is that the source of the problems in the world and our society lies with those who are intolerant, bigoted, and narrow-minded.

It is crucially important to bear in mind that the fundamental assumption of this point of view is that tolerance in and of itself is a virtue.

---

31. McKnight, *The King Jesus Gospel*, 93.
32. Yancey, *Vanishing Grace*, 15.

It espouses "diversity for diversity's sake."[33] In other words, as S. D. Gaede so aptly points out in *When Tolerance is No Virtue*, undergirding much of the current thought on multiculturalism and inclusivism is "not some sense of what is ultimately just or true but a very deep ontological and moral relativism."[34] The argument typically runs like this: Since every cultural perspective is equally valid, every idea or perspective ought to be included. "Indeed, to be exclusive about truth . . . is bad, while to be inclusive of all truth claims is good."[35] Yancey rightly says of this perspective: "Nowadays the principle of tolerance rules above all others, and any religion that claims a corner on truth is suspect."[36]

At a personal level, this perspective is most like the prodigal son. It chooses the path of "self-discovery" and "self-actualization." It says, "No one, not even God, has a right to tell me what to do. I am the only person who can decide what is right or wrong for me. I am the captain of my ship."[37] For those in this camp, "political correctness" means that one should not do or say *anything* that certain groups would find offensive. In other words, when it comes to issues such as sexual orientation, each group gets to define what is offensive for itself.[38]

However much some in this camp portray Jesus as on their side, this is not the view of "hospitality," "love," or "grace" that he teaches. His statement, "I have not come to call the righteous, but sinners to repentance" (Lk 5:32) is not consistent with the contemporary postmodern view of inclusivity and "political correctness." Jesus' words presuppose that there is something of which sinners must repent. Each of the characters in our stories takes specific steps to repent of attitudes and behavior he knows to be morally

---

33. Newman, *Untamed Hospitality*, 30.

34. Gaede, *When Tolerance is No Virtue*, 37.

35. Ibid.

36. Yancey, *Vanishing Grace*, 23. In *A Queer Thing Happened to America*, Brown shows how those who disagree with the "gay agenda" are portrayed in the mainstream media as intolerant and bigoted. He writes: "To be sure, many homosexual men and women have been subjected to all kinds of abuse and, sadly, they often continue to be the objects of vicious and even violent hatred. Homophobia does exist, despite the overuse of that word today, and in the strongest possible terms, I decry hateful acts and words directed again the gay and lesbian community. But let's be candid here. Things have shifted so dramatically—they have literally been turned upside down—that it now appears that no matter what you say and no matter how carefully and graciously you say it, if you dare to differ with the GLBT agenda, if you believe that it is immoral for a man to have sex with another man, if you do not support same-sex marriage, then you are an extremist, a bigot, a Nazi, and a jihadist" (55).

37. Keller, *Prodigal God*, 31.

38. Gaede, *When Tolerance is No Virtue*, 21–22.

wrong. When we minimize sin and the need for repentance, we cheapen and diminish God's grace. His great love becomes mere sentimentality.

Logically, if tolerance of a plurality of truths is made an ultimate virtue, it would seem to lead to moral apathy. If there are no truths worth defending, what basis is there for expressing moral outrage? As G. K. Chesterton once observed, "tolerance is the virtue of the man without convictions."[39] But, of course, it is not possible for those holding this position to be totally consistent. Some of the most passionate (and intolerant) people can be advocates of inclusivism on the left who fervently believe in the "moral correctness" of their cause. This can be seen, for example, in threats by some liberal activists to prosecute as "hate speech" those who preach the tradition moral line on gay sex. These activists have a specific point of view which they think is so obviously true that it justifies censoring religious dissent on it."[40]

"Us Versus Them"

But there is another approach which *also* distorts the biblical meaning of hospitality and grace. This is the approach which divides the world into two groups—the good people (like us) who are deserving of hospitality and the bad people who are the real problem in society and are therefore undeserving of hospitality.

Like the Pharisees in Jesus' day, those who espouse this view strongly believe that our society needs to be restored to its biblical roots. But this very effort to "restore America's Christian foundations" often inspires a judgmental spirit that endangers the very spirit of grace we are called to dispense to a needy world.[41] Yancey gives the all-too-typical example of a Christian radio personality who blamed an historic flood in Colorado which damaged 18,000 homes on legislators who "encourage decadent homosexual activities, vote to kill as many babies as possible, and pass laws approving abominable idolatries such as marijuana."[42]

Such pronouncements of moral condemnation tend to create an "Us versus Them" mentality that short circuits Jesus' call to bring grace and mercy into the world. All too often, it mimics the attitude of the Pharisee who prays: "God, I thank you that I am not like other people—robbers, evildoers, adulterers—or even like this tax collector" (Lk 18:11). Jesus condemns the religious leaders for creating a burdensome system of rules which allow

---

39. Ibid., 27.
40. See Hasson, *The Right to Be Wrong*, 38.
41. Yancey, *Vanishing Grace*, 226.
42. Ibid., 227.

them to feel morally superior while they themselves do not lift one finger to ease the burdens of others (Lk 11:46). We, too, can create similar moral boundaries which allow us to criticize certain behaviors at a distance. Today's Pharisees might condemn "sins" such as drunkenness, drug addiction, laziness, premarital sex, teen pregnancies, and abortion but do nothing to alleviate the pain which contributes to these social ills.

Philip Yancey observes that in today's culture war Christians devote enormous energy to judging those "outside the church," such as the homosexual community.[43] In reading the New Testament, however, we are struck by how much attention is given to sins *inside* the church. Among the long list of behaviors *within the church* which Paul censures (in addition to various forms of sexual immorality) are hatred, slander, discord, jealousy, selfish ambition, greed, dissensions, factions, and envy (Gal 5:19–21; 1 Cor 6:9–10). In the first chapter of Romans, Paul singles out homosexual intercourse because he regards it as providing a particularly graphic image of the way in which human fallenness distorts God's created order. But he does not seem to regard homosexual acts as worse than any of the other manifestations of unrighteousness listed in the passage—including envy, deceit, maliciousness, and even gossip and slander (Rom 1:29–31).[44] One can legitimately question why it is that these particular sins are rarely mentioned by Christians in their pronouncements of God's judgment. Could it be because some sins hit closer to home? Those who speak in apocalyptic terms of America's spiritual and moral decline rarely include themselves or their circle of friends in this assessment. It becomes another "us" versus "them" demarcation.[45]

Ending the Culture War

There is a third alternative. In the present culture war we should respect *as much as is possible* the other's freedom to follow their conscience, *even*

---

43. Yancey, *Vanishing Grace*, 228.

44. See Hays, *The Moral Vision of the New Testament*, 388. Witherington observes that in Romans 1:26–27 Paul clearly identifies sexual activity between people of the same gender, whether male or female, as a sin. But "neither Jesus nor Paul thinks that the sin of homosexual behavior should be treated as a special case. They do not call this an 'abomination,' as it is called in the Old Testament. They are equal-opportunity critiquers of heterosexual sin and homosexual sin (remember what both of them say about adultery), as indeed they are of many other kinds of sin. Paul makes it perfectly evident that all sorts of sins, if persisted in, can keep Christians from entering the dominion and from inheriting eternal life" (*New Testament Theology and Ethics, Vol. One*, 269–70.)

45. Moore, *Onward*, 202.

when we're sure they are wrong or misguided. Does this make us relativists? No. Respect for conscience allows for conflicting truth claims without denying them or relativizing them.[46] This is not the postmodern view that it's intolerant to call anybody wrong. Rather, it is to say that individuals have the God-given freedom—within broad limits—to follow what they in their fallen condition believe to be true, even when they are in error! In the story of the prodigal son, this is the father's gracious response to the son's folly. The biblical perspective provides for the freedom of conscience for all, including those who differ and dissent from the biblical worldview.

At the same time, individual freedom is not absolute. Since there are people with truly bad consciences who are bent on doing harm, there are points where the government must step in to protect its citizens. Government must enact laws which have the goal of preserving public well-being, safety, and common morals.[47] A just society cannot be achieved simply by securing freedom of choice. Whether we are arguing about surrogate motherhood, same-sex marriage, welfare, or affirmative action, justice is inescapably judgmental. It necessarily involves assumptions about values. To achieve a truly just society, then, we have to reason together about the meaning of the common good.[48] In a pluralistic society, the goal of a moral consensus can only be realized through persuasion, not unhealthy coercion. Christians living in a democracy are free to urge fellow citizens to adopt Christian values which they feel are for the social good insofar as these values are translatable into the world at large.[49] Christians can also point to the destructive consequences of radical moral relativism, both for individuals

---

46. Hasson, *The Right to be Wrong*, 15.

47. Ibid., 16.

48. Sandel, *Justice*, 281.

49. Crump, *I Pledge Allegiance*, 84–85. In *After the Election*, Sanders argues for an "open public square" with the accepted boundary conditions of the freedom of religion and the non-establishment of religion. Within these two boundaries the relationship between church and state should include religious language and religious activities that contribute to the "good" of society without any obligation of "conversion" or "participation." Steven Waldman similarly argues in his national bestseller, *Founding Faith: How Our Founding Fathers Forged a Radical New Approach to Religious Liberty*, that both liberal secularists and religious conservatives misunderstand America's "founding faith." He shows how the Founding Fathers forged a radical new three-part creed: 1) Religion is essential to the flourishing of the Republic. 2) To thrive, religion needs less help, not more, from the state. And 3) God gave all humans the right to full religious freedom. "The Founding Faith, then, was not Christianity, and it was not secularism. It was religious liberty—a revolutionary formula for promoting faith by leaving it alone" (xvi). See also Sweetman, *Why Politics Needs Religion: The Place of Religious Arguments in the Public Square*.

and for society as a whole.⁵⁰ But others in our society are equally free to reject such appeals.

The British theologian and cultural critic, Os Guinness, has written a number of helpful books on the culture war and the current state of American politics. He urges us as Americans to respond to the current cultural divide by adopting a positive freedom, which is the power to do what you ought to do. This kind of freedom requires a vision of truth, ethics, and the common good. Positive freedom is based on trust, character, promise-keeping, self-restraint, alignment with reality, and a commitment between parties to the principles of the union. Guinness criticizes the incessant culture warring which trivializes important issues, demeans the participants, and undermines civil dialogue. He puts forth the vision of a "civil public square"—as opposed to a "sacred public square," which gives a preferred place in public life to one religion; and a "naked public square," which seeks to eliminate all public expressions of religion.⁵¹

> *The vision of a civil public square is one in which everyone—people of all faiths, whether religious or naturalistic—are free to enter and engage public life on the basis of their faiths as a matter of "free exercise" and as dictated by their own reason and conscience; but always within the double framework, first, of the Constitution, and second, of a freely and mutually agreed covenant, or common vision for the common good, of what each person understands to be just and free for everyone else, and therefore of the duties involved in living with the deep differences of others.*⁵²

Within this covenant-based model of government there can be respect for each other's freedom without surrendering one's own allegiance to the truth. We are free to express our beliefs and values in the public square and insist that others are wrong, even as they are free to do the same.⁵³ Chris-

---

50. Extreme forms of postmodernism argue that what one chooses does not matter, only the freedom in choosing. Middleton and Walsh point out that the autonomous postmodern self leads to a decentered self which is driven and directed by nothing but its own arbitrary (and changing) preferences. "Choice thus becomes not an owning of responsibility but an escape from allowing oneself to be held accountable" (Middleton and Walsh, *Truth is Stranger Than It Used To Be*, 59). The ultimate result is the undermining of freedom itself.

51. Guinness, *The Case for Civility*, 77–131. .

52. Ibid., 135.See also the following writings by Guinness: *A Free People's Suicide: Sustainable Freedom and the American Future*; *Last Call for Liberty: How America's Genius for Freedom Has Become its Greatest Threat*; "Making the World Safe for Diversity: Religious Liberty and Social Harmony in a Pluralistic Age;" and "The Golden Triangle of Freedom."

53. Hasson, *The Right to be Wrong*, 146–47.

tians should seek to be "salt and light" in society, not as Christians trying to impose their morality on everyone else but as good citizens who "seek the welfare of the city" (Jer 29:7).[54]

Unlike those on the left who create a division between the "tolerant" and "intolerant" and those on the right who divide society into the "good" and the "bad" people, Jesus distinguishes between the humble and the proud (Lk 18:14). Timothy Keller fittingly remarks that "the prerequisite for receiving the grace of God is to know you need it."[55] When a newspaper posed the question, "What's wrong with the World?" the Catholic thinker G. K. Chesterton responded in a brief letter: "Dear Sirs: I am. Sincerely Yours, G. K. Chesterton."[56] Or as Pogo the comic strip character states: "We have seen the enemy; and the enemy is us." This is the attitude of the tax collector who cries out: "God, have mercy on me, a sinner!" (Lk 18:13). When we see that we are all broken people in a broken world we can begin to understand and appreciate the full scope of God's hospitality. Russell Moore says it well:

> We overcome, not because we're a moral majority or a righteous remnant, but because we're blood-covered sinners who know that if the gospel can change us, it can change anyone. We speak with kindness and persuasion not because we're weak but because the gospel is strong. We speak the truth, with conviction and with gentleness, as those who have nothing to prove.[57]

---

54. Olson, *How to Be Evangelical without Being Conservative*, 55–56. There is, for example, rational justification for recognizing the legal limits on individual freedom when it comes to the issue of same-sex marriage. We can agree, argues Skillen, that every person should receive equal treatment and protection under the law. However, legalizing same-sex marriage gives legal precedent for other forms of marriage such as bigamy and polygamy which further undermine the institution of marriage. "If marriage is grounded in the right of individuals not to be discriminated against in their choice of a partner, then what rational purpose is left for denying civil rights protection to those who want to join with more than one partner in marriage?" (*The Good of Politics*, 159–63). Concerning the debate over abortion, it is not politically realistic or even justifiable for Christians to push for legislation that criminalizes all abortions. But we can and should appeal to the principles of the "sanctity of life," consistent nonviolence, and a preferential option for the vulnerable; as well as legal president that protects the rights of the unborn to press for laws that restrict abortions and/or make them unnecessary. See Sider, *Just Politics*, 121; and Camosy, *Beyond the Abortion Wars*, 159–67.

55. Keller, *The Prodigal God*, 45.

56. Ibid., 46.

57. Moore, *Onward*, 204.

11

Outcasts as Honored Guests at the Great Banquet

IN the late 1960s I was discipled by an older Christian. Some of the most memorable experiences in those years of my young adulthood were the trips that we took to the inner city of Chicago to witness to the homeless who lived in flophouses that dotted Madison Street. At times, the stench that came from the garbage, urine, and rat-infested rooms was almost unbearable. I remember, in particular, one incident. An elderly resident had been beaten up by a younger man. One eye was so badly damaged that it required immediate medical attention. After much cajoling, this elderly man finally agreed to let us take him to the ER at a nearby hospital. When we visited him weeks later, he was deeply grateful that we had taken the time and effort to provide the help he so desperately needed.

On one other occasion, we decided to have a picnic for a group of homeless men. We transported them in vans from the inner city to a park in one of the northern suburbs, where we fed them grilled hot dogs and hamburgers and various side dishes. Then (for those who were able) we played a few games of volleyball before taking them back to the city. Some of the men could not recall when they had seen so much green grass in one place! This was a life-changing event—perhaps as much for my friend and me as it was for the homeless men we served.

Years later, when I was professor of sociology at Trinity International University (Deerfield, IL) I made it a point to arrange tours of the inner city of Chicago for my students. These tours usually included walks down the same street where my friend and I had witnessed to the homeless about the love of Christ years before. By then, the flophouses had been torn down. But the homeless were still there. In recent years, Madison Street has undergone a transformation. The homeless and the various ministries and shelters that served them have been pushed out to make way for gentrification, or the movement of wealthier people into the community. Upscale condos and apartment buildings and large houses with well-manicured lawns line the newly paved streets.

But the problem of homelessness has not gone away. The homeless have simply been pushed into other areas of the city. The composition of the homeless has also changed. A recent study indicates that as many as 10,000 families in Chicago may be impacted by homelessness.[1] Many homeless continue to live on the streets and back alleys of our cities and communities.

In Jesus' parable of the great banquet (Lk 14:1–24) we are told, "When you give a luncheon or dinner, do not invite your friends, your brothers or relatives, or your rich neighbors . . . But when you give a banquet, invite the poor, the crippled, the lame, the blind, and you will be blessed. Although they cannot repay you, you will be repaid at the resurrection of the righteous (vss 12–14). What do these words of Jesus say about who should be part of our fellowship? What do they say about our relationships with those our society views as outcasts and are pushed to the margins?[2]

A New Social Order

One of the unique features of Luke's Gospel is that in his genealogy he traces the ancestry of Jesus as the Messiah back to Adam, who is described as "the son of God" (3:23–38). Jesus is thus presented as the "last Adam," who opens up a new future for the whole human race (1 Cor 15:22, 45).[3] As I have repeatedly emphasized throughout this book, this inauguration of a new order which is signified in the events of the Last Supper (and the meals of hospitality preceding it) involves both a new attitude and new social practices. As John Howard Yoder states, "The promised coming change involves social and personal dimensions *inseparably*, with none of our modern speculative tendency, to dodge the direct claim on us by debating whether the chicken or the egg comes first."[4] This again becomes apparent when we examine Jesus' parable of the great banquet in Luke 14:1–24.

---

1. Brown, "Study Finds 10,000 Families in Chicago Experienced Homelessness Last Year." See also UChicago Urban Labs, *Ending Family Homelessness Report*.
2. Broome, "Who's at the Table?," 6.
3. See Grassi, *Informing the Future*, 201–202.
4. Yoder, *The Original Revolution*, 17.

This parable of Jesus takes place during a Sabbath dinner in the home of a prominent Pharisee (14:1). It is actually told in four segments, or units: 1) the healing of a man from dropsy (14:1–6); 2) a message in the form of a parable to the guests on appropriate attitudes and behavior in selecting seats (14:7–11); 3) a message to the host on issuing invitations (14:12–14}; and 4) the actual parable of the great banquet (14:15–24).[5] The overall emphasis of this passage is on God's kingdom as a community of justice. This theme is consistent with the fact that throughout Luke the marginalized are the center of Jesus' ministry.[6] A closer look at what Jesus says in each of these segments, particularly in relation to the Jewish and Greco-Roman culture of his day, forces us to think about our own meal practices—who gets invited, how they are served, and what we hope to achieve in terms of social honor, status, or approval.[7]

God's Kingdom as a Community of Justice			
14:1–6	14:7–11	14:12–14	14:15–24
Healing a man from dropsy	Parable for guests	Message to host	Parable of Great Banquet

Table 3 The Theme of Luke 14:1–24

Treatment of the Sick on the Sabbath (14:1–6)

Luke's description of the setting for this parable gives us a sense of the drama that is about to unfold. Dinner on the Sabbath was a rather special meal to which guests were often invited. The host of this particular meal is a prominent religious leader or ruler, who Jesus indicates (14:12–13) regularly invites people like himself to noon meals or lunches (*ariston*) and dinners or large banquets (*doche*). Such meals were often festive occasions and presupposed the possession of considerable wealth and leisure.[8] On this occasion, the other guests include other prominent Pharisees and experts in the law who carefully watch or scrutinize Jesus' every action (14:1–3).

Also present at this meal is a man with dropsy, or an abnormal swelling of the body. Seeing this man in front of him, Jesus heals him and sends him on his way (14:4). This action violates rabbinic law which prohibits healing on the Sabbath in all instances where there is not a danger to life (which

---

5. LaVerdiere, *Dining in the Kingdom of God*, 95–96.
6. See Gorman, *The Death of the Messiah*, 108.
7. Chester, *A Meal with Jesus*, 81.
8. LaVeridiere, *Dining in the Kingdom of God*, 89.

this was not). In addition, it was commonly believed that the man's illness was the result of God's judgment.[9] Socially, the man is considered to be an impure, dishonored, and marginalized person who is among the "poor, the crippled, the lame, and the blind" who are mentioned later in the chapter.

This, of course, is not the only instance in which Jesus heals on the Sabbath. But it is doubly significant in that this particular healing takes place in the context of a meal, which by its very nature expresses solidarity among the participants. In this singular act, then, Jesus both shows that the real meaning of the Sabbath is to protect life and health (see Mk 2:23-28; Lk 6:1-5) and expresses meal solidarity with a person considered to be on the fringes of society.[10]

Swapping Chairs: Social Honor and Shame (14:7-11)

Following the healing of the man with dropsy, Jesus notices how the guests jockey for places of honor at the table (14:7). In the Greco-Roman culture (as well as Jewish culture) dinner parties ideally expressed the three main values of *koinonia* (or intimacy), friendship, and pleasure. But these ideals of egalitarian comraderie were strictly limited by a ranking system in which equality was sought and expressed only with those within one's own social class. Each guest was normally assigned a place at the table in relation to other guests according to their social ranking or status.[11] As Ben Witherington describes this ranking system:

> The normal protocol was for the more high-status persons, including of course the host, to get the better seats and the better food and drink. The pecking order was so often rigid that one could tell where one stood with the host by how close to the host one was seated, with the guest of honor reclining on the couch with or next to the host. The closer to the host, the more important and honorable you were thought to be.[12]

It is in this cultural context that Jesus tells a parable which plays into feelings of honor and shame that were so much a part of everyday life. "When someone invites you to a wedding feast, do not take the place of honor, for a person more distinguished than you may have been invited. If so, the host who invited both of you will come to you and say to you,

---

9. Bock, *Luke*, 391.
10. LaVerdiere, *Dining in the Kingdom of God*, 101.
11. See Gospell, *The Poor, The Crippled, the Blind, and the Lame*, 187-95
12. Witherington, *Making a Meal of It*, 36.

'Give this man your seat.' Then, humiliated, you will have to take the least important place. But when you are invited, take the lowest place, so that when your host comes, he will say to you, 'Friend, move up to a better place.' Then you will be honored in the presence of all your fellow guests." Jesus concludes with the words, "Everyone who exalts himself will be humbled, and he who humbles himself will be exalted" (14:8–11).

Jesus is giving more than practical advice or a lesson on humility. His words bring to mind the "great reversal" envisioned in Mary's Magnificat (1:46–55) and the Beatitudes and Woes (6:20–26). When the kingdom of God is finally established, "those who choose now to sit with the poor and lowly are destined for promotion while those who sit now with the rich and powerful will find themselves ordered down to the lowest places."[13] God's treatment of us is impacted by how we treat others.[14]

Swapping Guests: Ethic of Reciprocity (14:12–14)

Our meals reflect our vision of life. They express our views on acceptable behavior and social status, and what we consider to be important or unimportant. The social norms of Jesus' day called for a strict adherence to the ethics of reciprocity, a gift-and-obligation system of social relations in which there is an ability to respond in kind to acts of hospitality. These expectations of reciprocity naturally extended to the table.[15] The host's guest list in our story therefore includes people of similar social status who are able to repay his hospitality. Within the Jewish culture, alms for the poor were of course encouraged. But within both the Jewish and Roman settings, eating with someone outside one's own social class was frowned upon.

As for those with disabilities—the crippled, the lame, and the blind—the response of the social elite was generally one of contempt, ridicule, and devaluation. This was particularly true within the Greco-Roman world.[16] In fact, there is evidence from ancient sources that people with physical and sensory impairments and other physical anomalies were used to provide entertainment at social events and public banquets. In these contexts, people with unusual physical characteristics often became targets of derision and the brunt of people's jokes.[17]

---

13. Byrne, *The Hospitality of God*, 123.
14. Bock, *Luke*, 393.
15. Green, *The Gospel of Luke*, 550.
16. See Gosbell, *The Poor, the Crippled, the Blind, and the Lame*, 114.
17. Ibid., 215–217.

Within the Jewish tradition, those with physical disabilities or limitations were often coupled with the widows and orphans and other vulnerable members of the Israelite community who were to be treated with compassion and justice. People with disabilities, however, were prohibited from serving as priests (Lev 21:16–23). We should bear in mind that behind these Levitical instructions is the Israelite view that the Holy of Holies is God's dwelling place and that those who would be in God's presence must be without defects of any kind. Implicit in this view is the expectation that the future restoration of human beings to a holy state on a renewed earth will involve physical as well as moral restoration. To be holy is to be whole.[18] But by the Second Temple period of Jesus' day the religious elite had extended this principle of ritual purity to non-priestly activities. All persons with disabilities were considered ritually impure and prevented from fully participating in various cultic activities such as annual pilgrimages.[19]

Jesus' ministry runs completely counter to the values of the social and religious elite of the Roman Empire. At the very beginning of his ministry he proclaims that his mission is to bring good news to the poor, proclaim freedom for the captives, restore sight to the blind, and release the oppressed (Lk 4:18–19; cf. 7:20–22), thereby fulfilling the prophecy of Isaiah (Isa 61:1–2; 58:6). He provokes the ire of the religious leaders by healing a crippled woman on the Sabbath (Lk 13:10–17). Following the cleansing of the temple, he heals the lame and the blind (Matt 21:12–14). These healings are not simply demonstrations of Jesus' power. They are about his ability to bring people to wholeness and a glimpse of the age to come when God's presence will fill the earth.[20]

He also turns the social norm of reciprocity on its head by calling for his dinner host to invite to his lavish banquets those least able to repay him for his hospitality—the poor, the crippled, the lame, and the blind. This selfless generosity will not go unrewarded; however, this repayment will not take place in this life but in the next (14:12–14). Jesus' table ethic of grace, love, and justice thus creates a new society that is countercultural. The behaviors Jesus demands eliminate the distance between rich and poor, insider and outsider.[21]

---

18. Alexander, *From Eden to the New Jerusalem*, 153.
19. Gosbell, *The Poor, the Crippled, the Blind, and the Lame*, 166–67.
20. Alexander, *From Eden to the New Jerusalem*, 153–55.
21. Green, *The Gospel of Luke*, 553.

Who's in and Who's Out (14:15-24)

All of the foregoing narrative units are intended by Luke to lead up to the main parable. In this parable Jesus relates the story of a banquet host who is shunned by his peers. In response to the lame excuses given by the first invitees for not accepting his invitation to a great banquet, the host then issues invitations to a very unconventional group of people—the poor, crippled, lame, blind and others who are considered to be outsiders in the society of Jesus' day.

This parable might be viewed as a picture of God's future salvation. It is a response to the question of who the "blessed" are who will eat at the feast of the kingdom of God (14:15). Jesus makes it clear that the long-awaited messianic banquet is fast approaching (see Lk 5:33-34). He is the banquet host (14:16) who invites us to this great banquet. But there are many "religious" people who give flimsy excuses for rejecting God's gracious offer of salvation to sinners (see Lk 5:31). Like the Pharisees, they do not recognize their need for God's grace. Such people, Jesus warns, will never have the opportunity to get a taste of his banquet (14:24). Instead, the only ones who are invited are the spiritually poor, blind, lame, and crippled who acknowledge their utter dependence on God's grace for their deliverance. In contrast to the exclusiveness of the Pharisees, Jesus gives us a picture of the inclusiveness of God's kingdom, which is open to all. There are no limits to God's grace.

But the larger context does not allow us to simply "spiritualize" this parable. The previous verses make it clear that Jesus is also talking about the proper treatment of those who are *physically* poor, lame, crippled, and blind (14:12-14). It is these people who live in the outskirts of the city and are often subjected to mockery and derision by those wielding power and wealth. Himself shunned by the initial invitees who are among the religious and social elite, the host invites the most unlikely persons to be honored guests at his banquet. As one commentator maintains, the host envisioned in this parable of the great banquet extends hospitality to the utterly destitute. He creates a new social order in which the boundaries that normally exclude people like himself from people like them are rendered totally unimportant. "He initiates a new community grounded in gracious and uncalculating hospitality."[22] In God's kingdom, the world's ordering of things is turned upside down.

---

22. Ibid., 562.

The Messianic Banquet and the Great Reversal in the Kingdom of God

John Lennon's *Imagine* is the best known and most successful song of his solo career. Written in 1971 at the height of the Vietnam War, it expresses his vision of an ideal world:

>Imagine there's no heaven
>It's easy if you try
>No hell below us
>Above us only sky
>
>Imagine all the people living for today
>Imagine there's no countries
>It isn't hard to do
>Nothing to kill or die for
>And no religion too
>
>Imagine all the people living life in peace, you
>You may say I'm a dreamer
>But I'm not the only one
>I hope someday you'll join us
>And the world will be as one
>
>Imagine no possessions
>I wonder if you can
>No need for greed or hunger
>A brotherhood of man
>
>Imagine all the people sharing all the world, you
>You may say I'm a dreamer
>But I'm not the only one
>I hope someday you'll join us
>And the world will be as one.

However misguided the worldview underlying Lennon's song, it reflects a universal yearning for justice and a world of peace and harmony. But what we imagine is more often like a dream, a figment of the imagination. When we awaken, we are jarred into the reality of new global evils—of rampant, uncaring, and irresponsible materialism and greed on the one hand; and raging unthinking religious fundamentalism on the other.[23]

The Messianic Banquet

Eight hundred years before Jesus, the prophet Isaiah similarly proclaims the coming of a "day of salvation," a time of universal peace when the poor and needy will find relief from the ruthless and powerful and there will be no hunger:

> You have been a refuge for the poor,
> a refuge for the needy in distress . . .
> so the song of the ruthless is stilled
> On this mountain the Lord Almighty will prepare
> a feast of rich food for all peoples,
> a banquet of aged wine,
> the best of meats and the finest of wines.
> On this mountain he will destroy
> the shroud that enfolds all peoples,
> the sheet that covers all nations;
> he will swallow up death forever.
> The sovereign Lord will wipe away the tears from all faces;
> he will remove the disgrace of his people from all the earth.
> The Lord has spoken.
> In that day they will say,
> "Surely this is our God,
> we trusted in him, and he saved us.
> This is our Lord, we trusted in him;
> let us rejoice and be glad in his salvation."
> (Isa 25:4–9)

As we have seen, this passage looks backward to the exodus when God rescued his people from the ruthless power of the Egyptians and brought them into a covenantal relationship with him on Mount Sinai (Exod 19:1–6: 24:1–18). Isaiah also looks forward to the final messianic kingdom, when justice will be established on the earth (42:4).

The following passage further emphasizes the fact that in God's future kingdom there will be provision for everyone without any price tag:

---

23. Wright, *Simply Christian*, 3, 8.

> Come, all you who are thirsty,
> come to the waters;
> and you who have no money,
> come, buy and eat!
> Come, buy wine and milk
> without money and without cost.
> Why spend money on what is not bread,
> and your labor on what does not satisfy?
> Listen, listen to me, and eat what is good,
> and your soul will delight in the richest of fare.
> (Isa 55:1-2)

These passages highlight our total inability and helplessness, and total dependence on God's grace. In God's kingdom the menu has no prices on it; nor does the principle of reciprocity or ability to repay have any meaning or significance, since the purchase price has already been paid by the suffering servant.[24] This, of course, is the meaning of Last Supper, which is not simply a farewell meal between Jesus and his disciples. Jesus' reference to the cup of the "fruit of the vine" which he will not drink again until the kingdom of God comes (Lk 22:17-18) is a *prophetic sign* of the great messianic banquet and the kingdom of God, which is inaugurated by his death and resurrection and will come in its fullness when he returns.[25]

The Great Reversal

Jesus' violation of the social conventions of his day—particularly as embodied in meal practice—involves a criticism of the way the "law" of the Scribes and Pharisees is used to prop up the social and political system of power that lies behind their concept of morality. In other words, his criticism of the "law" is not simply an attack on the legalism of the Pharisees and other religious elite. It is also a criticism of the way the law is a social convention used to protect the current distribution of political and economic power.[26]

Jesus' practice of table fellowship and his kingdom vision of meal hospitality, then, are a challenge to the existing social structures; they represent a great reversal of the everyday patterns of life in a secular society. Jesus is "toppling the familiar world of the ancient Mediterranean, overturning

---

24. See Chester, *A Meal with Jesus*, 59. See also Motyer, *Isaiah*, 387.
25. Pitre, "Jesus, The Messianic Banquet, and the Kingdom of God," 151-52.
26. See Brueggemann, *The Prophetic Imagination*, 87.

its socially constructed reality and replacing it with what must have been a scandalous alternative."[27] This "great reversal" is a theme that is found throughout Luke's Gospel. It can be seen, as we have already indicated, in Mary's Song, which envisions a day when the powerful rulers are brought down from their thrones, the hungry are filled with good things, and the rich are sent away empty (Lk 1:52–53). It is also evident in the story of Lazarus, in which the initial contrast between the extravagance of the rich man and Lazarus who eats scraps from the rich man's table is later reversed, with Lazarus resting in the bosom of Abraham and the rich man tormented by the fire of hades (Lk 16:19–25).

Christians today live in the "overlap" between the present and future kingdom, or the "now and not yet" of God's kingdom. While we eagerly wait for the kingdom of God to arrive in its fullness, we are nonetheless called to presently live by the values of the kingdom. Our very identity and mission flow out of our citizenship in this age-straddling kingdom of God.[28] Yet today, the church also struggles with the seduction of power and social prestige which was prevalent among the religious and social elite of Jesus' day. Many churches and ministries appear to be more influenced by culture and political ideology than by the radical and countercultural demands of Jesus. His parable of the great banquet raises the central question whether, or to what extent, the church's prophetic voice has been drowned out by the culture and politics of the day.

The Lord's Supper and Countercultural Hospitality

It remains for us to further consider the relationship between Jesus' teaching on hospitality in Luke's Gospel and God's hospitality as contained in the Lord's Supper. In addition, what are the implications of this connection for our own identity and vocation, both as individual believers and collectively as the church?

God's Grace and Our Response

Two concepts that are often associated with God's grace toward us is that it is "unmerited" and that it is "boundless." In other words, there is absolutely nothing we can do to earn or merit God's grace. It is totally undeserved. And secondly, there are no limits or "boundaries" to God's grace. There is

---

27. Chester, *A Meal with Jesus*, 85.
28. Schaeffer, *Living in the Overlap*, 53.

nothing we have done which is not covered by God's grace. God completely accepts each and every one of us just as we are. This is the wonderful, matchless, and radical grace of God that we celebrate in the Communion or the Eucharist. However, beyond the fact that this ordinance is rooted in a "meal" or "supper" that Jesus had with his disciples before his sacrificial death on the cross, we generally don't think to ask why we call it the "Lord's Supper" or the "Lord's Table," and why this is significant for us as a community of individuals saved by God's grace.

We have seen in this chapter that God's lavish grace which is poured out on his people and the world he created is pictured in terms of a great banquet to which all—rich and poor, young and old, the sick and disabled, people from every tribe and nation and of every race—are invited. The "Lord's Table" anticipates this gathering of diverse people to the banquet of God in the new heaven and new earth. God's hospitality is, as I have tried to show, reflected in Jesus' own table fellowship with the sinners and social outcasts of his day, in his parables, and, finally, in his Last Supper with his disciples.

This linkage between God's immeasurable grace and his hospitality (which is portrayed in terms of eating and drinking at his table) has a number of implications for the church as the body of Christ. First, it means that God's grace or hospitality always precedes and is the foundation for human hospitality. The church must consistently and actively declare the message of God's love. First and foremost, God is to be glorified for his mercy and grace. But, secondly, it means that the church is, in a real sense, called to be the presence of Jesus in the world. It is a "community of hospitality" and reconciliation.[29] Finally, the association of grace with hospitality means that there is a deep link between the *verbal content* of the good news of God's grace and its *concrete embodiment* in boundary situations involving guests and hosts. That is, just as Jesus' response to the sinner, stranger, and other outcast figures demonstrates God's immeasurable hospitality toward those who in human terms are undeserving of his care and attention, the same must be true for those of us who claim to be his followers.[30]

We should also bear in mind that the type of hospitality that Jesus calls us to is not simply a matter of showing compassion to the needy. Nor is hospitality just about the benefit that comes to the marginalized. It is fundamentally concerned with the health and identity of the church itself. Reorienting the church toward what has been called "marginal mission" builds and strengthens the church. This approach to the church's mission

---

29. Boersma, *Violence, Hospitality, and the Cross*, 206–7.
30. Ibid., 216–17.

embodies a spiritual vision of what the church is called to be and do in the world which is in stark contrast to the worldly preoccupation with success, comfort, and security.

Furthermore, our response to persons with disabilities cannot be separated from other social issues. Not only is this evident in Jesus' teachings. Statistically, disability intersects with the problems of poverty, race, abuse, and discrimination in our society. About 30 percent of African-American families affected by disability live in poverty. One in five of persons with disabilities have less than a high-school education. Almost 60 percent are either unemployed or underemployed. Seventy percent report abuse; and almost half report experiencing isolation, social ostracism, and loneliness. Those with fewer resources receive less care and are more likely to be abused. Helping persons with disabilities cannot therefore be limited to constructing a ramp for easier access to the church building. In addition to physical barriers, there are frequently also social, economic, cultural, and emotional barriers that have to be overcome. This process is often messy and complicated.[31]

The church today is faced with an incredible challenge as well as opportunity. There are, of course, churches that strive to integrate the gospel with an ethic of hospitality. They should be encouraged and celebrated. Yet, realistically, it is easy to feel overwhelmed by the magnitude of the issue. Jesus' call for us to live a countercultural lifestyle of hospitality to our fellow brothers and sisters in the church, and even more radically to strangers and the marginalized outside the boundaries of the community, goes against our most natural inclinations. We have limited patience for people with problems that aren't quickly or easily fixed and often avoid those with chronic disabilities.[32] A selfish pursuit of the outward trappings of success and upward mobility embodied in the "American dream" often takes precedence over following Jesus' example of identification with the poor and socially marginalized. Consequently, we distance ourselves from those who are different from us and stigmatize "those people" whom we consider to be outsiders. Jesus welcomed the stigmatized without a concern for social acceptance or conformity to social norms. Yet, all too often, we are guilty of uncritically adopting societal stereotypes of individuals or groups labeled as dangerous, risky, worthless, unimportant, or pollutants.[33] We prefer to close our doors to the stranger and our borders to the alien, whom we view as a

---

31. These statistics come from a presentation by the Banquet Network entitled "Jesus and the Margins: Race. Poverty, and Disability" (2019).

32. Heuertz and Pohl, *Friendship at the Margins*, 100.

33. Jipp, *Saved by Faith and Hospitality*, 39.

burden and major headache (and worse) rather than someone who bears God's image. We tend to see the migrant, the refugee, and the homeless through the lens of utilitarian calculus rather than as those for whom Christ died and with whom we might share his love, in both word and deed.

Evangelicals rightly speak out in support of the rights of the unborn; but many of us are silent when it comes to promoting justice for the oppressed and socially ostracized. The late cardinal Joseph Bernardin of Chicago made the simple argument that the ethic of life is a "seamless garment" which cannot be sustained in one situation and eroded in another; concern for the dignity and sanctity of human life applies to all, both the born and the unborn.[34] The violence of abortion is often made more palatable to the conscience by the use of clinical language like "fetus" or "the product of conception" which renders invisible the baby in the womb. The children of immigrants fleeing violence are likewise made invisible when they are placed in cages and become mere statistics in the battle over the "right" to protect our boarders. "No matter how civilized we may believe ourselves to be," warns Russell Moore, "we can see what happens when a child happens to be in the category of both unpopular and defenseless, and the results are tragic."[35]

Perhaps one of the most persistent attitudes that we have toward poor and marginalized people is the belief that lack of effort or some other moral deficiency is more often than not to blame for their plight; and that there are large numbers of poor who simply don't deserve help.[36] We assume that we can easily distinguish between the "undeserving poor" and the "deserving poor"—although research shows that issues of poverty and homelessness are generally the result of the interaction between poor personal decisions and a complex set of social factors, including family breakdown and abuse, lack of significant social relationships, unavailability of affordable housing, inadequate employment opportunities, poor health, and discrimination.[37] Our morally based classifications of poor people tend to create a mentality of "them" versus "us." In political rhetoric and even in daily conversations, the poor become "outsiders, strangers to be pitied or despised, helped or punished, ignored or studied, but rarely full citizens, members of a larger community on the same terms as the rest of us."[38] To use the words employed by Senator Dan Quayle in his 1988 vice presidential debate with

---

34. See Sider, *Just Politics*, 126–27.
35. Moore, "What's the Real Issue behind the Abortion Debate?," 3.
36. See Pew Research Center, "Fairness of the Economic System."
37. Elliott, *Why the Homeless Don't Have Homes and What To Do about It*, xxi, 8–9.
38. Katz, *Undeserving Poor*, 116.

Senator Lloyd Bentsen, they are "those people." Most importantly, the "myth of the underserving poor" becomes a way of writing certain people off and denying our common status as objects of God's unconditional love.[39]

Jesus' teaching on radical hospitality shows us that grace is the road to love. As Timothy Keller observes, those who fully grasp the gospel of God's grace and become spiritually poor invariably find their hearts gravitating toward the materially poor. To the degree that God's grace shapes our self-image, we will identify with those in need, even those whom society deems unworthy.

> [We] will see their tattered clothes and think: "All my righteousness is a filthy rag, but in Christ we can be clothed in his robes of righteousness." When [we] come upon those who are economically poor, [we] cannot say to them "Pull yourself up by your bootstraps!" because [we] certainly did not do that spiritually.[40]

Placing Limits on Hospitality

Still, questions remain. How can the above vision of unconditional hospitality be reconciled with the fact that we have limited resources of money, time, and energy which force us to establish boundaries and priorities? Those who give freely are often overwhelmed by need. How can we say "yes" to everyone without so diluting what we have to give that it becomes ineffective? If we welcome every troubled person, including inevitably those who take advantage of our hospitality, how will others to whom we have responsibilities be affected? And don't we have to be careful about our own needs, both physically and emotionally?

In commenting on these questions, Christine Pohl wisely states that "ignoring limits can be a form of arrogance, a refusal to recognize finiteness."[41] Various Scripture passages acknowledge that in a world distorted by sin there will be those who abuse hospitality; they emphasize the importance of wisdom, discernment, and discretion in offering hospitality as a result. (2 John 9–11; Jude 4, 8, 12, 19; 1 Tim 5:3–16; 2 Thess 3:10–12). However, such passages need to be balanced against other statements by both Jesus and Paul which enjoin liberality and compassion (Matt 5:42; Lk 6:30; 2 Cor 9:13; Gal 6:10). As Pohl rightly states, "in hospitality, hosts must find an appropriate balance of boundaries and freedom that allows them to

---

39. See Charlesworth and Williams, *The Myth of the Undeserving Poor*, 82.
40. Keller, *Generous Justice*, 102–3,
41. Pohl, *Making Room*, 132–34.

sustain the practice. Boundaries, restriction, and guidelines will vary with the kinds of guests, type of setting, needs of hosts, and the availability of resources."[42]

The problem is that Scripture passages are often taken out of context and wrongly used to make moralistic judgments about the poor and immigrants in general. On the issue of immigration, for example, Romans 13 can be legitimately used to the support right of nation-states to protect the integrity of their borders, provided it is done in a way the respects the due process of law and the rights and dignity of individuals and families. Certainly, there are legitimate issues regarding the protection of our citizenry and limits of resources. But, as I have stated previously, this passage is often wrongly used to justify fear mongering, xenophobic rhetoric, stereotypes, and intolerant policies that violate biblical principles of love and compassion for the stranger.[43]

I will cite another example. Paul's words in 2 Thessalonians 3:10 ("If a man will not work, he shall not eat") are given to ensure that scarce resources within the Christian community are not squandered needlessly. Paul's further motivation is a broader concern to preserve a practice of generosity and care among the Thessalonian Jesus groups (2 Thess 3:13).[44] We can agree with Steve Corbett and Brian Fikkert that we should not do for persons what they can do for themselves. They add that in some cases we should withhold handouts, but offer help in finding long-term solutions.[45] This advice is consistent with Paul's instructions and provides a safeguard against dependency. But Paul's words cannot be used to justify broad policies of eliminating or cutting food stamps, as some argue. Nor can they be used to justify not helping a homeless person on the supposition that he or she is lazy, since in most cases we don't have the slightest idea of what has led to that person's current situation. Our response to requests for help will vary depending on the situation. In many cases, discernment may be needed in *what* or *how* best we should give, but not necessarily in *whether* to give. Dependency is often created not by charity per se, but by limiting our giving to handouts and failing to take additional steps of rehabilitation and development which truly empower the poor.[46]

We need both grace and wisdom because of potential abuses of hospitality; but grace must always be primary. While there will always be risks

---

42. Ibid., 139.
43. Jipp, *Saved by Faith and Hospitality*, 125–26.
44. See Bruce Longenecker, *Remember the Poor*, 149.
45. Corbett and Fikkert, *When Helping Hurts*, 106.
46. Ibid., 105.

of misuse or distortion in giving, attempts to eliminate those risks often diminish the value and essential character of giving itself.[47] In a message entitled "From Exclusion to Embrace," Yale professor Miroslav Volf offers some helpful insights on the priority of grace over judgment. The *will* to embrace another person, he says, is always unconditional. It is a fundamental obligation that is based on the unconditional love of God who died for the ungodly. "The will to give ourselves to others and 'welcome' them, the will to readjust our identities to make space for them, is prior to any judgment about others, except that of identifying them in their humanity."[48] This will is "absolutely indiscriminate and strictly immutable," transcending any moral mapping of the social world into "good" and "evil." This does not mean that welcoming the stranger is unqualified. Genuine embrace of another cannot take place until truth and justice have been established. But, *and here is the crux of the matter*, what is the ultimate goal of discerning the truth? Is it simply that of ensuring that everyone gets what one deserves? Or is the larger goal that of healing relationships? It must, Volf contends, be the latter if we are to strive for love.[49]

---

47. Pohl, *Making Room*, 149.
48. Volf, "From Exclusion to Embrace: Reflections on Reconciliation," 3
49. Ibid.

12

Fellowship, Breaking Bread, and Sharing Possessions

Discerning readers of Luke's account of the church in the book of Acts are impressed by how the early believers transcended many of the false polarities we see in the church today[1]—divisions, for example, between those who stress doctrinal correctness or orthodoxy and those who emphasize the work of the Holy Spirit; or the conflict between those who focus on personal salvation and those who identify the church more with social engagement and community formation. The book of Acts does not create a dichotomy between personal spirituality and life lived in community; or between personal faith and social-cultural engagement. Nor does it create a division between the "teaching of the apostles" and life lived under the power of the Holy Spirit.

The emphasis of conservative (evangelical) Christians on the transformation of individuals through Christ and the power of God's saving grace is an important corrective to the tendency of some "liberal" congregations to turn Christianity into a religion of "good works." This finds support in even a cursory reading of Acts. But, as Anthony Robinson and Robert Wall have argued in their commentary on Luke's account of the early church, the contemporary preoccupation with a privatized faith which focuses almost exclusively on individual pursuits and well-being, as well as on personal salvation, over accommodates the gospel to a culture of individualism. It misses the larger story of God's community, which takes form in the world and provides a new vision for those who share in it.[2]

1. Robinson and Wall, *Called to Be Church*, 5.
2. Ibid., 2–6.

The book of Acts might rightly be described as a "culture forming narrative" that aims at the construction of an alternative way of life which runs counter to the life patterns of the Greco-Roman world.[3] Luke narrates a salvation that is intensely personal and is rooted in sincere repentance and faith; but this individual salvation is not divorced from a public pattern of life that witnesses under the power of the Holy Spirit to the present dominion of the resurrected Lord of all.[4] As we will see, this culture-forming life of the early church is directly related to how it understands and practices the Lord's Supper.

Acts and the Gospel Story

Recent studies have demonstrated that the primary purpose of Luke's narrative in Acts is to persuade other Jews that Jesus is the Messiah spoken of in the Old Testament and that the church is the fulfillment of prophecies regarding the restoration of Israel.[5] The book of Acts opens with Jesus instructing the disciples concerning the kingdom of God (1:3). In this way, Luke links the narrative of Acts with the gospel story, in which Jesus announces the fulfillment of God's promise to restore the kingdom to Israel (Lk 4:43; 9:27; 13:29). This same reference to the kingdom is made at the very end of the book (Acts 28:31). This suggests that the subtext or *underlying theme* of the entire narrative is the triumph of God's reign through the risen Christ who is present in the church.[6] *The Gospels tell us how the story of Israel comes to completion in the story of Jesus; the book of Acts tells us how Jesus' story continues through the story of the church.*[7] The risen and exalted Christ "continues his mission by the Spirit in and through the church, which is both the *place* where Christ is at work and also the *instrument* through which Christ works."[8]

---

3. Rowe, *World Upside-Down*, 4.

4. Ibid., 154.

5. See Pao, *Acts and the Isaianic New Exodus*, 249–50; see also Hesselgrave, *The JustMissional Church*, 258.

6. Robinson and Wall, *Called to be Church*, 32

7. See McKnight, *The King Jesus Gospel*, 155–56.

8. Goheen, *A Light to the Nations*, 124.

Figure 5: Israel, Jesus, and the Church

One of the ways in which the book of Acts portrays the continuation of Jesus' work through the church is in the practice of hospitality—particularly in the form of sharing meals and possessions. In this account of the early church, Luke reminds us that the church's internal witness to Christ's kingdom centers on table fellowship and the sharing of material goods (*koinonia*) even as its external witness focuses on proclamation of faith in Christ and his lordship (*kerygma*).[9] Both of these aspects of kingdom witness are closely tied to the practice of the Lord's Supper—or the breaking of bread (2:42).

Joshua Jipp points out that there are several ways in which the "Summary Statements" of Acts 2:42–47 and 4:32–35 portray the early Christian community as the place where Jesus is present and "remembered" through food and hospitality.[10] First, the breaking of bread (2:42, 46) and sharing of possessions (2:33–45; 4:32–35) are presented as partial fulfillment of Jesus' promise that his apostles will eat and drink at his table in the kingdom (Lk 22:30). Second, the repeated reference to "breaking bread" (2:42, 46; 27:35) recalls Jesus' acts of breaking bread (Lk 9:16; 22:19; 24:30, 35), which express both his hospitality for people (Lk 9:12–17) and his sacrificial presence with his people (Lk 22:19–22). Finally, as I will show in greater detail, the fellowship, provision of food, and sharing of possessions with the poor mirror Jesus' own identity as host of the hungry (Lk 9:12–17) and provider of hospitality to *all* people (Lk 15:1–2).[11]

To see more clearly these connections between the Lord's Supper, the kingdom of God, and hospitality through the church, we have to first look at how Acts describes the early Christian community as the renewed "people of God" animated by God's Spirit.

---

9. Robinson and Wall, *Called to Be Church*, 71.
10. Jipp, *Saved by Faith and Hospitality*, 28–29.
11. Ibid., 29.

The Church as a Renewed People of God

Those who hold a classic dispensational view of the Bible maintain that when Scripture uses the word *Israel* it is always without exception a reference to the literal physical nation of Israel. There is, in other words, no sense in which the Israel as the people of God revealed in the Old Testament is continued or "replaced" by the church as the people of God in the New Testament.[12]

It seems clear from a careful reading of the book of Acts, however, that Luke views the early Christian movement as a continuation of God's redemptive plan—a plan which began with the call of Abraham and continued through the creation of his covenant with the nation of Israel.[13] That is, he sees the church as a continuation of the faithful remnant of Israel, the "renewed people of God" and the recipient of God's redemptive promises to Israel. Luke portrays the early church as a community of people among whom God's reign has begun. In this sense, the growth of the church can be viewed as the expansion of vital and dynamic "communities of the kingdom."[14]

The Coming of God's Spirit on a Restored Israel (the Church)

The dramatic event that marks the beginning of the church as the reconstituted people of God is, of course, the coming of the Holy Spirit at Pentecost (Acts 2:1–13). The term "Pentecost" literally means the "fiftieth day." It was the term used by the Jews who were scattered throughout the Roman Empire to refer to the day-long harvest festival more commonly known as the "Feast of Weeks" (Exod 23:16: 34:22; Lev 23:15–21; Deut 16:9–12). This sheds light on why Luke describes the Holy Spirit as coming down on God-fearing Jews from every nation who are staying in Jerusalem (Acts 2:5–11). This is a clear reference to Isaiah's prediction of the ingathering of exiles as the reconstituted nation of Israel (Isa 43:5–7).[15]

Pentecost was one of three pilgrimage feasts during which the entire household of Israel gathered together in Jerusalem—fifty days after the Passover to celebrate God's goodness to the nation.[16] The significance of

---

12. See Donaldson, *The Last Days of Dispensationalism*, 37–38. I will discuss the dispensational view of the "end times" in greater detail in part four of this book.

13. Ibid., for a description of this non-dispensational view. (42–43)

14. Snyder, "Church Growth," 209–31; Glasser, *Announcing the Kingdom*, 274–76.

15. Pao, *Acts and the Isaianic New Exodus*, 130–31. See also Hesselgrave, *The Just-Missional Church*, 264 and 277–78 (note 16).

16. Robinson and Wall, *Called to Be Church*, 51.

this connection between the events of Pentecost and the Jewish religious calendar would have been obvious to Luke's audience. Fifty days after the initial Passover, God renewed his covenant with Israel at Mt Sinai by giving the Torah and declaring it to be a kingdom of priests and a holy nation (Exod 19:1–6). *The giving of God's Spirit on this Pentecost is therefore a fulfillment of his promise of a new covenant when his law will be written on people's hearts* (Rom 8:2; cf. Jer 31:31).[17]

Following the dramatic events of Pentecost, Peter gives two speeches. In the first, he addresses the large group of Jews who are gathered together in Jerusalem (Acts 2:14–36). In this speech he directly connects the dramatic outpouring of the Holy Spirit at Pentecost with the messianic prophecy of Joel, which places the gift of the Spirit in the "last days" (Joel 2:17). This is a term used in the Old Testament to refer to the new era of the kingdom when Israel would be blessed (Isa 2:2; Hos 3:4–5). To further make his point, he presents the resurrection and ascension of Christ to God's right hand (2:32–33) as the initial fulfillment of Jewish expectations concerning the coming of the Davidic kingdom (Ps 110:1).

In a second speech Peter describes Jesus' resurrection and the healings performed by the apostles through faith in Jesus as a fulfillment of what God had foretold through the prophets (Acts 3:11–26). But he also distinguishes between a current period of "refreshing," which people can enjoy if they repent, and the *final* restoration of all things promised by the Old Testament prophets. Perhaps recalling the words of the angels after Jesus' ascension (Acts 1:11), he states unequivocally that Christ will remain in heaven until the time comes for God to "restore everything," as he has promised through the prophets (3:21). Evidently, then, Peter distinguishes between two phases of God's kingdom—the "now" and the "not yet." Presently, the community of believers (the church) gives a "preview" of the future final kingdom when all people will be under Christ's rule of justice and righteousness.[18]

---

17. Ibid.

18. See Bock, "The Reign of the Lord Christ," 56–57. Bock notes that in the Septuagint translation by Symmachus, Isaiah 32:15 uses a similar term (refreshment) to describe the pouring out of God's Spirit from heaven. This suggests that the repentant are promised "refreshing" in this age as they are promised the Spirit in this age in Acts 2:38. Peter therefore suggests that God's kingdom comes in two distinct *but related* phases. For individual Israelites to share in the second final stage of "restoration" as well as the benefits of the first stage they must repent (Ibid., 58). See also Keener's discussion in *Acts: An Exegetical Commentary, Vol 2*.

The Church as a Witness to the Kingdom

Luke makes it clear in the opening chapters of Acts that because of the work of the Holy Spirit in the lives of believers the Christian community is informed by six fundamental characteristics: 1) mission (1:8); 2) power (2:1–4; cf. 4:7); 3) submission to the Lordship of Christ (2:36); 4) faith and repentance (2:37–41); 5) transformational fellowship (2:42–47; 4:32–36); and 6) social-cultural engagement (2:47; cf. 4:18–20). Each of these elements are integrated into whole-life discipleship and mission.

Today's churches often equate "mission" with a particular "program" or "department" in the congregation's life. In the book of Acts, however, the whole church is a missionary outpost or beachhead that bears witness in both word and deed to the new creation in Christ.[19] The church in Acts does not "have" a mission; it is defined by mission—that is, mission is a natural extension of the entire life of the congregation.

One author has described the missionary expansion of the early church in terms of the exponential spread of the gospel through "webs of relational ties," beginning with Jewish communities in Jerusalem, then into Gentile communities, and finally in major trade centers throughout the Roman Empire.[20] In each case, movements of renewal and revival are generated by public witness to Jesus' resurrection and lordship, an outpouring of the Holy Spirit, private and public repentance, and divine empowerment for love, unity, and fellowship. In story after story, the book of Acts

> portrays a movement that is turning people in large numbers "from the power of Satan to God" (Acts 26:18) and socializing them into a community that lives by very different norms—the norms defined by Jesus' life and teachings." Such a movement—when lived with integrity—inevitably has an explosive effect in the surrounding culture.[21]

Personal transformation through the Holy Spirit leads to small group renewal and structural change, which in turn results in social and cultural engagement and the conversion of large numbers of people (2:41, 47). It is from this perspective that we should understand the early church's practice of hospitality in the form of common meals and the sharing of possessions.

---

19. Robinson and Wall, *Called to Be Church*, 43–44.
20. See Viv Grigg, "The Spirit of Christ and the Postmodern City."
21. Hays, *The Moral Vision of the New Testament*, 128.

The Lord's Supper, Common Meals, and Shared Possessions

Luke's description of worship, fellowship, and hospitality in the early church raises some important questions. What was the nature of the communal meals or "love (agape) feasts" practiced by the first-century Christians (see Jude 12)? Were they distinct from or part of the observance of the Lord's Supper? And what about Luke's reference to the practice of sharing of possessions or "having everything in common" (Acts 2:44–45; 4:32)? What did this community of goods consist of? Was it a kind of "social experiment," and a temporary response to a local need faced by the Jerusalem church?[22] Or does Luke present it as a practice to be emulated in some way?

The First-Century Setting

In responding to the above questions, we have to keep in mind that first-century Jerusalem (and Greco-Roman society in general) was quite different from that of modern industrial and post-industrial societies. There was not a large middle class, at least in the sense that we have it today. A majority of people in the early urban centers were farmers, laborers, artisans, wage earners and the poor who lived at or below the substance level, or the minimum level needed to survive.[23] One author has described the ancient urban poor as "ill-fed, housed in urban slums or not at all, ravaged by sickness," and with little hope of social betterment.[24] Some estimate that 15 percent of the typical urban population were "expendables"—those for whom the rest of society had no use, such as beggars, widows without families, and orphans.[25] Perhaps 35 to 40 percent of the population were economically stable or had moderate surplus. And 2–3 percent were the "social elites" who controlled a large percentage of the wealth.[26]

In this society, people survived by means of family connections, or by being part of a "kin-group network" where reciprocal sharing took place with those who are part of the in-group. Any wealth that was generated would not be utilized to generate more wealth; rather, it would be shared among the in-group. In a subsistence setting, sharing goods within one's extended family system or clan *was* a form of insurance or investment for the future. If the giver and his household fell on hard times, they could count on

---

22. See Blaiklock, *The Acts of the Apostles*, 61
23. See Longenecker, *Remember the Poor*, 45–53.
24. See Keener, *Acts: An Exegtical Commentary, vol. 2*, 1056
25. Ibid., 1012.
26. Ibid. See also Longenecker, *Remember the Poor*, 53.

others within their family or kin network to help out. It is also natural that those living in extended households would eat together daily.[27]

Since, for a variety of reasons, many of the first Christians had to leave their natural kin-group they re-created one with fellow believers. In other words, the previous kin-group defined by blood relations was replaced by a new fictive kin-group defined by those who followed Jesus as Messiah. The community of believers became, quite literally, a surrogate family—certainly in a spiritual sense, but in the physical and social sense as well. Reta Halteman Finger describes the crucial importance of these new family relationships for the early believers: "The reconstitution of the fictive kin-group meant physical as well as spiritual survival, since without it the lack of relationships and connections doomed first-century Mediterraneans to destitution and starvation."[28] But the connection of believers to one another in the sharing of resources as part of a new family was not just a matter of physical survival. Finger further states: "They would have seen their community as the first fruits of the New Age, the reign of God on earth, ushered in by Jesus and carried on through his Spirit in their daily relationships with each other."[29]

Worship, Shared Meals, and the Lord's Supper

Luke gives us a picture of what worship looked like in the early church (Acts 2:41–47). Biblical scholars have noted that the expression "they devoted themselves" (lit. "they were continuing steadfastly") in 2:42 can also be translated "they regularly took part in worship."[30] There were basically four elements in this worship life: 1) teaching; 2) fellowship; 3) breaking bread; and 4: prayers. Fellowship (*koinonia*) is closely associated with "breaking bread," which refers to common meals. There was, in other words, a very close connection or relationship among the community members—a practice of mutual support and participation in each other's lives that included regular shared meals together.[31]

It is likely that worship in the early church was divided between meetings in the temple (2:46) and meetings in homes of more well-to-do individual believers. Corporate prayer involving the *entire church* in Jerusalem probably took place in the temple courts, which were large enough

27. Finger, *Of Widows and Meals*, 140–41; 277.
28. Ibid.
29. Ibid., 132.
30. Gehring, *House Church and Mission*, 80.
31. Ibid.,

FELLOWSHIP, BREAKING BREAD, AND SHARING POSSESSIONS

to accommodate significant numbers of people. Instruction in the teachings of the Apostles (2:42) most likely occurred in conjunction with the common meal, which was shared among smaller groups of believers in private homes.[32] In this way, the early Christians not only continued Jewish customs. They also continued Jesus' practice of table fellowship. Hospitality was offered within the overlap of household and church. Such hospitality, which took place when the church regularly met for worship, "helped foster family-like ties among believers and provided a setting in which to shape and to reinforce a new identity."[33]

The question is whether the common meal or "the breaking of bread" (2:42, 46) is also a reference to the Lord's Supper. This seems definitely to be the case, since the same term is used elsewhere by Paul to specifically refer to the Lord's Supper (20:7, 11; 1 Cor 10:16; 11:20, 23–25). Furthermore, there is a connection backward to Jesus' "breaking bread" in the Last Supper (Lk 22:19; Mk 14:22–25) and his meal with the disciples following his resurrection during which he "broke bread" (Lk 24:13–35). Therefore, "the 'breaking of bread' and the Lord's Supper (in the Pauline letters) originate from a common source leading back to the Last (Passover) Supper Jesus celebrated with his disciples in Jerusalem."[34]

The importance of this cannot be stressed enough, since it shows that among the early believers there was a *close connection between worship and praise of God (2:47), participation in the Lord's Supper, and the practice of hospitality. For the first Christians these elements could not be separated.* Luke describes the "breaking of bread" in the early church as occurring on the "first day of the week" (Acts 20:7–8, 11). Many commentators argue on the basis of this reference that the communal meal was only a weekly occurrence. However, elsewhere Luke describes the distribution of food as occurring on a daily basis (6:1; cf. 2:46).[35] It seems more probable, then, that the common (or "agape") meal took place daily while the specific practice of the Lord's Supper as *part* of the agape meal occurred weekly, on Sunday when the believers came together for worship. No doubt the agape meals included the lowest classes of Jerusalem society—the "expendables" and the poor—who were also considered as part of the family of God in which socioeconomic class distinctions no longer mattered.[36] Luke says that there

32. Ibid., 83; See also Keener, *Acts: An Exegetical Commentary*, vol. 1, 1010–11.

33. Pohl, *Making Room*, 32, 42.

34. Gehring, *House Church and Mission*, 84. Also Keener, *Acts: An Exegetical Commentary*, vol. 1, 1003–4.

35. Finger, *Of Widows and Meals*, 257.

36. This is indicated by the Luke's account of the neglect of Hellenistic widows in the daily distribution of food which was addressed through the selection of seven men to

was not a needy person among them (4:34). "And the most immediate and effective way for their basic needs to be met and their cross-class status to be shared would have been through the daily communal meal."[37]

They Had Everything in Common

We now come to what is the most controversial and debated aspect of this passage. Luke indicates that a significant part of the hospitality of the church in Jerusalem is that: "All of the believers were together and had everything in common" (2:44). They did not claim their possessions as their own, but shared everything they had (4:32). For many of us who adhere to the capitalist belief that private ownership of possessions is the absolute norm, this practice of the early Christians smacks of socialism or communism. For this reason, many commentators have sought in various ways to qualify Luke's statement.[38]

However, Luke describes this community of goods in glowing terms, as evidence of the outpouring of God's Spirit.[39] To grasp what Luke is saying here it is important to bear in mind that his central point of emphasis is that "much grace was upon them all" (4:33). Atonement through the cross as the fullest manifestation of God's grace makes possible *shalom*, or peace with God, others, and creation. Humanity's most fundamental need is reconciliation with God, who created us and has a wise design for human flourishing.[40] As Robinson and Wall comment, the early believers are able to "let go" of their possessions because they have been "taken hold of" by something else—God's grace or hospitality, which they have experienced by his Spirit. "Generosity is made possible because God has been generous to them. Something else, namely the Spirit, is filling their lives and hearts, thus

---

serve tables (Acts 6:1–7). Pagan writers by the second century associate large numbers of widows and orphans with the Christian movement. There may have been a disproportionate number of Hellenistic widows compared to their Judean counterparts who were poor because they lacked the same level of local extended kin networks on whom they could depend. See Keenan, *Acts: An Exegetical Commentary*, vol. 2, 1266–67.

37. Finger, *Of Widows and Meals*, 135.

38. A common view is that this "communism of goods" was a temporary expediency that was not widespread and led eventually to an impoverishment of the Jerusalem church. This is why Paul had to later organize a "collection" for the "poor" in Jerusalem (I Cor 16:1–4). See, for example, Blaiklock, *The Acts of the Apostles*, 61, 69. However, Luke makes it clear that the direct cause of the later crisis in the Jerusalem church was a severe famine, not the liquidation of its capital (Acts 11:27–30).

39. Keener, *Acts: An Exegetical Commentary* vol. 2, 1176.

40. See Cole, *God the Peacemaker*, 67.

allowing hands to freely share the goods and possessions that we so often imagine will fill and secure our lives."[41]

The experience of God's grace through his Spirit is the basic dynamic in the Christian life. It leads directly to powerful witness by the apostles: "With great power [they] continued to testify to the resurrection of the Lord Jesus . . ." (4:33). Without the resurrection, God's plan of salvation would be incomprehensible, for a dead Christ cannot open the kingdom to anyone.[42] The essence of the apostolic witness is that God has made the crucified Jesus both Lord and Christ, or Savior (2:36). But to limit our obligation to evangelism or verbal proclamation unduly limits our response to God's grace. The *practical effect* of God's grace and the power of Jesus' resurrection in the lives of these early believers is a practice of communitarian sharing, which results in there being no needy persons among them (4:34). This "anti-poverty program" is adopted by the early church as the "new Israel," in fulfillment of the Old Testament covenant ideal that "there should be no poor among you" (Deut 15:4). The practice of selling possessions and giving the proceeds "as there was need" is also viewed as a continuation of Jesus' teachings on possessions (Lk 3:11; 12:33; 18:22) and a fulfillment—or at least the "first fruits"—of Jesus' promise to bring "good news" to the poor and the oppressed (Lk 4:16–21; cf 7:18–23).[43]

Toward a Theology and Ethic of Sharing

The question we are faced with is how to apply the practice of sharing by the Jerusalem church to our own lives as Christians living in the twenty-first century. As Christine Pohl points out, in sharing with others in need we are often brought face-to-face with the reality of our own limited resources— whether in terms of time or money.[44] Given our own financial obligations (bills, credit card debts, student loans, rising food and gas prices, putting children through college, etc.) we worry that we will not have enough resources for ourselves. Yet, although we often *act as if* resources are scarce and fear that we will not have enough, the reality in most cases is that we live with abundance and not scarcity. In other words, "The problem may have much more to do with our willingness to respond than with our resources."[45] This can be particularly true in a capitalist economy, which

41. Robinson and Wall, *Called to Be Church*, 82.
42. Cole, *God the Peacemaker*, 152–54.
43. Hays, *The Moral Vision of the New Testament*, 124.
44. Pohl, *Making Room*, 130.
45. Ibid., 135.

constantly bombards us as consumers with the message that "you never have enough." The "economics of scarcity" can cause us to close our eyes to the prevalent needs around us and serve as a barrier to sharing what we do have. To state the issue more directly, one of the primary impediments to sharing may be that we are too often distracted by and too busy participating in a consumer capitalist economy which traps us in an endless cycle of buying and consuming.[46]

The Lure of Luxury

James Twitchell, author of *Living it Up: Our Love Affair with Luxury* and professor of advertising at the University of Florida, describes an experiment he conducted with some of his students. First, he asked them to identify data from E.D. Hirsh's best-selling *Cultural Literacy: What Every American needs to Know*—terms like *gross national product*, *Emancipation Proclamation*, and *irony*—listed under the rubric: "What Literate Americans Know." Naturally, Twitchell says, the students were "abysmal, functionally illiterate." Then, he gave them a long list of the "best of the best," and asked them to identify—names like Georgio Armani (men's wear designer); Loro Piana (knitwear); Paul and Shark (boating wear); Galliano (women's wear designer); Porche 911 (sports car); Yamaha YZF-Ri (sport bike); Hermes (handbags); and La Perla (lingerie). The students passed *this* test with flying colors. In our postmodern world, the knowledge of history and science has been replaced by knowledge of luxury products, brand names, and consumption (what to buy and what not to buy).[47]

Luxury spending in the United States has been growing more than four times as fast as overall spending—and this spending is being done by younger and younger consumers. More and more, says Twitchell, we are becoming part of "a mass class of upscale consumption" where we understand each other, not by sharing religion, politics, or ideas, but by the brands we share. This is why there are Starbucks on street corners in poor neighborhoods; why Gen Y-ers clutch bottled water with French names; why fake Rolex watches are sold on street corners and on the internet; why Ferrari makes golf bags and Porsche makes watches; why Ralph Lauren puts his name on eyeglasses and bras; and why the Cape Cod Potato Chips brand has achieved the status of a "gourmet food," just like David's cookies and Dove Bars.[48]

46. Jipp, *Saved by Faith and Hospitality*, 148.
47. Twitchell, *Living it Up*, 3–6.
48. Ibid., xiv–xv;14.

But why the lure of luxury items and brand names? According to Twitchell, it is because we are not just buying things; we are buying meaning and a story. The solution to the modern angst is to fill up the self at the mall.[49] "You are what you can get, and you get what you can get by shopping for it. What you are is not what you make but what you consume."[50] In other words, we are consuming an image which confers status and social position. What we buy gives us a place in the world. "By adding value to material, by adding meaning to products, by branding things, by telling a story," Twitchell argues, "advertising performs a role historically associated with religion. . . . Commercialized luxury has colonized much of the space one held as sacred."[51]

In the musical play *Fiddler on the Roof* the main character is a poor milkman named Tevye. Overworked and underpaid, he cries out to God: "I realize that it's no great shame to be poor; but it's no great honor either. So would it have been so terrible if I had a small fortune?" He then goes on to sing, "If I Were a Rich Man," fantasizing that:

> The most important men in town would come to fawn on me!
> They would ask me to advise them. . . .
> And it won't make one bit of difference if I answer right or wrong.
> When you're rich, they think you really know!

In our culture, we equate our net worth with our self-worth and consider those who have more to be more important than those who have less.[52] This is why the poor buy lottery tickets they can't afford in hopes that they will win the mega millions jackpot; and why the average millennial expects to become a millionaire at some point and retire at an early age.[53]

However, we know that money and things do not bring us the security we crave. As the writer of Proverbs states: "The rich man thinks of his wealth as an impregnable defense, a high wall of safety. What a dreamer!" (Prov 18:11 TLB).

---

49. Ibid., 68–74.
50. Ibid., 106.
51. Ibid., 156.
52. Hostetler, *American Idols*, 25–26.
53. Burnett, "The Average Millennial Expects to Become a Millionaire,"

Possessions, Idolatry, and Faith

It is clear that our possessions have symbolic significance; they are an extension of ourselves into the world and into the lives of other persons. We say, for example, that "the clothes make the man," or "the style expresses the person." Luke Johnson puts it this way: "What we wear, eat, dwell in, drive, and use all express who we are and what we are.... The way we use, own, acquire, and disperse material things symbolizes and expresses our attitudes and responses to ourselves, the world around us, other people, and, most of all, God."[54] This is true of all of us, regardless of how much or how little we have. Certainly, a certain amount of food and a certain adequacy of clothes and shelter are necessary. Jesus says that we are to pray, "Give us this day our daily bread." And he promises that God, our heavenly Father, will provide for our needs. But for every person, rich or poor, money and possessions are not simply "out there" as neutral objects. They are also "in here," inextricably wrapped up in our sense of identity and self-worth. This issue of "meaning," which is significantly influenced by culture and society, is all-important when we consider what the Bible says about possessions and sharing with others.[55]

The central issue, then, is what is the source of meaning, power, self-worth, and personal identity? What is it without which life would not be worth living? What is my source of hope? What is it, when the rubber meets the road, which functions as my god? "Where we identify the source of our life and power (our *being*) and our worth," says Johnson, "is for us our center, and our center organizes the patterns of our perceptions from which our actions flow. Where the center is, there is our god."[56] From a biblical perspective, the choice we have is quite clear. Either we trust in God or we trust and identify ourselves with something in the material world. G. K. Beale states bluntly: "We either commit ourselves to God, identify with his name and become like his character, or we commit ourselves to some object of the creation and become like that thing."[57] This idea of becoming what we worship or commit ourselves to is implicit in the Old Testament description of idolatry as exchanging the glory of God for the image of an idol (see. Ps 106:19-21). When the Israelites ran after worthless idols made of wood, they lost their capacity to reflect God's character of love, justice, and mercy (Jer 2:11, 34; 7:5-11; Mic 5:12-6:8). In similar fashion, when we use

---

54. Johnson, *Sharing Possessions*, 39-40.
55. Ibid., 41-42.
56. Ibid., 50-52.
57. Beale, *We Become What We Worship*, 304-5.

FELLOWSHIP, BREAKING BREAD, AND SHARING POSSESSIONS

possessions to project an image of success or importance or view money as our source of security, we are denying God and exalting a modern Baal in his place.[58] Pursuing the idol of material success also blinds us to the needs of others around us.

Biblically, all we have is a gift from God; it is not "ours" in the first place. What we possess we possess as God's stewards. In fact, if the earth is "his" and all that is in it is "his" (Ps 24:1), in the final analysis there is a sense in which we do not own *anything*. We owe our very life to God. We are therefore fooling ourselves "when we think that we not only 'own' things, but can find in what we own our life and security."[59] The awareness that all that we have is from God both causes us to respond in thankfulness to God for his gracious provision and frees us from the tyranny of possessing. Furthermore, our attitude toward possessions not only symbolizes our fundamental response to God, in either faith or idolatry. How we respond to other people, with either a clinched fist or generosity, is also the way we respond to God. If our response is motivated by idolatry, the movement will be toward self-aggrandizement and injustice; if it is one of faith, our orientation will be towards appropriate sharing of possessions in love and according to the other's needs.[60]

Based upon these observations and the example of hospitality of the early Jerusalem church, we can therefore draw the following practical conclusions. First, all believers are enjoined to share with others as they are able. The poor widow who shared little out of her poverty was more generous and exhibited greater faith than the wealthy who shared out of their abundance (Lk 21:1–4). Second, economic relationships within the body of Christ should be characterized by mutual love, equity, freedom, and compassionate solidarity, and not by competition and social or status hierarchy.[61] Third, a guiding principle in the church should be from each according to his ability to each according to his need (Acts 2:44–45; 2 Cor 8:3–12 cf. Deut 15:7–8). Therefore, no church member should go without life's necessities. However, giving should be voluntary and under the motivation and direction of the Holy Spirit.[62] Finally, sharing is a mandate of faith and clinging to what one has is incompatible with both love and faith in God. But this mandate does not mean imitating the practice of the early church; the ways in which it is

---

58. Hostetler, *American Idols*, 195.
59. Johnson, *Sharing Possessions*, 58.
60. Ibid., 88, 100.
61. Jipp, Saved by *Faith and Hospitality*, 159–60.
62. See Crump, *I Pledge Allegiance*, 155–66.

expressed are as diverse as life's circumstances.[63] Christians and churches should think creatively about ways in which our economic arrangements and patterns of table fellowship can be redeemed and ordered toward love for God and love for others.[64] In this respect, following the example of Jesus and the Jerusalem church "necessarily presupposes a set of economic practices, ideas, and relationships supportive of the proper ends of the church, which is the kingdom of God as it unfolds in human history."[65]

---

63. Johnson, *Sharing Possessions*, 138.

64. Jipp, *Saved by Faith and Hospitality*, 173. For a further discussion of the "economics of discipleship" see Budde and Brimlow, *Christianity Incorporated*, 155–78.

65. Ibid., 157.

Part Four

The Wedding Supper

13

The Wedding Supper and the Biblical Hope

WE humans are by nature meaning-seeking creatures. Particularly in times that are disturbing or disorienting, religion is used to frame our experiences in terms of "plausibility structures"—narratives or systems of meaning that "make sense" of reality.[1] The question for Christians is, what type of narrative do we use to frame or give meaning to our experiences? Historically, the answer to this question has been expressed in terms of the biblical "hope"—a term that is associated with our final salvation or redemption that is assured because of Christ's resurrection. Peter describes God's ultimate purpose for Christians as a "new birth into a living hope through the resurrection of Jesus Christ from the dead and into an inheritance that can never perish" (1 Pet 1:3–4).

So far, so good. But when we dig deeper we realize that there is quite a bit of confusion about the ultimate hope of Christians—and of the world. In *Jesus the Bridegroom*, Brant Pitre describes the nature of this confusion in this way: The New Testament often describes the union between Christ and his church through the cross in terms of a marriage. But as every married couple knows, the wedding day is not the end but rather the *beginning* of a spousal relationship. In an ordinary Jewish wedding, after the wedding banquet and the sealing of the marriage covenant, the bridegroom takes the bride home to live with him. In the case of Jesus, however, something strange happens. Shortly after his wedding is inaugurated through his death and resurrection, Jesus the bridegroom *leaves* by ascending into heaven (Acts 1:1–11). What are we to make of this? As Pitre asks, "What kind of bridegroom marries his bride and then (literally) 'takes off'?"[2]

1. The term comes from Peter Berger, *Sacred Canopy*.
2. Pitre, *Jesus the Bridegroom*, 114–15.

The answer, of course, is that in the biblical story, although the wedding of Jesus, the Messiah, and his bride, the church, has begun (or been inaugurated), it is not yet complete. As I have noted repeatedly throughout this book, Jesus himself expresses this distinction between the "now" and the "not yet" in the Last Supper when he states: "I will not drink again of the fruit of the vine until that day when I drink it anew in the kingdom of God" (Mk 14:25). As we will see, this promise takes the form of a "new wedding covenant."[3] So, when and how does the story end? How is the union of God and his people brought to ultimate fulfillment? What is the exact nature of the biblical hope or vision of the future?

It will become apparent as we proceed that it is here where there is a lack of clarity (and disagreement) over what the Bible actually teaches. As Pitre states: "While many people think of the end of the world (primarily if not exclusively) as a time of tribulation, apostasy, deception, and the coming of the Antichrist, the New Testament also describes the end of time in another way: *as the eternal marriage of Jesus and his bride in a 'new heaven and a new earth'* (Rev 21:1–2)."[4] I will argue in this chapter and the chapters that follow that this *ultimate hope also has implications for change, rescue, and transformation within the world in the present.*[5] But, first, we have to look at some common misconceptions that people have of "heaven" and its association with the biblical hope.

Heaven and the Biblical Hope

Kathi and I love to travel. Frankly, we don't do as much of it as we would like. But when we are able to get away, we enjoy seeing new places, whether they be historical sites or settings that display the beauty of nature. We also look forward to visiting family and friends in various parts of the country. But, to be honest, after a week or two of being on the road, we are usually anxious to return home—to get back to the regular routine, eating meals at our kitchen table, and sleeping in our own bed. As the saying goes, "There's no place like home." Undoubtedly, many readers are familiar with this feeling.

---

3. Ibid., 48–49. See also Long, *Jesus the Bridegroom*, 202–3.
4. Ibid., 115.
5. See Wright, *Surprised by Hope*, 5.

Heaven in the Popular Imagination

The Bible likewise describes Christians as "travelers" or "sojourners" who look forward to going home to their final resting place. King David, for all his wealth and power, describes himself as a "guest" or "alien," and his days on earth as a mere shadow (1 Chron 29:15; Ps 39:12). And the writer of Hebrews describes Christians as strangers and exiles on earth who are seeking a homeland (Heb 11:13–14). If we are honest with ourselves, however, many of us try to satisfy this homesickness by investing in pleasures of the here and now.[6] In his classic work, *The Weight of Glory*, C. S. Lewis describes us as half-hearted creatures who satisfy ourselves with "mud pies" of drink, sex, and ambition when we are offered infinite joy. We are far too easily pleased.[7]

Yet every person experiences well-being in this world as fleeting and uncertain. When we or others we know and love experience a heart-wrenching divorce or face a life-threatening illness; and when we are confronted with the persistence of terrorism, the rise of ruthless dictators, and the possibility of nuclear war, we have the deep sense that we (and this earth) were made for more. This sense that the present world is not all there is to life is expressed in the song by Los Lonely Boys entitled "Heaven," which has been widely played on both pop and country music stations:

> In this crazy world, how far is heaven . . .
> Cause I know there's a better place
> Than this place I'm living.[8]

Best sellers such as Anthony DeStefano's *A Travel Guide to Heaven* and Don Piper's *90 Minutes in Heaven* are indicative of the fascination that Americans have with heaven. Polls consistently show that between 80 and 90 percent of Americans believe in heaven; and a recent Gallup poll reported that 77 percent rate their chances of "going to heaven" as "good" or "excellent."[9]

Most Americans, including many Christians, picture heaven as the ultimate resort. DeStefano, the CEO of Priests for Life, a Catholic antiabortion organization, describes heaven as "Disney World, Hawaii, Paris, Rome, and New York all rolled up into one." God, he says, is the "king of all travel agents" who has spent 4.6 billion years creating his incredible resort—a

---

6. See Fitzpatrick, *Home*, 36.
7. Lewis, *Weight of Glory*, 26.
8. Smith, *Heaven in the American Imagination*, 2.
9. Ibid.

never-ending vacation, great big family reunion, and ultimate adventure for travelers of all ages.[10] This image of heaven in the popular imagination is reinforced by books such as Erwin Lutzer's *One Minute After You Die*, which maintains on the basis of Revelation 21:16 that heaven "will be composed of 396,000 stories (at twenty feet per story) each having an area as big as one half the size of the United States!" Lutzer continues: "Divide that into separate condominiums and you have plenty of room for all who have been redeemed by God since the beginning of time."[11]

Bringing Heaven to Earth

Contrary to the beliefs of many Christians, however, the Bible does not portray the Christian's ultimate hope as disembodied souls flying off to some distant paradise where they will spend eternity. Admittedly, this is a difficult topic to address. Our own personal desires and longings to be reunited with loved ones who have passed away often strongly influence our perceptions of heaven. While this is understandable, the Bible actually does not say much about what happens when we die. There are some passages in Scripture (i.e., Lk 23:42–43; 2 Cor 5:1–10) which do suggest that in their postmortem state, believers experience a spiritual mode of existence in heaven.[12] Paul seems to indicate that immediately following death, believers go to be "with Christ" (Phil 1:23). Revelation also indicates that martyrs of the faith are in the present heaven (6:9–11). It is reasonable to assume that the same is true of loved ones and will be true of us when we die.[13]

But this "glorious interlude," or what is often referred to as the "intermediate state," is not the final state.[14] Our ultimate hope—and the emphasis of Scripture—is that God is going to redeem *this* world, including you and me.[15] When all is said and done, as Paul makes clear in 1 Corinthians 15, our spiritual bodies will be reunited with our resurrected bodies in a "new heaven and new earth." The picture of the *ultimate end* in Revelation 21–22

---

10. Ibid. 109.
11. Lutzer, *One Minute After You Die*, 83.
12. For a discussion of alternative views of the intermediate state, see Bird, *Evangelical Theology*, 317–25; 664–65. See also Burke, *Imagine Heaven*, 60–61. Alcorn argues on the basis of 2 Corinthians 5:2–4 that there may be "intermediate bodies" with some sort of physical form in the present or intermediate heaven. (*Heaven*, 57–59) Others argue, however, that 2 Corinthians 5:1–10 describes Paul's expectation of a redeemed humanity in a new creation. See Middleton, *A New Heaven and a New Earth*, 230–31.
13. Alcorn, *Heaven*, 65–67.
14. Bird, *Evangelical Theology*, 328.
15. Ross and Storment, *Bringing Heaven to Earth*, 60.

is not one of ransomed souls making their way to a disembodied heaven "but rather the new Jerusalem coming down from heaven to earth, uniting the two in a lasting embrace."[16] *The essence of the Christian hope, then, is in a very real sense the expectation of the final marriage of heaven and earth, of God and his creation. This is what is celebrated in the Lord's Supper! The Eucharist is a condensed summary of the final climax of redemption when heaven is brought to earth.*[17]

How we view heaven has profound implications for how we approach life on *this* earth. To the extent that Christians view the Christian hope in terms of "going to heaven," of salvation that takes us *away from* this world, argues N. T. Wright, then there will be little motivation for us to see the biblical hope as having much to do with change or new possibilities within the present world.[18] But the language of heaven as it is presented in the New Testament runs counter to this type of thinking. God's kingdom in the preaching of Jesus, Wright continues, "refers not to postmortem destiny, not to our escape from this world into another one, but to God's sovereign rule coming 'on earth as it is in heaven.'"[19] To understand why there is often so much confusion in this area we need to delve briefly into the controversy over what the Bible says about the "end times."

The "End Times" Debate

There is perhaps no area of biblical teaching that is the source of as much disagreement and debate among Christians as biblical eschatology, or what is often referred to as "end times" prophecy. As one biblical scholar notes, "Among the areas dividing the Christian ranks, few have been as explosive as those surrounding the doctrine of 'last things,' or eschatology."[20] This debate has significantly shaped the attitudes that Christians have toward the future of the earth. In what follows I will briefly address three key questions concerning the "biblical hope" that have preoccupied Christians: 1) Does the Bible teach the future "rapture" of the church? 2) What is the relationship of the "millennial kingdom" mentioned in Revelation 20 to the new heaven and new earth (Rev 21–22)? And 3) will the earth be destroyed at Christ's return? I will suggest readings of some key passages which correct misconceptions that many Christians have of the "end times"—misconceptions

16. Wright, *Surprised by Hope*, 19.
17. See Vanhoozer, *Faith Speaking Understanding*, 160.
18. Wright, *Surprised by Hope*, 5.
19. Ibid., 18.
20. Grenz, *The Millennial Maze*, 23.

which result in the idea of an otherworldly destiny in heaven that displaces the biblical teaching of God's renewal of *this* earth.[21]

A Secret Rapture?

I remember viewing the evangelical film *A Thief in the Night* (1972) when I was a young teen. The movie centers on the story of Patty, a young woman who is not raptured and is therefore faced with the prospect of going through the tribulation. This was a scary thought for adolescents like me. The same theme of being "left behind" is depicted in the wildly popular *Left Behind: A Novel of the Earth's Last Days* (1995), a sixteen-volume series that at last count has sold close to 80 million copies. The series has been adapted into four movies; and it has inspired a flood of apocalyptic merchandise and a number of spin-off series.

The *Left Behind* novels are a popularized version of the doctrine of the "secret rapture" held by dispensationalists. This is the belief that at the second coming of Christ, true Christians who have died together with the believers who are alive will meet the Lord in the air; they will then be taken into heaven, where they will stand before "the judgment seat of Christ" and celebrate the "wedding supper of the Lamb" (Rev 19:1–10).[22] Most dispensationalists believe that the rapture will occur prior to the "great tribulation," which will last for seven years (*pre-tribulation*); but some argue that the rapture will take place at the halfway point, or three-and-one-half years into the tribulation (*mid-tribulation*). At the end of the tribulation, Christ will return to the earth with his saints to set up the millennial kingdom, or what is often referred to as the "thousand-year reign" of Christ.

Critics of traditional dispensationalism agree with the common observation within this point of view that "there is something desperately wrong with this world which only God can fix." But the subtle danger of the Left Behind perspective, they argue, is that this honest and realistic assessment of this world often leads to fatalism and an identification of the "biblical hope" with the "rapture" of Christians into heaven.[23] The idea of the church's rapture is promoted by numerous dispensational authors and TV preachers, with some making wild speculations regarding the timing of the second coming and the end of the earth. It should be emphasized that date

21. See Middleton, *A New Heaven and a New Earth*, 283.

22. Grenz, *Millennial Maze*, 98–99. See also LaHaye, *Revelation Unveiled*, 289–97 and MacArthur, *Because the Time is Near*, 281–93.

23. Isaac, *Left Behind or Left Befuddled*, 111–12; Middleton, *A New Heaven and a New Earth*, 301.

setting is engaged in by only a minority of dispensationalists. Nonetheless, it is these representatives of the dispensational worldview which receive the most attention. Many of these teachers engage in what some refer to as "newspaper exegesis"—claims that certain current events are a "fulfillment" of biblical prophecy concerning the "last days." This apocalyptic mindset has had a significant impact on people's attitudes towards the present world. Middleton argues that the "resolute focus on the church's imminent exit to heaven has the effect of inclining believers in the rapture to treat the future (and thus the present) of the earth as unimportant." Concern for this world takes a back seat "since there is little theological ground in a rapture-oriented eschatology for ecological or social responsibility."[24]

To be fair, it should again be stressed that there is a range of emphases among dispensationalists who believe in a "pre-tribulational rapture." It would be wrong to view dispensationalism as a static and monolithic viewpoint.[25] There is a growing number of "progressive" or "moderate" dispensationalists who endorse a more "holistic" understanding of redemption.[26] Even those who might be considered "traditional" dispensationalists have supported efforts to address the physical and material needs of people such as hospitals, orphanages, and agricultural projects, although most view such efforts as primarily a means to realizing the main objective of saving people's souls. On the whole, however, we can say that the belief in the rapture among traditional dispensationalists is reflective of the view that God cares more about the salvation of human souls than he does about the renewal of *this* earth. Many believe that the present earth is simply a "halfway-house" which will be eventually destroyed and replaced by the new heaven and new earth. If our ultimate hope is a release from this earth (through death or the rapture) and if the present earth is going to be obliterated anyway, why should we be concerned about the pollution of our air and oceans or put much effort into "saving" this planet?[27]

I believe that this picture of the believer's hope is inconsistent with a number of passages in the New Testament which depict the eternal destiny of the redeemed in terms of a renewal of earthly life.[28] In his sermon

---

24. Ibid., 305.

25. Grenz, *The Millennial Maze*, 93.

26. See Blaising and Bock, *Progressive Dispensationalism*, 46–47.

27. Bouma-Prediger, "Eschatology Shapes Ethics," 16–18. Hunt rightly states that much of current "end-times" theology gives a pass—a "get out of jail free" card—for caring about the environment. "After all, why do we need to make sure our oceans are clean and air is breathable if Jesus is just going to set it all on fire and start over again?" (*Unraptured*, 136).

28. Middleton, "A New Heaven and a New Earth," 73; 86–91.

following Pentecost, Peter refers to the future fulfillment of God's promise to "restore everything" (Acts 3:21); and in his epistle he encourages his readers to look forward "to a new heaven and a new earth, the home of righteousness" (2 Peter 3:13). The apostle Paul refers to the time when God will fulfill his purposes "to bring all things in heaven and on earth together under one head, even Christ" (Eph 1:9–10). Drawing on the language of Exodus 2:23–24, which portrays the Israelites as groaning in their bondage under Pharaoh, in Romans 8:19–23 he looks forward to the day when all of creation will be liberated from its bondage to decay (vs 21). This comprehensive scope of redemption is further emphasized in Colossians, which describes salvation in terms of the reconciliation of "all things" on earth and in heaven to God through Christ (1:19–20). Furthermore, since Christ has *already* disarmed evil powers and authorities and because God's ultimate victory is assured (Col 2:15; Rev 21:5), we ought to share in God's restless yearning for renewal of the cosmos.[29]

Dispensationalists generally appeal to two passages in support of the idea of a rapture. The first is Jesus' description in Matt 24:37–41 of what will happen when the Son of Man returns. Verses 40–41 read: "Two men will be in the field; one will be taken and the other left. Two women will be grinding with a hand mill; one will be taken and the other left." It is often assumed that the persons who are "taken" in these verses are believers who go to heaven to be with the Lord. But a careful reading of the entire passage reveals that Jesus is drawing a comparison with those *unbelievers* at the time of Noah who were eating and drinking and knew nothing about what would happen to them "until the flood came and took them all away" (vss 38–39). It was Noah and his family who were "left behind" on earth. The phrase "took them all away" describes judgment. So, in drawing this parallel between the days of Noah and the day when he returns, Jesus is actually referring to the *unrighteous* who are taken away to judgment![30]

The second "proof text" for the rapture is 1 Thessalonians 4:13–18. In this passage, Paul is offering encouragement to the early church by affirming that those believers who have died prior to Christ's return will not be disadvantaged, but will be the first to be raised. Then comes the key verse: "After that, we who are still alive will be caught up together with them in the clouds to meet the Lord in the air. And so we will be with the Lord forever" (vs 17).

While at first blush this passage might seem to offer strong support for a rapture of the church, a number of things can be said in response. First, down through the history of the church this text has been simply viewed as

---

29. Mouw, *When the Kings Come Marching In*, 111.
30. Middleton, "A New Heaven and a New Earth," 95.

describing the return of the Lord. It says nothing about a twofold coming of Christ or about believers being taken to heaven. The idea of two phases or episodes separated by a tribulation—a snatching away of the church followed by a public second coming—must be "read into" the text.[31] Second, Paul is using somewhat different language to say what he is saying in 1 Corinthians 15:23–27, 51–54 and Philippians 3:20–21 regarding the *transformation* of our physical bodies to be like Jesus' glorious body. In describing believers as being "caught up . . . in the clouds to meet the Lord in the air" (vs 17), Paul is using symbolic language borrowed from the prophet Daniel, who describes how the persecuted people of God are vindicated over their enemies by being raised up on clouds to sit with God in glory (Dan 7).[32] Finally, in his use of the term *apantesin* ("to meet") Paul may be also drawing on the Greco-Roman custom of *apantesis* ("meeting"). According to this custom a delegation was sent outside the city to receive a dignitary; they then *returned* with him, escorting him in grand procession into their city. The implication is that believers will escort Christ the king *back to* earth.[33]

What about the Millennial Kingdom?

The foregoing discussion leads naturally to the question of the millennial kingdom. Historically, there have been three primary views among Christians: *postmillennialism, amillennialism,* and *premillennialism*.[34] I will briefly return to this debate in chapter fifteen. Here, I will simply note that since the early twentieth century the view known as "dispensational premillennialism" has become the dominant view among evangelicals. According to this view, a clear distinction must be made between two phases of God's program for salvation history—1) his program for Israel, which focuses on the land of Palestine and involves the literal fulfillment of God's promises to Israel in a physical millennial kingdom; and 2) his program for the

---

31. Isaac, *Left Behind or Left Befuddled*, 56; 70.
32. See Wright, *Surprised by Hope*, 131–32.
33. Middleton, *A New Heaven and a New Earth*, 223–34.
34. The debate centers on the meaning of Revelation 20:1–6. Proponents of postmillennialism argue that the physical return of Christ will occur *after* an earthly golden age which takes place through the church, an era of peace and righteousness which Revelation 20 pictures in terms of a thousand-year reign of Christ. Advocates of the view known as amillennialism (which is probably better termed "inaugurated millennialism") maintain that the millennium (or thousand-year reign of Christ) started at Christ's resurrection and will be concluded directly before his final coming. Finally, adherents of premillennialism expect the return of Christ *prior* to the thousand-year period mentioned in Revelation 20. See Grenz, *The Millennial Maze*, 24–5.

church, which centers on heaven and the spiritual blessings that God has for those who acknowledge Christ as Savior.[35] However, most evangelicals are "dispensationalists by osmosis," meaning that they have absorbed dispensational views through the immense popularity of the Scofield Reference Bible and popularized versions of dispensationalist eschatology such as Hal Linsey's *Late Great Planet Earth* without fully understanding or accepting the entire dispensationalist schema.[36] A growing number of evangelical scholars reject the rigid distinction that traditional dispensationalists make between Israel and the church.[37]

While most of the "end times" debate among evangelicals has centered on the timing and nature of the millennium, a crucial question concerns the nature of the relationship between the millennial kingdom and the "new heaven and new earth" described in Revelation 21–22. Middleton observes that when an "otherworldly" orientation is combined with a temporary earthly millennium "all the biblical promises and descriptions of the redemption of the cosmos (and there are many) tend to be squeezed into this thousand-year rule of Christ, which leaves the final state to be reinterpreted as 'heaven.'"[38] Many evangelicals of all persuasions have tended to emphasize the *radical discontinuity* between the earthly millennium and the final destiny of the redeemed, which is viewed as spiritual and otherworldly in nature.[39] However, a number of evangelical scholars (including both amillennialists and premillennialists) have rejected this radical dualism of heavenly and earthly states in favor of a "new creation" picture of redemption.

---

35. Ibid., 26; 96.

36. Middleton, *A New Heaven and a New Earth*, 302–303.

37. Some more moderate (or "progressive") dispensationalists hold that *some* of the promises to Israel are fulfilled in the church. They reject the sharp distinctions that more traditional dispensationalists make between Israel and the church. But they still maintain that the state of Israel is the focus of the millennial kingdom. Another viewpoint known as "historic premillennialism" also rejects the rigid distinction between Israel and the church and instead argues that the church is the "spiritual Israel." Moreover, they hold to a postribulational rapture as opposed to the pretribulational rapture that is taught by most dispensationalists. Grenz, *The Millennial Maze*, 122–23; 128–31

38. Ibid., 286.

39. See Moore, *The Kingdom of Christ*, 92–93; 232. Blaising notes that many Christians and Christian theologians have subscribed to the "spiritual vision model" of eternity, which maintains that the final state of resurrected believers will be heaven. This view is based on the belief that "heaven is the highest level of ontological reality. It is the realm of spirit as opposed to base matter. This is the destiny of the saved, who will exist in that nonearthly, spiritual place as spiritual beings engaged eternally in spiritual activity" ("Premillennialism," 161; 185–86).

In this "new creation" model, the ultimate biblical hope is not a static and timeless eternity in "heaven" but a totally "new earth."[40]

Will the Earth Be Destroyed or Renewed at Christ's Return?

The final question then is this: What will happen to the present earth at Christ's return? As Randy Alcorn frames the issue: "Will the present Earth and the entire universe be utterly destroyed, and the New Earth and new universe made from scratch? Or will the original universe be renewed and transformed into the new one?"[41] Many biblical scholars argue that this earth will not be replaced by a totally new one; rather it will be cleansed of sin and re-created, reborn, renewed, and made whole. If God has to annihilate the present world and start over from scratch, they argue, then Satan will have won a great victory, for he will have succeeded in so devastatingly corrupting the present earth that God can do nothing with it but to blot it totally out of existence. But the Bible teaches that Satan has been decisively defeated through the cross![42]

Yet the question remains, if God's plan is to redeem *this* world, what about those passages in the New Testament which seem to teach that the entire cosmos will be destroyed at the return of Christ? Some who have difficulty with the idea of the renewal of this earth point to passages which describe heaven and earth as "passing away" (Matt 24:35; Mk 13:31; Lk 21:33; Rev 21:1) and to Peter's picture of the destruction of heaven and earth in the "day of the Lord" (II Pet 3:10–11). John MacArthur argues in this vein that: "The new heaven and the new earth will not merely succeed the present universe. They will be something brand-new and fresh. God must create a new heaven and a new earth because the first heaven and the first earth passed away."[43]

While it is not possible to give an extended treatment of this issue here, I will simply make the following points. First, the word "new" in the expression "new heaven and new earth" (Rev 21:1) indicates the creation of a universe which, though it has been gloriously renewed, still stands in continuity with the present one.[44] Paul uses the same word (*kainos*) in 2 Cor

---

40. Moore, *The Kingdom of Christ*, 51–52. It should be pointed out, however, that there are a continuum of views between the "spiritual vision" model of eternity and the "new creation" model. See also James, *New Creation Eschatology and the Land*, 1–26.

41. Alcorn, *Heaven*, 151.

42. Ibid., 152–53.

43. MacArthur, *Because the Time Is Near*, 315.

44. Alcorn, *Heaven*, 155.

5:17: "If anyone is in Christ, he is a new creation; the old has passed away, behold, the new [*kaina*] has come" (RSV). Here, when Paul says that the old has "passed away" he is not saying that there is an obliteration of the person. The new Christian is still the same person as before, although the old life has ended. By analogy, the "passing away" of the present heaven and earth has the idea of radical transformation or change in their present condition, not of destruction followed by replacement.[45]

2 Peter 3:10–11 further explains this transformation of the present world in terms of the image of refinement by fire. John Piper states: "What Peter may well mean is that at the end of this age there will be cataclysmic events that bring this world to an end *as we know it*—not putting out of existence, but wiping out all that is evil and cleansing it by fire and fitting it for an age of glory and righteousness and peace that will never end."[46] It is worth pointing out that in the oldest manuscripts the last part of verse 10 reads: "the earth and everything in it will be laid bare (or exposed)." In other words, "God's fire of judgment will consume the bad but refine the good, exposing things as they really are."[47]

Jesus the Bridegroom and the Last Supper

We can now return to the theme of the wedding supper mentioned earlier in this chapter. The promises made to Israel in the Old Testament as well as the promise in the New Testament of the fullness of our participation in eternal life are fulfilled in the coming of a new heaven and a new earth (Rev 21:1). It is only in a redeemed and transformed creation that we will experience full personal renewal and full restoration of our relationship with creation, with others, and, most importantly, with God, our Creator.[48]

Earlier in this book, we noted how the ancient Jews referred to YHWH, the God of Israel, as the divine "bridegroom."[49] We have also seen how God is depicted as the bridegroom of Israel in the Song of Solomon. Throughout the Old and New Testaments, the concept of the "wedding feast" is used as a metaphor for this final renewal and restoration of creation. More

---

45. Middleton, *A New Heaven and New Earth*, 206.
46. Piper, *Future Grace*, 376.
47. Alcorn, *Heaven*, 155.
48. Grenz, *Millennial Maze*, 214. Some argue that the promises in the Old Testament regarding the particular physical territory of Israel are fulfilled in the final state as *part of* the restoration of the earth. See James, *New Creation Eschatology and the Land*, 95–134.
49. Pitre, *Jesus the Bridegroom*, 8.

specifically, the image of the bridegroom returning to his bride is used to depict the renewal of God's "marriage covenant" with his people. In this sense, the story of salvation in the Bible is a divine "love story" between God and his people—and indeed between God and his entire creation. As Pitre perceptively remarks:

> From an ancient Jewish perspective, the God of Israel is also a *Bridegroom*, a divine person whose ultimate desire is to be united to his creatures in an everlasting relationship that is so intimate, so permanent, so sacrificial, and so life-giving that it can only be described as a *marriage* between Creator and creatures, between God and human beings, between YHWH and Israel.[50]

This is why at the very end of the book of Revelation the "new Jerusalem" is depicted as "coming down out of heaven from God, prepared as a bride beautifully dressed for her husband" (Rev 21:2; cf. 22:17).

In the Gospels, Jesus describes *himself* as the divine bridegroom coming for his bride; and he depicts the final age of salvation in terms of the image of a wedding feast. In fact, I hope to show that the Last Supper is in many respects a wedding banquet—the inauguration of a *new wedding covenant* that looks forward to the final wedding celebration spoken of by the prophets.[51] In his emphasis on the forward-looking nature of the Lord's Supper, Paul likewise indicates that only when Jesus comes again (1 Cor 11:26; cf. 1:7) will the meal be fulfilled as we dine with him in the "wedding supper of the Lamb" (Rev 19:9).[52] In the next chapter, then, I will examine the theme of the wedding banquet and Jesus as the bridegroom in the Gospel of John. The focus will be on the story of Jesus' miracle of turning water into wine in the wedding at Cana (Jn 2:1–12). In chapter fifteen, I will discuss the meaning and significance of the "wedding supper of the Lamb" in the book of Revelation.

---

50. Ibid., 9.
51. Ibid., 49. See also Long, *Jesus the Bridegroom*, 202–203.
52. Johnson, *1 Corinthians*, 209.

14

The Wedding at Cana

THE past two Christmases (2017 and 2018), Kathi and I have attended concerts put on by the Master Singers of Milwaukee. The concerts were held at St Joseph's Chapel. Neither of us have ever been drawn to Catholic liturgy, and there are some legitimate criticisms of Catholic worship with its emphasis on ritual and symbolism. But in these particular instances, we have to say that the physical splendor of the chapel, the poetry and theological depth of the lyrics, coupled with the harmony and beauty of the music itself, had a great impact on us. At times, we were both so deeply moved by the music that it brought tears of joy to our eyes. Parenthetically, these experiences have also heightened our awareness of the theological shallowness of some of the contemporary worship songs that are sung in many of our evangelical churches today.

In the prologue to his Gospel, John states: "The word became flesh, and made his dwelling among us. *We have seen his glory*, the glory of the One and Only, who came from the Father, full of grace and truth" (Jn 1:14). These words echo through thousands of churches around the world at Christmas time, with the result that this verse is one of the most famous and well known of Bible passages. They are words that speak of the manifestation of God's glory through the incarnation and the cross.[1]

In the next chapter, John describes an episode that is commonly referred to by preachers at weddings—Jesus' miracle of turning water into wine at a wedding at Cana. The astute reader will note that John concludes this account of Jesus' first miracle with a comment that connects it directly with the prologue: "This, the first of his miraculous signs, Jesus performed

---

1. Wright, *Following Jesus*, 33.

at Cana of Galilee. He thus *revealed his glory*, and his disciples put their faith in him" (2:11).

What is the significance of this connection? This miracle is one of many miraculous signs that point to Jesus' divinity and elicit faith (Jn 20:30). But, when one thinks about it, there are any number of other miracles that Jesus could have performed to kick off his ministry if all he wanted to do was demonstrate his power and authority. John is clear, however, that it is *this* miracle of turning water into wine at a Jewish wedding that Jesus uses to set the stage for the rest of his ministry. Why?[2] Furthermore, in what respects did Jesus reveal his glory in performing this particular miracle?

Jesus' First Miracle and John's Theology in Historical Context

I have argued throughout this book that the story of Jesus as presented in the Gospels must be viewed as part of the larger story, or "metanarrative" of creation, fall, redemption, and new creation in Scripture. The gospel stories present Jesus as the fulfillment of Old Testament messianic hopes and aspirations through his life, death, and resurrection. I have also emphasized that this story of Jesus as presented in the Gospels cannot be divorced from its larger historical context. This is particularly true of this account in John's Gospel. When we view Jesus' miracle of turning water into wine within its larger Jewish context, it becomes apparent that it is more than a startling event at a Jewish wedding.[3]

Let's look again at the historical context as it relates to John's use of theological symbols. We will then turn briefly to how this particular story fits into the theme of "new creation" in his Gospel.

Reviewing the Historical Context of John's Theology

We in the West tend to conduct theology in the abstract. "Bible study" is generally viewed as a "religious" exercise, which is separate from economics and politics. But an adequate understanding of Jesus and the Gospels must be based on the recognition that in the ancient world religion, politics, and economics were inseparable. The Roman emperor, who ruled over the entire Mediterranean world, was considered to be the "son of god" and was therefore worshiped in state temples and shrines.[4] Moreover, the temple-state

---

2. Pitre, *Jesus the Bridegroom*, 35.
3. Ibid., 29
4. Horsley and Hatcher, *John, Jesus, and the Renewal of Israel*, 13–14

in Jerusalem in many ways served as the local instrument of imperial rule. Under Herod, the high priestly aristocracy at the head of the temple was dependent and submissive to Rome; it was therefore, effectively, the face of Roman imperial rule in Palestine.[5]

Among the Jewish people at the time of Jesus there was widespread discontent, which was expressed not only in resistance to the Roman rulers and their religious cronies in Jerusalem but also in a longing for renewal in their land.[6] In John's Gospel, there are a number of symbols that Jesus uses to highlight and respond to this hope for deliverance, restoration, and renewal. The raising of Lazarus, for example, not only points to Jesus' own resurrection. It also points to the fulfillment of this longing for restoration to new life; it affirms Jesus' self-identification as the "resurrection and the life" and is an assertion that in his mission the long-awaited restoration of God's people has begun (Jn 11:17–44).[7]

As we have seen, another prominent and long-standing symbol in the Jewish religious tradition is the wedding, which represents the marriage or union between the people and their God. The account in the Gospels of the dispute over fasting (Mk 2:18–20; Matt 9:14–15; Lk 5:33–35) indicates, for example, that the idea of a future wedding feast had become a prime symbol which reflected the people's hopes for a future celebration of a union between God's anointed one (the bridegroom) and the renewed people of Israel (the bride). Jesus' miracle of turning water into wine at the wedding at Cana (along with other "signs") points to the fulfillment of these aspirations within the Jewish tradition for the new life, a "new age" of divine restoration and provision.[8]

Turning Water into Wine and the "New Creation"

The reader will recall from our discussion in chapter six that a main theme in John's Gospel is the "new creation." John begins his Gospel as though he is writing a new Genesis, a new creation story.[9] And in his passion narrative he sets the crucifixion and resurrection within the context of the "new creation." So John begins and ends with a focus on the theme that God is bringing about a new creation through the divine incarnation ("In the beginning was the Word. . . . The Word became flesh and made his dwelling among

---

5. Ibid., 18.
6. Ibid., 34.
7. Ibid., 148.
8. Ibid., 149.
9. Wright, *Following Jesus*, 35.

us. We have seen his glory . . .") and Jesus' death and resurrection.[10] In fact, all of the "signs" in John's Gospel (the healing of a paralyzed man at the pool—John 5:2–9; the healing of a man born blind—John 9:1–7; the raising of Lazarus—John 11:1–44, etc.) have an element of new creation in them.[11] By deliberately connecting Jesus' first miraculous "sign" of turning water into wine at a Jewish wedding with the prologue as a display of "God's glory," John is, in effect, saying that Jesus is the divine bridegroom who will fulfill the prophecies of a new creation, when God's glory will be fully manifested.

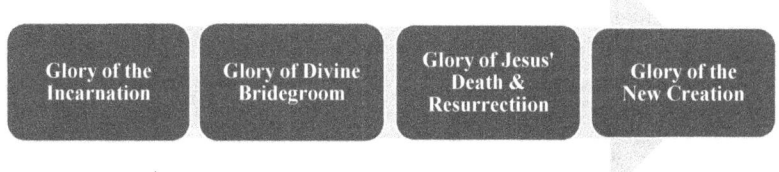

Figure 6: Jesus' Glory as the Divine Bridegroom

Jesus the Bridegroom, John the Baptist, and Ancient Jewish Marriage Customs

Jesus' identity as the "bridegroom of Israel" in John's Gospel can be better understood by looking at the role of John the Baptist and his relationship to Jesus. In the early days of Jesus' ministry, when he is forming his own band of followers (Jn 1:29–51), John's disciples approach their master to find out what he thinks of this Jesus (3:26). John responds by describing himself as a "friend" of the bridegroom who is "full of joy when he hears the bridegroom's voice" (3:28–30). What is the meaning and significance of these words? In what sense is John the bridegroom's "friend," and why is this important?

John as a "Friend" of the Bridegroom

To answer these questions, we need to look at Jewish marriage customs in the time of Jesus. As is the custom in our day, it was customary in Jesus' day for the Jewish bridegroom to select a close "friend" to act as his "best man." But, unlike today, a marriage back then was an arrangement entered

10. Emerson, *Christ and the New Creation*, 57.
11. Ibid., 58.

into by two families. There was first a "betrothal," with the wedding itself following after a period of at least a year. Arrangements for the betrothal were made by the heads (most often the fathers) of the families of the young man and young woman. But in these negotiations the fathers acted through deputies or representatives of the families. When consent was reached, the deputies and fathers drank together as a "sign" that the "marriage covenant" was agreed to by the two parties. The betrothal was viewed as a binding agreement that could only be broken by divorce or death. It is clear from this that the bridegroom's friend had a very significant role in the everything that took place before the wedding, since it was his negotiations as a "friend" or representative of the bridegroom and his family that played a crucial part in gaining consent of the father of the bride-to-be.[12]

This picture of the "friend" or "best man" who speaks on behalf of the bridegroom sheds significant light on the role of John the Baptist, who identifies himself as the "voice" (1:23) and the "friend" of Jesus, the bridegroom (3:29). John acts in the narrative as the deputy or friend of the bridegroom "sent by the groom's father to initiate proceedings that will lead, it is hoped, to betrothal and marriage."[13] We have seen that John's words in 1:23 ("I am the voice of one calling in the desert, 'Make straight the way for the Lord'") are taken directly from a passage in Isaiah, which is an invitation for Israel to reunite with her estranged husband (Isa 40:3).

John and the "Voice" of the Bridegroom Messiah

During the wedding ceremony itself the bridegroom's friend or "best man" has a further role to play. In Jesus' day, the wedding ceremony began with a joyous procession of the young woman from her father's house to the home of the bridegroom, which was usually the ancestral home or home of the patriarch (father). According to Jewish custom, it was the job of the best man to bring the bride to the groom at the time of the wedding. In some cases, the groom led the bride to her new home. In other instances this role would be given to the best man, with the groom later arriving to the house in his own procession. In either case, this was when she was considered finally married.[14]

This Jewish context helps explain the words of John the Baptist: "The bride belongs to the bridegroom. The friend who attends the bridegroom waits and listens for him, and is full of joy when he hears the bridegroom's

---

12. See Coloe, *Dwelling in the Household of God*, 29–31.
13. Ibid., 33.
14. Ibid., 32. See also Pitre, *Jesus the Bridegroom*, 33.

voice" (3:29). The scene is the bride's house. Everyone is waiting for the bride to be led to her new home, accompanied by her bridesmaids, family, and friends. The best man listens for the bridegroom's voice so that he can initiate the procession. Then the celebration can begin.[15] It is possible that John the Baptist's words are an allusion to Jeremiah 33:10–17. In this passage, the prophet connects hearing *"the voice of gladness, the voice of the bridegroom and the voice of the bride"* (vs 11 ESV) with the coming of the Davidic king, who brings righteousness and justice to Israel (vss 14–17). Just as Jeremiah talks about the joy of the days when the king will come, so too John speaks of his own personal joy when he hears the voice of the bridegroom (the Messiah), whom he then reveals or "makes known" to Israel (1:31).[16]

So far, however, the picture in John's Gospel of Jesus as a bridegroom is incomplete. This portrait of Jesus' person and mission comes more clearly into focus when we look at Jesus' own words and actions during the wedding at Cana.

The Wedding at Cana: Jesus the Bridegroom and Mary

When we first read John's account of Jesus' miracle of turning water into wine, it appears that he is simply telling us a story about Jesus' response to the lack of wine at a wedding. Having enough wine at a wedding was crucial. If the bridegroom ran out of wine at his wedding, the consequences would be disastrous for him socially and possibly even legally. He would be shamed publicly and could even be considered a disgrace to the family.[17]

But there are indications in the passage that Jesus' miracle is more than an act of compassion in a potentially very embarrassing situation for the banquet's host. Our first clue that there is a deeper meaning to this miracle is John's initial statement that the wedding took place "on the third day" (2:1). Secondly, the bride is never mentioned and the groom appears only briefly at the end of the episode. Furthermore, there are no words of gratitude by the host as the primary beneficiary of the miracle. Nor are there the expressions of amazement by onlookers that we see with many of other miracles performed by Jesus. It is also a bit odd that when the wine runs out, Mary brings this problem to the attention of Jesus, not the host or headwaiter. Then, there is Jesus' response: "Woman, what does this have to do with me? My hour has not yet come" (2:4 ESV). Why does he respond in this fashion, and then seemingly do an abrupt about-face by turning the six large jars of

---

15. Martin and Wright, *The Gospel of John*, 77.
16. Pitre, *Jesus the Bridegroom*, 31–32.
17. McGill, "God's Getting Married," 57.

water into wine? And why would he mention his "hour" at a wedding? As Brant Pitre remarks, when we examine these elements in the light of ancient Jewish Scripture and tradition, we find that there is much more to this story than first meets the eye.[18]

Jesus and the Wine of YHWH's Banquet

Let's look first at the exchange between Jesus and his mother Mary. To begin with, while Jesus' response to his mother might sound to us like a show of disrespect, it really isn't. The title "woman" was a typical way of addressing women in antiquity (see Jn 4:21; 8:10; Matt 15:28). In this instance, it is Jesus' way of distancing himself from an exclusively mother-son relationship.[19] Jesus' initial response (lit. "what to me and to you, woman") is a Semitic expression that creates a distance in interest or understanding between two parties.[20] So, in some sense Jesus is indicating a lack of understanding on her part. But in what sense?

For a possible answer we have to return to the symbolic significance of wine. John indicates that Jesus turned a very large amount of water—between 120 and 160 gallons—into wine (2:6). Such a large quantity would exceed the amount needed for a wedding banquet, suggesting that John intends to give a deeper meaning to this miracle.[21] Pitre points out: "From an ancient Jewish perspective, the sheer amount of wine provided by Jesus would call to mind the fact that in Jewish Scripture, one of the marks of the future age of salvation is that it would be characterized by superabundant wine."[22] Amos says that when God brings about the final salvation of his people, "New wine will drip from the mountains and flow from the hills (Amos 9:13). Joel declares that, "In that day the mountains will drip new wine" (Joel 3:18).

As we have observed throughout this book, the Jewish Scriptures picture the age of salvation in terms of a wedding feast in which there is eating and drinking. And it is God as the bridegroom who provides the wine for the banquet. The irony in John's account is that while it was the bridegroom's responsibility to furnish the wine for the wedding celebration, it is Jesus who actually does so. And the wine he provides when the previous wine runs out is the "best wine"—thus reversing the customary practice of

---

18. Pitre, *Jesus the Bridegroom*, 36–7.
19. Martin and Wright, *The Gospel of John*, 57–8.
20. Ibid., 57.
21. Ibid., 59.
22. Pitre, *Jesus the Bridegroom*, 42.

bringing out the most expensive wine first and then the cheaper wine when the guests have had their fill (2:9–10). In a real sense, the bridegroom at the wedding comes off as an imposter compared to Jesus, who truly fulfills the role of a bridegroom![23] Pitre sums up the significance of John's portrayal of Jesus in this way:

> When we combine the prophecies of the wine of YHWH with the prophecies of YHWH the Bridegroom, Jesus' actions at Cana lead us to conclude that . . . [he] is also beginning to suggest that the prophecies of *the divine bridegroom* are being fulfilled in him. . . . In other words, by means of the miracle at Cana, Jesus is beginning to reveal, in a very Jewish way, the mystery of his divine identity.[24]

The Significance of Mary's Word's and Jesus' Response

This brings us to the role of Mary in this episode. Many commentators have been puzzled by her words to Jesus, "They have no more wine." A common interpretation is that it is an implicit request to rectify a problem by doing something phenomenal.[25] But this interpretation does not make much sense in light of Jesus' response, "My hour has not yet come." A more plausible approach is to view Mary's role as symbolic. Knowing that Jesus is the Messiah, she is indirectly suggesting that this may be the occasion him to fully reveal his identity as the divine bridegroom spoken of by the prophets and demonstrate his power and glory to the world.[26] Jesus' response to her indicates that she (like the disciples) does not fully understand or grasp the implications of what she is asking. In effect, he is saying (or intimating) to Mary something like: "It is not yet time for me to provide the wine of the banquet of YHWH. I will provide that supernatural wine, but only at the hour of my passion and death." Nonetheless, he performs a "sign" that *points forward* to the "hour" of his crucifixion, when his glory will be fully revealed.[27]

We can see echoes of this "dialogue" between Mary and Jesus in the Old Testament prophets. Mary's assertion—"They have no more wine"— brings to mind Isaiah's use of the imagery of a lack of wine to describe the

---

23. McGill, "God's Getting Married," 64–65.
24. Pitre, *Jesus the Bridegroom*, 45.
25. See Keener, *The Gospel of John, vol. 2*, 503.
26. McGill, "God's Getting Married," 60.
27. Pitre, *Jesus the Bridegroom*, 47.

utter devastation of a world system based wholly on human resources apart from God:

> The new wine dries up and the vine withers;
> all the merrymakers groan. . . .
> No longer do they drink wine with a song. . . .
> In the streets they cry out for wine;
> all joy turns to gloom,
> all gaiety is banished from the earth.
> (Isa 24:7, 9, 11)

But Isaiah does not stop with this image of people running out of wine.[28] At the end of this passage, he describes "that day," when a Davidic king will come to "punish the powers in the heavens above and the kings on the earth below" (24:21) and establish his reign in Jerusalem (vs 23). In the next chapter, he describes the age of salvation in terms of a "banquet of aged wine" for "all people" that will undo the effects of the fall (Isa 25:6–9).

The Wedding at Cana and the Last Supper

In this final section, my purpose is to show how the Cana miracle sheds light on the meaning of the Last Supper. But, first, we have to look more closely at the ways this particular story anticipates Jesus' death and resurrection—which, of course, is the means through which God forgives and redeems his people and fulfills his purposes for creation.

Pointers to Jesus' Death and Resurrection

There are several allusions to Jesus' death and resurrection in this account. The first, as we have already intimated, is Jesus' reference to "my hour" (2:4). The second is John's description of this episode as occurring on the "third day" (2:1). And the third is John's conclusion that this miracle is the *first* of Jesus' "miraculous signs" in which he "revealed his glory" 1:11). Let's look briefly at each of these references.

Jesus' mention of "my hour"—or time—in this account is the first of eight incidents in the Gospel of John where Jesus uses term in reference to himself (2:3; 7:30; 8:20; 12:23; 12:27; 13:1; 17:1; 19:27). In each of these occurrences, Jesus is clearly referring to his impending crucifixion and resurrection. The most important of these mentions of an "hour" is the last one,

---

28. Ibid., 40.

which occurs just before his death. It is no accident that in the very next two verses *after* this final reference to "that hour," (19:27) Jesus receives wine vinegar, or common wine, when he exclaims "I am thirsty" (17:28–30).²⁹ This scene *mirrors* the very first mention of Jesus' "hour" in the wedding at Cana, after which he provides wine in abundance.³⁰

Cana Wedding	Jesus' Passion (Cross)
"My hour has not yet come" (Jn 2:4)	"From that hour [of the cross]" (Jn 17:15–27)
Jesus provides wine in abundance (2:8–10)	Jesus receives wine vinegar (17:28–30)

Table 4. The Cana Wedding and Jesus' Passion

This brings us to the other ways in which John's account of the Cana miracle gives hints of Jesus' death and resurrection. When John begins his account by saying that the wedding was on "the third day" (2:1), there are indications that he is doing more than simply giving a chronology of events. The next significant event where reference is made to the "third day" is Jesus' cleansing of the temple, when Jesus declares that the temple will be destroyed and raised up "in three days" (2:19). Jesus is, of course, referring to his own death and resurrection—his "hour." And it is *this* third day toward which the Cana wedding directs the reader.³¹

In the Old Testament, the tabernacle and later the temple is God's home. It is the place where heaven and earth are joined together—the place of sacrifice and atonement where people were to go to meet God.³² In the temple scene, John indicates that God's presence shifts from the Jerusalem temple to the person of Jesus. "Just as the glory of God filled the tabernacle (Exod 40:34–35), so the glory of God now tabernacles in Jesus."³³ And the final "miraculous sign" where God's glory is *most abundantly* revealed is Jesus' death and resurrection (Jn 2:11, 18–29). In this way, John weaves together various symbols—the wedding, bridegroom, wine, the temple, etc.—symbols which point to Jesus' death and resurrection and the *ultimate*

---

29. The Greek word *oxos* refers to common wine or wine vinegar. Martin and Wright point out that the Romans give Jesus common wine, or sour vinegary wine to mock him (Luke 23:36). They offer Jesus something undrinkable to drink when he cries out in thirst (*The Gospel of John*, 323).

30. McGill, "God's Getting Married," 60–61.

31. Ibid., 57.

32. Wright, *Following Jesus*, 38.

33. See Beale and Kim, *God Dwells Among Us*, 82–83.

fulfillment of Jewish eschatological hopes for the reunion of God and his creation.

The Last Supper as a Wedding Banquet

We can now see more clearly the manner in which John presents the Last Supper as a wedding banquet. Here, again, we return to Jesus' mention of the "hour" of his death. Throughout his account of Jesus' ministry (2:3; 7:30; 8:20) John uses this term to refer to an event in the future, as something yet to come ("his time had not yet come"). But, then, during the week of his passion, which culminates in Jesus' Last Supper with his disciples and his death, John uses the term to indicate the hour *has arrived* (12:23; 13:1). In other words, John is indicating that this is the time—or hour—when Jesus will finally fulfill his role as the divine bridegroom. This mention of "the hour" coupled with the fact that this meal is portrayed as a "love feast" in which Jesus expresses his total self-sacrificial love for his disciples (13:1) suggests that John is presenting the Last Supper as a wedding banquet in which Jesus is the bridegroom and the group of disciples (soon to become the church) is the bride.[34]

John is not the only one who subtly uses the marriage metaphor to describe the Last Supper. His readers were undoubtedly familiar with the Synoptic Gospels, in which the idea of Jesus as a bridegroom is a recurring theme (Matt 9:15; 25:1, 5–6, 10; Mk 2:19–20; Lk 5:34–35).[35] In the Synoptic accounts of the Last Supper, Jesus' reference to the cup of wine as the "blood of the covenant" (Matt 26:27; Mk 14:24) or the "new covenant in my blood" (Lk 22:20) is a clear reference to the "new covenant" in Jeremiah 31. In this passage, as we have observed, Jeremiah combines the image of a banquet with a marriage metaphor to describe the restoration of the relationship between Israel and her God.[36] He is describing a *re-enactment* of a *marriage covenant* between God and Israel which was first initiated on Mount Sinai after the first exodus. So in using this language at the Last Supper, Jesus is describing the meal as a wedding banquet which establishes a *new marriage covenant* between God and his people. The twelve disciples together represent the bride of God—the renewed people of Israel. Just as God wed himself to the twelve tribes of Israel at Mount Sinai through the blood of the old covenant, so now Jesus celebrates the new marriage covenant between

---

34. Pitre, *Jesus the Bridegroom*, 47–48).
35. McGill, "God's Getting Married," 65.
36. See Long, *Jesus the Bridegroom*, 203.

himself and the twelve disciples, which is sealed by the shedding of his blood on the cross.[37]

Of course, as Jesus himself intimates, this marriage union between God (Jesus) and his people is not yet complete. In fact, the Cana wedding is itself a dramatization of the *final fulfillment* of Jewish expectations of reunion between God and his people by means of a great wedding feast at the end of the age.[38] In Revelation, John depicts this final marriage covenant as the "wedding supper of the Lamb" (Rev 19:7–9; 20:1–3). This is the subject of the next chapter.

The Return of the Bridegroom

Before we examine the wedding supper of the Lamb in Revelation, however, we need to look briefly at two passages in the Gospels which, either implicitly or directly, refer to the return of Jesus as the divine bridegroom.

I Go to Prepare a Place for You (Jn 14:1–3)

In contrast to modern-day weddings, in which the couple will purchase a home or apartment *after* they are married, in first-century Judaism it was the duty of the bridegroom to prepare a home for his bride to live in *before* the wedding celebration. As one Jewish scholar says: "The groom would go out to receive the bride and bring her into his house; in fact, the wedding ceremony was essentially the groom's introduction of the bride into his house."[39]

In the view of some, this ancient Jewish custom may provide the context for understanding Jesus' well-known words to his disciples:

> In my Father's house are many rooms; if it were not so, would I have told you. I am going there to prepare a place for you. And if I go and prepare a place for you, I will come back and will take you to be with me that you also may be where I am. (Jn 14:2–3)

In this passage Jesus may be implying that he is the bridegroom who will be taking his bride into his Father's house. "If this suggestion is correct," says Pitre, "then it seems that at the Last Supper Jesus is explaining his imminent departure in a very Jewish way. Although he and the twelve disciples

---

37. Pitre, *Jesus the Bridegroom*, 50–51.
38. McGill, "God's Getting Married," 67.
39. Quoted in Pitre, *Jesus the Bridegroom*, 117.

have celebrated the wedding feast of the new covenant, he must leave them for a time, in order to prepare the eternal 'dwelling place' (Greek *topos*) into which he will one day bring his bride to be with him forever."[40] Many biblical scholars see Jesus' reference to his "Father's house" as an allusion to the "heavenly temple," which is described in Revelation as the new heaven and new earth or the "dwelling place" (lit. "tabernacle") of God, where he will dwell with his people (21:3; cf. Jn 1:14; 2:16-21). From this perspective, what Jesus is referring to is *not* the "interim heaven" that believers go to immediately after they die, but the "final heaven," the new heaven and new earth or "heavenly temple," which will be created at the divine bridegroom's second coming and in which there will be a multitude of rooms for his bride, the church.[41]

Preparing for the Return of the Bridegroom (Mt 25:1-13)

In the parable of the ten virgins, Jesus explicitly compares his second coming to the belated and unexpected arrival of a Jewish bridegroom at his wedding (Mt 25:1-13). Jesus is describing the coming of the kingdom of God and the final judgment in terms of the sudden return of the bridegroom and the readiness, or lack of readiness, of the wedding guests (ten virgins) to meet him. Those who are prepared (the five "wise" virgins) go with the bridegroom into the joy of the marriage feast, while those who are unprepared (the five "foolish" virgins) are barred from entry.

Again, we need to bear in mind the social context and the marriage customs of Jesus' day. No doubt, he is drawing on the customs associated with the ancient wedding procession. As opposed to modern-day weddings, which climax with the *departure* of the bride and groom for their honeymoon, ancient Jewish weddings (as we have noted) often climaxed with the *arrival* of the bridegroom with his entourage at the wedding feast, when he came to take the bride to himself. As Pitre states, "it seems clear that in the ancient Jewish context, the procession of the bridegroom to meet his bride was a proverbial image of the joyful climax of a wedding celebration."[42]

Jesus is making several points in this parable. First, the bridegroom's delay, the drowsiness and sleep of the virgins, and their being roused at midnight to meet the bridegroom (25:5-6) illustrate our total ignorance

---

40. Ibid., 118.

41. Ibid. See also McKnight, *The Heaven Promise*, 47-48; and Middleton, *A New Heaven and a New Earth*, 217; 228-29.

42. Pitre, *Jesus the Bridegroom*, 119-20.

concerning the time of his coming (25:13).[43] This ignorance should lead to constant readiness to the very end. Jesus therefore compares two kinds of people: those who are prepared for the final judgment (i.e., those who have enough oil for their lamps) and those who are not (i.e., those whose oil runs out). But he is talking about more than spiritual readiness, although that is crucial. In the Sermon on the Mount, Jesus describes the man who obeys his teaching as "wise" and the man who does not as "foolish" (7:24–27). He also uses lamplight to represent the "light" of good works (5:13–16). In this parable, then, taking enough oil to keep the torches burning represents "good works" in obedience to Jesus' teaching. In other words, Jesus is saying that watching through preparedness means doing good works.[44]

For some, the expectation of the great wedding banquet in heaven leads to escapism. But, as Scot McKnight argues, a right understanding of heaven and its promises should lead to a positive engagement with culture and the present world:

> Too much focus on the future Heaven or on life in the here and now misses the dual emphasis of the Bible—and indeed of our lives. Heaven people ought to be the most zealous about care for creation, love of others, peacemaking, and social justice. Heaven people have tasted the grandeur of Heaven, and therefore they long for Heaven to begin its work now on earth. But these same active workers can also be those who long for the fullness of God's presence and the perfection of God's people in the new Heaven and the new earth.[45]

The core of the heaven promise is that in the new heaven and new earth God will make all things right. This is essentially what Jesus is saying in the Last Supper, when he indicates to the disciples that, as the bridegroom of the future wedding banquet, he will drink of the fruit of the vine *anew* with his followers "in my Father's kingdom" (Mt 26:29). The church, as the future bride of Christ, is called to embody, in advance, what will one day happen in heaven.[46]

---

43. Gundry, *Matthew*, 502.
44. Ibid., 499–502
45. McKnight, *The Heaven Promise*, 123.
46. Ibid., 129–30.

15

Revelation and the Wedding Supper of the Lamb

In *Reading Revelation Responsibly*, Michael Gorman rightly warns that interpreting the book of Revelation is a "serious and sacred responsibility" which should not be entered into lightly. "Furthermore," he continues, "although Scripture is a living word from God that can bring a fresh message to people in changing contexts, with respect to Revelation it must be clearly stated that some readings are not only inferior to others, they are in fact unchristian and unhealthy."[1]

This wise counsel is confirmed by the ways Revelation has been misused by leaders of various sectarian movements. The founders of Mormonism (Joseph Smith), Millerism (William Miller), Seventh Day Adventism (Ellen White) and Jehovah's Witnesses (Charles Russell) employed Revelation to promote apocalyptic predictions of the end of the world and the return of Christ.[2] A more recent example is David Koresh, leader of the Branch Davidians in Waco Texas, who saw himself as the second coming of the Lamb (Messiah) who would lead the war against Babylon—a belief that tragically resulted in the death of many of his followers. In view of such serious misapplications of Revelation, Luke Johnson rightly laments: "Few writing in all of literature have been so obsessively read with such disastrous generally results as the Book of Revelation (= the Apocalypse)."[3]

For these reasons, before describing the wedding supper of the Lamb and what it means for us as Christians in the context of the Lord's Supper,

---

1. Gorman, *Reading Revelation Responsibly*, viii–ix.
2. See Koester, *Revelation and the End of All Things*, 14–15.
3. Quoted in Gorman, *Reading Revelation Responsibly*, 3–4.

we need to first understand the structure, purpose, and message of the book of Revelation as a whole.

A Futuristic or Timeless Message?

Down through the history of the church, interpreters have tended toward either of two hermeneutical options.[4] Some have viewed it as a timeless message about how God relates to people in every generation while others have interpreted it as primarily a message about the future of the world. These differing orientations are reflected in the ongoing debate between amillennialists, postmillennialists, and premillennialists over the meaning of the "millennium," or thousand-year reign of Christ, referred to in Revelation 20:4–6.[5]

A major representative of the "timeless message" perspective is St Augustine, who argued that Revelation applies to the interior life of Christians in all times and places.[6] In his great work *City of God* he describes the spiritual conflict between the earthly city and the heavenly city which characterizes all of human history and the church prior to the second coming of Christ. This was the dominant view in the church after Augustine and is the only eschatology that is either expressed or implied in the historic creeds of the Christian tradition.[7]

Those who adhere to a more "futuristic" interpretation of Revelation argue, on the other hand, that the visions in this book give us glimpses into events that will transpire in the days to come prior to the return of Christ. While this view has been held by Christian thinkers throughout the church's history, it has become especially popular among Christians (particularly evangelicals) since the First World War. Over the last 50 years there has been a significant increase in the numbers and popularity of books on the apocalypse, tribulation, and second coming. Hal Lindsey's *The Late Great*

---

4. See Koester, *Revelation and the End of All Things*, 2.

5. I have noted the main differences between these three viewpoints in a previous footnote. Traditional amillennialists view the millennium as a symbol of the present church age and a reference to the spiritual reign of Christ. Postmillennialists hold that the kingdom of God (or millennium) will come progressively through evangelism and social reform. Christ will return *after* the kingdom has been inaugurated. Premillennialists maintain that the second coming will occur prior to millennium. They argue that there will be a period of tribulation during the final period of the world as we know it (the "end times"), after which Christ will return to establish his thousand-year reign on earth.

6. Ibid., 7.

7. See Grenz, *The Millennial Maze*, 149; Berkhof, *Systematic Theology*, 708.

Planet Earth (1970) was the best-selling non-fiction book in the 1970's. By the turn of the century, it had sold an estimated 35 million copies and was translated into 50 languages. A quick search on Amazon reveals a plethora of other books claiming to give hidden insights into terrorism, oil shortages, turmoil in the Middle East, and other worldwide crises on the basis of John's apocalyptic visions.[8] According to a recent poll by Pew, a majority of evangelicals (58 percent) believe Jesus will return no later than 2050.[9]

In the view of others, however, the purpose of Revelation is not to fuel end-times speculation. The idea that John's visionary dream is a manual charting the chronology of a futuristic geopolitical scenario and the second coming of Christ is, from this perspective, a dangerous distraction from its true prophetic message for the church.[10]

The book of Revelation contains references to the past, present, and the future. On this all interpreters are in agreement. The crucial question is one of emphasis and the relationship between these three temporal aspects of the text. The very nature of Revelation as apocalyptic literature calls for hermeneutical humility and self-criticism. In this vein, Gorman observes that the challenge "is to hear Revelation addressed to us without manipulating its content to our own ends."[11]

I would suggest that a primary purpose of this book is to inspire its readers to hope, faithfulness, perseverance, and worship in the face of adversity, persecution, and evil in the world. The dominant title for Jesus that John uses throughout Revelation is "the Lamb," an image which occurs no fewer than 29 times. Most of these references occur in worship passages.[12] At the end of Revelation, John uses the picture of the "wedding supper of the Lamb" (19:7–10) to communicate both Christ's vicarious sacrifice on the cross and his ultimate judgment and victory over sin, evil, and death. The final triumph of the Lamb is the basis for the Christian's hope, which looks forward to the day when we will worship the "Lord God Almighty and the Lamb" (21:27) in a new heaven and new earth (Rev 21:1). John is urging his readers—and us—to be followers of the Lamb. As Gorman states,

> Revelation is (primarily) good news about Christ—the Lamb of God—who shares God's throne and who is the key to the past, present, and future—and therefore also about uncompromising

---

8. Webster, *Follow the Lamb*, 5.
9. Andersen, *Fantasyland*, 274.
10. See Webster, *Follow the Lamb*, 4, 8–9.
11. Gorman, "What Has the Spirit Been Saying?," 28.
12. Guthrie, "The Lamb in the Structure of the Book of Revelation," 64.

faithfulness leading to undying hope, even in the midst of unrelenting evil and oppressive empire.[13]

The Basic Plot and Structure of Revelation

Most people who read Revelation are drawn to the symbolic visions that make up the majority of the chapters of this book (chaps 4–21). It is often thought that by deciphering the "coded language" of the various symbols contained in John's visions we can "unlock" the meaning of Revelation and its significance for us today. In a recent popular treatment of Revelation titled *The Babylon Code,* the authors write: "Is it possible that God embedded a code in the Bible that could be cracked only in the end times? What if by decoding this prophetic cryptogram we could unlock the secret to both our salvation and our survival?"[14] The rest of the book is devoted to uncovering the "Babylon code" supposedly contained in this final book of the Bible.

But Revelation is not a theological crossword puzzle. Granted, the picture-language that John uses is often strange to us. So we may feel that it needs to be "decoded." At the same time, a focus on the separate visions often results in a failure to take a bird's eye view of Revelation as a whole and see it as a structural unity. We also need to be clear about the nature of apocalyptic language. The assumptions we make here profoundly affect the way we interpret and apply the various visions of Revelation.

The Visions of Revelation

Let's begin with a brief summary of John's visions. After an introduction (1–8), the book of Revelation is structured around four visions which are indicated by the expression "in the Spirit" (1:10; 4:1; 17:3; 21:10).[15] The first vision consists of the exaltation of Christ and his letters to the seven churches. The second vision pictures the heavenly throne room and the opening of the seven seals by the slain Lamb of God. This is followed by the blowing of the seven trumpets and the emptying of the seven bowls of God's judgment. The central theme in this second vision is the conflict between God and Satan, who is pictured as a fierce red dragon. Satan calls up two beasts that defy God and oppose the church. In the third vision, we see the rise of Babylon, the harlot, which has dominion over all of the kings

---

13. Gorman, *Reading Revelation Responsibly,* 12.
14. McGuire and Anderson, *The Babylon Code,* 8.
15. See Ladd, *Theology of the New Testament,* 670–71.

of the earth, but is finally judged and destroyed by God and the Lamb. The emphasis of this third vision is God's final victory over Satan and the powers of evil. The fourth vision centers on the "new heaven and new earth" and the final union between Jerusalem (the bride) and the Lamb of God (Christ, the bridegroom).

The Structural Unity of Revelation.

While the elaborate structure of Revelation is often confusing to readers, it is again critically important that we view this book as a structural unity. The book begins and concludes with a description of the Lord God (Christ) as the "Alpha and Omega" the "First and the Last" (Rev 1:8, 17–18; 22:13). It is this picture of the risen Jesus, who is alive forever and ever and holds the keys of life (1:18; 22:14), which frames the entire book.

Following a dramatic vision of the resurrected Christ (1:12–16)—his head and hair white like snow, his eyes like blazing fire, his feet like bronze glowing in a furnace, and his voice like the sound of rushing waters—John delivers his message to the seven churches (1:19–3:22). These letters are often treated separately from the material body (the apocalyptic visions) of Revelation. But it is better to see them as closely connected. "The symbolic visions of chapters 4–21," says G. K. Beale, "are parabolic portrayals of the more abstract, propositionally expressed exhortations, warnings and promises of the letters, so that the latter interpret the former and *vice versa*."[16] The use of the number seven (which is symbolic of completeness) in the reference to both the churches and lampstands strongly suggests that John intends these letters to be a final exhortation to *all churches in every time and place*.[17] The repeated use of the phrases "to him who overcomes" and "he who has an ear, let him hear" in each of these letters indicates that their primary purpose is to exhort believers to persevere, overcome compromise, and be faithful to the end. Revelation concludes with the same promise that those who overcome and persevere will inherit eternal life with Christ (22:7, 9, 11, and 14).[18]

---

16. Beale, *John's Use of the Old Testament in Revelation*, 316.
17. Emerson, *Christ and the New Creation*, 144.
18. Ibid., 146–47.

The Nature of Apocalyptic Language

The first word in the Greek text of Revelation is *apokalupsis* (1:1), which literally means "a revelation" or "an unveiling." In using this word, "John purports to reveal spiritual truth, to pull back the veil that separates the spiritual and the physical realms so that his churches can view their world from a spiritual perspective."[19] His purpose, in other words, is to give a divine perspective on the physical world we experience—to inspire hope and resistance in the face of evil and oppression by revealing truth about unseen present realities (God, heaven, Satan) and unknown future realities (judgment and salvation).[20]

A key feature of apocalyptic literature is dualism, both cosmic and temporal. *Cosmic dualism* expresses the idea that there are two opposing forces in the universe—one led by Satan who is the source of sin and evil and the other led by God who is the source of all that is good. Throughout human history, this cosmic warfare is manifested in terms of a conflict between the kingdom of God and the kingdom of Satan (or the world). *Temporal dualism* expresses the belief that human history is divided between the present age, during which there is evil, injustice, oppression, and persecution, and a coming age of goodness, justice, and peace. The future age will come solely through God who is active in his creation and will faithfully execute his plan for its final redemption. Revelation describes this cosmic struggle and the eventual triumph of God over evil in highly symbolic language.

As I have already mentioned, many people assume that Revelation gives us prophecy in the sense that it predicts in rather explicit detail "the way the present world will end." But this misconstrues the point of the book. To begin with, the plot of Revelation does not advance chronologically. As one commentator observes: "Although the visions unfold one after another in an orderly manner, the story advances by a spiral rather than a straight path, like a road that circles its way up a mountain, offering diverse vistas of the terrain below."[21] In some cases, multiple visions depict a single event. At other times, the forward movement of visions is disrupted by flashbacks. This, again, prevents us from viewing Revelation as portraying, in literal and linear fashion, the course of historical events.[22]

---

19. Stevenson, *A Slaughtered Lamb*, 90.
20. Gorman, *Reading Revelation Responsibly*, 15.
21. Williamson, *Revelation*, 25.
22. Koester, *Revelation and the End of Things*, 39; Gorman, *Reading Revelation Responsibly*, 22. This is the error made by many who interpret Revelation from a dispensational perspective. See, for example, LaHaye, *Revelation Unveiled*; and MacArthur, *Because the Time is Near*,

While a foretelling of future events is an important aspect of Revelation, the *purpose* of these predictions is not to give a *blueprint* of the "last days," so that we can match current events to specific visions in Revelation.[23] The symbolic language of Revelation is not the language of the newspaper but the language of poetry. It is "literal non-literalism."[24] *It is meant to give hope and comfort. But it also contains a warning to those who may be tempted to participate in or accommodate themselves to the very evil for which the oppressive system and its perpetrators will be judged.*[25]

The Victory of Jesus the Lamb

I have indicated that a central symbol that John employs in conveying this message of hope and warning is Jesus as the "Lamb." In what follows, I will survey a series of visionary texts which enjoin allegiance to Jesus, the Lamb, whose final victory and reign will one day be celebrated in the marriage supper of the Lamb. My focus will be on four groups of visions: 1) God and the Lamb (4–5); 2) the Beast and the Lamb (12–13); 5) Babylon and the Lamb (15–19); and the New Jerusalem and the Lamb (21–22).

The Central Vision: God and the Lamb (4–5)

The letters to the seven churches in chapters 2 and 3 are a sort of verbal corridor that lead from an entryway (the introduction) to the heavenly throne room, which is described in chapters 4 and 5.[26] Here, John returns to the series of visionary texts which make up the bulk of the book of Revelation. The unified vision of these two chapters, which focuses on the two main images in the entire book—the throne of God and the Lamb of God—in many ways serves as the central and core vision for the entire book.[27]

As John's vision develops, he sees that the One who is seated on the throne holding a scroll which is sealed with seven seals; this scroll contains the plan of God, the plan of salvation, the divine purpose for the restoration of God's entire creation.[28] The only one who has the authority to break

---

23. Stevenson, *A Slaughtered Lamb*, 95.
24. Gorman, *Reading Revelation Responsibly*. 20.
25. Ibid., 24.
26. This description is based on Wright's portrayal of John's visions in *Following Jesus*, 56.
27. Gorman, *Reading Revelation Responsibly*, 102–3,
28. Wright, *Following Jesus*, 56.

the seals and open the scrolls is the sacrificial Lamb, who by his death has conquered the powers of evil so that God's rescue plan for the entire cosmos can now be unrolled and put into dramatic operation. The promise is that those who have been made into a "kingdom of priests" will one day reign with the victorious Lamb, who sits on the throne in a new heaven and new earth (5:10; 21:5). According to Matthew Emerson, this tension between the "now" and the "not yet"—a theme which we recognize in the practice of the Lord's Supper—is found throughout the book of Revelation. Granted, Revelation is unique in that it does portray the last events of history that culminate in the final fulfillment of God's work of cosmic restoration. However, its point "is not to recount visions that only relate to the very end of history but is instead very much like the rest of the NT in that it relates both what has already happened, what is happening, and what will happen in the future."[29]

The picture of cosmic order and worship that is given in chapters 4 and 5 stands in tension with the Greco-Roman civic life of John's day, which centered on the imperial cult.[30] The imagery of worship pictured by John has many similarities to the various rituals associated with the Roman imperial court, such as the presence of attendants around the throne, and the giving of hymns, praises, and golden crowns by attendants and lesser kings.[31] Some of the Roman emperors, such as Caligula (A.D. 37–41) and Nero (A.D. 54–68), brazenly presented themselves as deities.[32] In contrast to this imperial cult, which also involved worship of imperial deities, John depicts the true worship of God and the Lamb. He pictures 24 elders falling down in worship before the Lamb and holding bowls of incense, "which are the prayers of the saints" (5:8). J. Nelson Kraybill notes that the emperor worship and other Roman religious ceremonies regularly employed a shallow bowl called a *patera* for pouring drinks. "Now, in the heavenly court, John sees such bowls being used to hand deliver prayers of the church to the throne of God."[33]

In contrasting the true worship of God and the Lamb with the false centers of worship in the Greco-Roman world, John also raises crucial questions regarding the Christian's relationship to the dominant culture. Here the issue is not so much *whether* to apply Revelation but *how* to apply it, since

---

29. Emerson, *Christ and the New Creation*, 149.
30. See deSilva, *Seeing Things John's Way*, 100–101.
31. Gorman, *Reading Revelation Responsibly*, 106.
32. Kraybill, *Apocalypse and Allegiance*, 86–88.
33. Ibid., 99.

this book already has a strong appeal for many Christians in the church.[34] Of particular significance is the way John juxtaposes the conquering Lion of Judah (5:5) with the image of the slaughtered sacrificial Lamb (5:9. 12). This imagery recalls, of course, the Passover Lamb of the exodus and the triumph of God over the might of Pharaoh's army in rescuing his people from their slavery in Egypt. In addition, this imagery of the slaughtered Lamb bears witness to Jesus' ransoming and redeeming death. But the emphasis of this passage is also on the *power* of the Lamb *through* his sacrificial death:

> Worthy is the Lamb, who was slain, to receive power and wealth and wisdom and strength and honor and glory and praise! (5:12)

In this passage, the centering image of the slaughtered and self-sacrificial Lamb (and not the ferocious Lion) receiving power conveys the truth that emperors such as Nero, who presumably control history, are upstaged by the Lamb of God.[35] This imagery of the victorious Lamb also redefines the nature and meaning of power. As those who "follow the Lamb wherever He goes" (14:4), Christians are reminded that ultimate victory comes as we follow the way of the cross.[36] The imagery in this passage of Christ's sacrificial death *as the way God rules the world* should cause us to re-examine the ways in which we are tempted to identify "God's will" with worldly uses of power and coercion, often on our terms. Revelation is often misread as a demonstration of this kind of divine coercive power in history and current events.[37]

The War: Dragon, Beast, and the Lamb (12–13)

The last half of Revelation (chaps 12–22) traces the final defeat of Satan, who in the cosmic battle with God and the Lamb is cast down from heaven to earth, and from earth to the abyss. In the course of this conflict between good and evil, Satan (the Dragon) operates through other agents, including two beasts (the Anti-Christ and the False Prophet) and the harlot (Babylon); but God and the Lamb eventually triumph over the efforts of these "destroyers of the earth."[38] This theme of the final defeat of Satan not only informs the structure and theological message of Revelation; it is also a completion

---

34. deSilva, *Seeing Things John's Way*, 313.
35. Kraybill, *Apocalypse and Allegiance*, 101.
36. Beale, *Revelation*, 115.
37. Gorman, *Reading Revelation Responsibly*, 111.
38. Koester, *Revelation and the End of All Things*, 116.

of the grand narrative of the Bible that begins with creation and the entrance of evil into the world through Satan (the serpent of Genesis 3).[39]

Chapter 12 opens with John looking into the heavens and seeing a woman clothed with the sun, with the moon under her feet and a crown of twelve stars on her head—a symbol of victory and rule (12:1; 10). The woman cries out in pain as she is about to give birth. Beside her is an enormous red dragon who is poised to devour the baby once it is born. The woman does give birth to a male child, who will "rule the nations with an iron scepter" (12:5). This is an obvious allusion to Psalm 2:9, which uses the same language to describe the rule of the Messiah over the kings of the earth. The monster's crude attempt to devour the child is thwarted with the child being snatched up to God and his throne (12:5). The following verses then describe the war in heaven between Michael and his angels and the dragon and his angels—a war which results in the dragon or serpent being hurled to the earth, where he continues to pursue the woman and makes war against the rest of her offspring (12:7–17).

Various interpretations have been given to this passage, which cannot be addressed in detail here. Briefly, we can say that John is here recounting the biblical story in highly symbolic language. There are many allusions in Revelation 12 to Genesis 3, which is also a story about a woman and a serpent/dragon.[40] John's description of the serpent of old (Satan) as the deceiver of the whole earth (vs 9) recalls the serpent's deception of Eve in the garden (Gen 3:1–6). One of the results of Eve's sin is the pain of childbirth (Gen 3:16), a curse which is echoed in John's narrative (Rev 12: 2). Genesis 3:15 predicts the ongoing enmity between the serpent and the woman and between the serpent's offspring and the woman's offspring. This same battle—both in heaven and on earth—is symbolically depicted by John. In John's story, the woman most likely represents the spiritual or faithful Israel. The child obviously refers to Christ the Lamb who defeats Satan by his blood (12:11); and the rest of the woman's offspring (12:17) are God's faithful witnesses (the church) who embody the pattern of Christ.[41]

Revelation 12 therefore is a description of the cosmic battle that began in the garden between Satan and Eve (Gen 3:15)—a battle that was won decisively by Christ in his death and resurrection (12:1–6), but which nevertheless continues on this earth with Satan's attacks on the church.[42] In the words of Gregory Stevenson, "Although it is a spiritual war, it is one that is

---

39. Emerson, *Christ and the New Creation*, 151.
40. Stevenson, *A Slaughtered Lamb*, 184.
41. Ibid., 185.
42. Emerson, *Christ and the New Creation*, 156.

waged within the very concrete structures of the social, religious, and political realities within which we live."[43]

Revelation 13–20 describes this earthly conflict in graphic detail. Most commentators identify the first beast from the sea (13:1) as the Roman Empire (or imperial power) and the second beast from the earth (13:11) with those who promote the imperial cult. But these symbols have ongoing significance for the church; the evil activities of Satan through his surrogates occur throughout the church age. The second beast is a "counterfeit of the church and the Spirit who empowers and indwells it."[44] The Bible warns of deceivers who infiltrate the church. Though they may appear to be "lamb-like," they take their cue from the surrounding culture and ultimately oppose the reign of God and Christ.[45] The subversion of much of the church by the Nazi propaganda and civil religion under Adolf Hitler is an example of the constant dangers posed by such political, social, and religious deception.[46]

Final Judgment: Babylon and the Lamb (15–19)

A great deal of ink and theological debate has been devoted to addressing a series of questions that emerge from a reading of these chapters of Revelation. What is the meaning of the seven bowls of God's wrath (15:1–16:21)? Who or what is represented by Babylon the great harlot who rides upon a seven-headed Beast (17:3)? To what is John referring when he speaks about the Battle of Armageddon (16:6; 19:11–21)? Obviously, space does not permit an extended discussion of these questions. I would simply repeat the warning that efforts to identify current events with specific apocalyptic images based upon a literalistic reading of Revelation too often causes readers to miss the larger message of the book.

---

43. Stevenson, *A Slaughtered Lamb*, 186.
44. Beale, *Revelation*, 271, 280.
45. Ibid., 280.
46. See, for example, Lutzer, *Hitler's Cross*. Lutzer observes that the land that gave us Luther and Bach also gave the world Hitler and Wagner. "The church that was called by God to stand against the evils of the Nazi regime came to embrace it. Swastikas, with the cross of Christ sometimes neatly woven in the center, adorned the churches. The broken cross of the political savior and the cross of the spiritual Savior would unite to lead Germany out of its abyss to the glorious heights of self-respect and unify the German-speaking areas of Europe. The Fatherland had been resurrected; the Germans could smile again." While this picture of the "holy union" may startle us, Lutzer continues, "in Hitler's day being a good Christian involved being a good German nationalist. God and country were practically one and the same. When the churchmen finally awoke from their spiritual and political slumbers, they discovered too late that they had been deceived" (128). We should not be so naïve as to think that today's church is immune from similar deception.

Take, for example, the images or scenes of divine judgment in Revelation. One author argues that the September 11, 2001 terrorist attacks followed by the stock-market crashes in Wall Street are escalating judgments or warnings that point to the possible fulfillment of end–time events.[47] Another author argues that the appearance of "four blood moons" points to a "world–shaking event" that could signify the beginning of the events culminating in the Tribulation.[48] Such pronouncements are theologically irresponsible for one simple reason: they presume to know the mind of God. As Gorman states:

> [C]orrelating specific disasters with intentional divine wrath and judgment is tantamount to claiming an intimate knowledge of the mind of God, and that is an act of incredible hubris, if not idolatry. Human beings—apart from a very few specifically inspired biblical prophets and seers—have not been granted insider information about the ways of God in executing the reserved power of judgment.[49]

The images of death and destruction in Revelation portray the *universality* and *finality* of God's ultimate eradication of evil *rather than the means by which God brings about that eradication.*[50]

In Revelation, Babylon, the great seductive and self-glorifying whore, is the personification of evil and idolatry in the world. "Babylon," writes the noted biblical scholar Bruce Metzger, "is allegorical of the idolatry that any nation commits when it elevates material abundance, military prowess, technological sophistication, imperial grandeur, racial pride, and any other glorification of the creature over the Creator."[51] Babylon makes war on the Lamb, and persecutes the saints (17:6, 14). But, in the end, it is the Lamb who overcomes; and it is "Babylon the Great" that will ultimately receive from God "the cup filled with wine of the fury of his wrath" (16:19). With the final destruction of this city, there is a voice from the throne saying, "It is done! (16:17). John is here giving an obvious play on words, as these are the very words uttered by Jesus on the cross when he cried out, "It is finished!" (Jn 19:30).

The fall of Babylon (18:1–8) prepares the way for the announcement of the Lord's reign (19:1–6) and the wedding supper of the Lamb (19:7–10).[52]

---

47. Cahn, *The Harbinger*.
48. Hagee, *Four Blood Moons*.
49. Gorman, *Reading Revelation Responsibly*, 152.
50. Ibid.
51. Quoted in Ibid., 130.

52. In my view, these verses depict the union of Christ with his righteous people at the end of history, for which they glorify God. See Beale, *Revelation*, 402–8. This raises the difficult question of how to interpret chapter 20, specifically the reference to the

The very attire of the bride, who has made herself ready for the bridegroom (the Lamb), contrasts sharply with that of the harlot (Babylon). The prostitute's wardrobe of purple and scarlet clothing along with glittering jewelry (17:4) represents her alluring charm and ability to entice and control people and nations; it also conveys the seductiveness of evil, immorality, wealth, and power. "Babylon represents those who have deserted God and replaced him with another lover."[53] By contrast, the bride of the Lamb is draped in fine linen, bright and clean (19:8) to represent faithfulness and the righteous and just actions of the saints.

John's intention in this passage is clearly to show the deep connection between the Last Supper and the wedding supper of the Lamb. Just as Jesus' last meal with his disciples symbolizes the fullest extent of his love (Jn 13:1), so at the end of the world there is a glorious reunion of the Messiah and the "the Bride, the wife of the Lamb." "Blessed are those who are invited to the wedding supper of the Lamb!" (19:9). Christians who have this hope don't, as Randy Alcorn says, fill their stomachs with stale leftovers and scraps fallen to the floor. They can smell the banquet that is prepared for them. They know what their mouths are watering for. They won't let the distractions of this world spoil their appetite.[54]

Hope Fulfilled: The New Jerusalem and the Lamb (21–22)

I have argued that, although there may be an intermediate state called "heaven," the Christian's ultimate hope is not that "I will go to heaven when I die." Nor, despite the emphasis that many Christians place on the doctrine of the rapture, does the biblical hope have anything to do with being "raptured into heaven." In fact, as one biblical scholar has remarked, John's final vision in Revelation depicts a "rapture in reverse," the descent of God and heaven to us![55] There is a final merging of heaven and earth into a "new heaven and a new earth" (21:1).

In describing this final marriage of heaven and earth, John gives his readers a vision of the Holy City (Jerusalem) coming down from heaven, "prepared as a bride beautifully dressed for her husband" (21:2). As I noted

---

thousand-year reign of Christ in 20:1–6. Space does not permit an extended discussion of the different views on these verses. Briefly, I would suggest that 16:14, 19:19, and 20:8 all refer to the same future battle with Satan, which results in his final defeat and judgment at the end of history. The millennium of 20:1–6 is therefore temporally *prior* to the events described in chapter 19. In these verses, the saints are pictured as ruling with Christ in his heavenly court prior to the last judgment and physical resurrection (Ibid., 423, 451). See also Bloesch, *Essentials of Evangelical Theology*, vol. 2, 189–204.

53. Alexander, *From Eden to the New Jerusalem*, 177–78.
54. Alcorn, *Heaven*, 472.
55. Quoted in Gorman, *Reading Revelation Responsibly*, 170.

in chapter two, this picture of the new heaven and new earth is followed by a description of the Holy City as garden-like (22:1-5) and in the shape of a temple (21:10-21). In other words, the bride of Christ (the Lamb) is represented by a merging of three biblical metaphors or symbols: 1) the new Jerusalem; 2) the new temple; and 3) the new Eden.

Why is this significant? Simply because these three images represent the culmination of Israel's story, the story of the "new Israel" (the church)—and indeed the entire story of redemption in the Bible. The reader will recall that Jerusalem is often depicted by the Old Testament prophets as the "bride of God," but also as an adulterous wife. But God's promises are fulfilled through the new Israel, which John describes as built on the foundation of "the twelve apostles of the Lamb" (21:12-14). Furthermore, there is a new temple, because in the new heaven and new earth "the Lord God Almighty and the Lamb *are* its temple" (21:22). Finally, the bride of the Lamb is identified with the new Eden because God's original purpose was to expand the boundaries of Eden (his first sanctuary) so that the entire earth could be filled with his presence. This original purpose is realized as the throne of God and the Lamb is now in the midst of his people and his glory is manifested throughout the new creation (21:11; 22:1-5).[56]

With these images, the divine love story—the story which we re-enact in the celebration of the Lord's Supper—comes full circle. The story which begins in the garden with the "marriage" of Adam and Eve ends with the eternal marriage of God and his people in Christ, the Lamb.[57]

Being Followers of the Lamb

Finally, a word should be said about what it means for us to be followers of the Lamb in the context of the message of Revelation.

The "Now" and "Not Yet" of God's Kingdom

Throughout this book I have described the gospel, or the story of redemption, in terms of the reign of God which will one day fill the new heaven and new earth. This is the vision that John gives us in Revelation 7:9-10:

> After this I looked, and there before me was a great multitude that no one could count, from every nation, tribe, people and language, standing before the throne and in front of the Lamb. They were wearing white robes and were holding palm branches

---

56. Beale and Kim, *God Dwells Among Us*, 138-40.
57. Pitre, *Jesus the Bridegroom*, 128.

in their hands. And they cried out with a loud voice: "Salvation belongs to our God, who sits on the throne, and to the Lamb."

In this passage, John is clearly also alluding to Jesus' triumphal entry into Jerusalem during the Passover, when the great throng of people meet him waving palm branches and shouting:

> Hosanna!
> Blessed is he who comes in the name of the Lord!
> Blessed is the King of Israel!
> (Jn 12:13)

Shortly after this event, Jesus predicts the ultimate defeat of the prince of this world (Satan) through his death and resurrection:

> Now is the time for judgment on this world; now the prince of this world will be driven out. (Jn 12:31)

This vision of God's reign is dramatized in the celebration of the Lord's Supper or Eucharist. In the present age, the kingdom of God is "now and not yet." It is critical that we keep this tension. For, as Russell Moore rightly warns, if we mistakenly bring the kingdom too near (already) we run the risk of utopianism and a politicized gospel. On the other hand, if we keep the kingdom too distant (not yet) there is the danger of cultural apathy or withdrawal from society. So the question is, "Where is Jesus ruling *now*, and *how*?" Jesus indicates that it does not come with shock and awe, but in secret and hidden ways, like yeast working its way through a loaf of bread (Mt 13:22).[58] The enthroned Lamb of God, who takes away the sins of the world (Jn 1:29), presently reigns *primarily in and through* his church (Eph 1:22–23), which is called to be a signpost of the kingdom. "The priorities of the King, seen in the ultimate restoration of creation, become the priorities of the colony of the kingdom: the church."[59] The "new heaven and new earth" is therefore not reserved solely for the future. Although we must still live in terms of the "not yet," at the very center of the church's story is the unique task of cultivating "new Edens" and "new Jerusalems"—places of healing and restoration in our cities, towns, and neighborhoods.[60] We therefore need to ask ourselves what it might look like for the present-day church to live out the vision of God's reign, which will be realized in its fullness at the end of human history. *This is our driving metanarrative.* If

---

58. Moore, *Onward*, 58–9.
59. Ibid., 63.
60. See Leong, *Race and Place*, 73.

it is not, then we are living our lives according to some other fundamental worldview that undermines our loyalty to Jesus Christ.[61]

The Political Implications of Revelation

The message of Revelation also has political implications. The primary objects of Revelation's prophetic critique are imperial idolatry (civil religion) and injustice (in the form of military, economic, political and religious oppression) which is manifested in the Roman Empire. For the readers who are impoverished and intimidated by Rome's power, John's message is one of hope and encouragement. But for those who prosper under the political regime, his visions are a summons to recognize the political, religious, and economic patterns that run counter to the claims of God.[62] Moreover, the imperial idolatry that John addresses is not limited to the Roman Empire. Revelation is a powerful critique of all idolatries, injustices, and misguided allegiances which are daily with us. As Craig Koester states, John's visionary world "portrays the clash of powers in extraordinary form in order to evoke the kind of faith and resistance needed to follow the Lamb in ordinary life."[63]

Many of us who are Christians like to think that we are immune to the wiles of political hucksters and demagogues. But history teaches us how easily political ideology and civil religion centered on an authoritarian personality can drive the gospel rather than the other way around. Earlier, I alluded to the support of most German Christians for Hitler following the First World War. For a large percentage of German Protestants, the political life of the nation was entangled with their religious life. Love for the Fatherland and loyalty to its leaders were regarded as patriotic and Christian virtues. Nazi flags were prominently displayed in church sanctuaries along with the cross. Belief in Christianity was so closely intertwined with nationalism that it was difficult to say where the one began and the other ended.[64] Hitler enjoyed wide support among evangelicals for his opposition to homosexuality, abortion, and Communism. Very few Christians, however, actively opposed his policies of anti-Semitism, eugenics, and euthanasia.[65]

In *Fascism: A Warning*, former U.S. Secretary of State Madeleine Albright further describes Hitler's rise to power. Hitler capitalized on the anger, resentment, and fears of the German people. Rather than appealing to

---

61. See Stassen and Gushee, *Kingdom Ethics, 1st ed.*, 63.

62. Gorman, *Reading Revelation Responsibly*, 33; See also Koester, "Revelation's Visionary Challenge to Ordinary Empire," 5.

63. Ibid., 18.

64. See Barnett, *For the Soul of the People*, 11; 309.

65. Baranovski, "The Confessing Church and Antisemitism," 90–109.

abstract theories and objective arguments, he used extremist rhetoric to rile public sentiments against perceived threats, promised a new era of German ascendancy, and did not hesitate to tell what he later described as "colossal untruths." Continues Albright: "He was delighted, not dismayed, by the outrage his speeches generated abroad.... [He] lied shamelessly about himself and about his enemies. He convinced millions of men and women that he cared about them deeply when, in fact, he would have willingly sacrificed them all. His murderous ambition, avowed racism, and utter immorality were given the thinnest mask, and yet millions of Germans, were drawn to [him] precisely because he seemed authentic."[66] Hitler's rise to the status of a ruthless dictator did not occur overnight. Rather, Fascism took hold incrementally, step-by-step in a way that was almost imperceptible to many Germans, including Christians, until it was too late. Albright perceptively asks: "Is the United States immune to this malady—or susceptible?"[67]

Recently, a large electronic billboard on Interstate 170 in St. Louis County, Missouri caught the attention of drivers. It featured a picture of President Trump, with the Bible verse, "The Word became flesh . . ." (Jn 1:14). The top right of the billboard featured the cross superimposed on the American flag and the words: "Make the gospel great again"—an obvious play on Donald Trump's famous political slogan.[68] While this controversial ad was quickly removed, it illustrates how the gospel can be idolatrously identified with the nation and messianic figures. Let me be clear that my purpose, here, is not to draw invidious comparisons between the American church today and the German church under the Nazi regime, or between

---

66. Albright, *Fascism*, 33–40.

67. Ibid. In *How Democracies Die*, Levitsky and Ziblatt identify four primary indicators of authoritarianism which threaten democracy: 1) rejection, in words and actions, of the democratic rules of the game; 2) denial of the legitimacy of opponents; 3) toleration or encouragement of violence; and 4) willingness to curtail the civil liberties of opponents, including the media (21–22). These authors point out that the erosion of democratic norms in America began in the 1980s and 1990s and accelerated in the 2000s. "Donald Trump may have accelerated this process, but he didn't cause it." Our present challenges are rooted in extreme partisan polarization (9). Historically, the Republican and Democratic parties have served as "gatekeepers" of democracy by keeping extremist figures out of the mainstream. Today, they argue, the Republican Party must find a way to win elections without appealing to white nationalism, or what Republican Arizona senator Jeff Flake calls the "sugar high of populism, nativism, and demagoguery" (223).

68. Smith, "Pro-Trump Billboard Quotes John 1:14," 1–6. An evangelical group on Facebook calling itself "Make the Gospel Great Again" claimed credit for the ad, saying "This is one of our efforts, yes! We are nationwide, bringing the good news of God re-taking his country, and making it a stronger, more Christian place . . ." A similar billboard was erected on I-35 about 5 miles north of Waco, Texas.

American politics and the rise of National Socialism. *They are not the same.* Moreover, as I have emphasized in this book, the tendency to associate the gospel with a particular political ideology is not unique to Christians on the political right. During his candidacy and then his presidency, Barack Obama was similarly (though perhaps less overtly) portrayed as a Christlike figure. Rather, my point is that the tendency to deify human power and systems—whether in the form of Nazism, Communism, Socialism, imperialism, nationalism, racism, or any other ism—always exists, but is not always self-evident. Hitler and his Nazi party were successful in large part because the Nazis appealed to the people's self-interest by promising national greatness and a better life.[69] Human nature in its sinfulness will always prefer self-serving ideologies, self-aggrandizement, and the accumulation of power for its own sake over the self-renunciation, self-sacrifice, and servanthood demanded by the gospel of Jesus Christ.[70]

In his discussion of the sustainability of freedom in America today, Os Guinness wisely warns us of the temptation to national hubris and the false belief that a nation's greatness and supremacy derives from its prowess and power. Such hubris always breeds insensitivities, particularly a blindness to the costs of human arrogance and dominance, both to ourselves and to others.[71] In their pursuit of power, Christians may be tempted to let the ends of security or control—and even freedom itself—justify the means. As Guinness further cautions: "Free people are always free to defend their freedom strongly. What they are not free to do is pretend that any and all means of defending freedom are right because they are done in the name of freedom."[72] We must therefore continually ask ourselves whether we are complicit in making moral evil seem good and if we are guilty of confusing our political loyalties with loyalty to God and the Lamb.

---

69. See Brustein, *The Logic of Evil*, 177–84.
70. Crump, *I Pledge Allegiance*, 108.
71. Guinness, *A Free People's Suicide*, 181–82.
72. Ibid., 191. While Guinness's words are intended for *all parties* in the present cultural and political war between liberals and conservatives in America, they are of particular relevance for the church.

Conclusion

The Lord's Supper and the Life of the Church

16

How Should We Define the Gospel?

O N the Easter Sunday of April 1, 2018, NBC aired the newest version of Andrew Lloyd Weber's *Jesus Christ Superstar*. In a *Christianity Today* article discussing this modern-day depiction of Christ's death, Peter Chattaway asks: "How should Christians respond to a catchy musical that casts a skeptical, and at times flamboyantly irreverent, light on the story of Jesus?"[1] When the controversial musical was first staged in 1971, it received mixed reviews among believers, with some criticizing it for being biblically inaccurate and sacrilegious, and others viewing it as means of reaching the "younger generation." According to a 1971 cover story in *Time* magazine, some of the first staged versions of *Jesus Christ Superstar* were unauthorized versions of the musical put on "by churches large and small from New Jersey to New Mexico, who were using *Superstar* to stir up their congregations." The most recent broadcast of *Superstar* by NBC joins other recent films with similar themes, like *Risen*, *The Shack*, and *Killing Jesus*. Whatever one might think of it, concludes Chattaway, many people who may not have gone to church on Easter Sunday morning will have watched a show about Jesus and heard Judas ask who Jesus really is. "It's a good question. Let's hope those who hear it will be open to the answer."[2]

But which Jesus? This questions is central, of course, to the meaning of the Lord's Supper. Broadly speaking, one might say that *Jesus Christ Superstar* mirrors fundamental divisions within American Christianity itself. On the one side, there is what one writer describes as a "Superstar Christianity," made up of those who are drawn to the musical's portrayal of Jesus' suffering

---

1. Chattaway, "NBC Resurrects 'Jesus Christ Superstar,'" 1.
2. Ibid.

and his ethical message of love, mercy, and justice.³ John Legend, the star of NBC's version of the musical, reflects this viewpoint when he states that the overriding message of the show is one of love: "[Jesus'] message was disruptive at the time. It was about disrupting the status quo. It was about looking out for the poor. It was about extending grace to people who may have been forgotten or cast aside, and so, hopefully that message still stays with us and is timeless and we can apply it to the way we see the world now."⁴ Those who adopt this perspective are concerned with social justice and economic welfare, inclusion, and forgiveness. Strict adherence to the "details" of Scripture is a lesser priority.

On the other side, there is a traditional "orthodox Christianity," which is concerned with scriptural authority and doctrine. Most in this camp are put off by the unbiblical and unsavory elements in the show (which are many) and its portrayal of Jesus as a mere human. They dismiss the musical for its irreverence, denial of scriptural teachings regarding personal morality (particularly homosexuality), and lack of reference to the forgiveness of sins through Jesus' death on the cross and his resurrection.

I would suggest that in various respects, this religious schism is evident in the rift between two perspectives within contemporary evangelicalism. On one side of this divide there are the advocates of the "emerging church" who emphasize Jesus' "gospel of the kingdom." On the other side, there are those who stress an individualistic gospel of personal salvation.

The Emerging Church and "Superstar Christianity"

Granted, there are many aspects of *Jesus Christ Superstar* which *any* Christian would find objectionable and offensive. For example, it presents Mary Magdalene as a prostitute who is in love with a very human Jesus. Nonetheless, I suspect that there are adherents of what is often referred to as the "emerging church" who look past these distasteful elements of the show and identify with the more positive aspects of its ethical message. Proponents of this movement are sharply critical of a focus on the cross as a way to "escape hell" and "go to heaven when I die." Brian McLaren speaks for many advocates of the emerging church when he states:

> But now I wonder if this gospel about how to get your soul into Heaven after death is really only a ghost of the real gospel that Jesus talked about, which seems to have something to do with

---

3. See Henne, "Superstar Christianity," 1.
4. Butler, "John Legend: 'Jesus Christ Superstar' is all about Love," 1.

God's will being done on earth now, not just in Heaven later. . . . Yes, I believe that the gospel has facts that deal with forgiveness of sins, but I feel unfaithful to Jesus to define the gospel by that one fact when I see our contemporary churches failing to address so many other essential gospel concerns—justice, compassion, sacrifice, purpose, transformation into Christlikeness, and ultimate hope.[5]

McLaren argues that societal systems are guided by a "framing narrative," a story which unifies, integrates, and motivates a people and provides a framework in which we live, act, desire, and dream. A framing story is either healthy or unhealthy and destructive. When the framing narrative is characterized by greed, injustice, class conflict, sexual irresponsibility, religious bigotry, ethnic hatred, nationalistic militarism and other manifestations of sin, the entire system becomes dysfunctional, self-destructive and suicidal.[6] Jesus confronts society's suicidal machine with a radical "reframing" story—the gospel or "good news" of God's kingdom which brings hope, healing, joy, and opportunity. But we have adopted a gospel of personal salvation which domesticates Jesus' gospel, or a "counter-narrative" of love, justice, and peace. In the words of McLaren, "We have in many ways responded to the big global crises of our day with an incredible, shrinking gospel."[7]

A Realized "Here and Now" Kingdom

We can, in my view, agree with McLaren's concern for "kingdom ethics." As Russell Moore argues, "Seeking first the Kingdom should not dampen Christian concern for social and political justice, but heighten it. After all, the priorities of the King—seen in his ultimate goal of the restoration of the creation—must become the priorities of the Kingdom colony, the church."[8] However, in his criticism of traditional Christianity for reducing the gospel to "personal salvation," McLaren tends towards another form of gospel reductionism. The *inaugurated* kingdom with tension between the "now" and "not yet" is largely reduced to a *realized* "here and now" kingdom. He and other emerging church leaders espouse a theology in which God's kingdom of justice and peace is manifested in society and culture through Christian

---

5. Quoted in Miles, "A Kingdom Without a King?," 8.
6. McLaren, *Everything Must Change*, 52–72.
7. Ibid., 244.
8. See the interview with Moore in "Moving Forward with a Kingdom Consensus," 1. See also, Moore, *The Kingdom of Christ*, 131–73.

activism.⁹ Thus, he maintains that the vision of the New Jerusalem in Revelation 21, like all prophetic visions, "seeks to inspire our imaginations with hope about what our world can actually become through the good news of the kingdom of God." The "new heaven and new earth" (Rev 21:1) means "a new way of living that is possible within this universe, a new societal system that is coming as surely as God is just and faithful."¹⁰ Rob Bell affirms that heaven is a real place where God's will is done and acknowledges that presently heaven and earth are not one.¹¹ At the same time, he maintains that "The goal isn't escaping this world but making this world the kind of place God can come to. And God is remaking us into the kind of people who can do this kind of work."¹²

A number of emerging church leaders who adopt this approach tend to deconstruct the role of the church in God's plan. For example, Doug Pagitt argues that while the church is called to be "the hermeneutic of the gospel" it is "not necessarily the center of God's intentions. God is working in the world, and the church has the option to join God or not."¹³ Others articulate the similar view that the kingdom of God is expressed and found most often *outside* the walls of the established church and religious structures.¹⁴ Bell argues that humanity's role within creation is to be engaged in creating a new social order with Jesus.¹⁵ Ultimately, there is little difference between this portrayal of the kingdom and the social gospel of the late nineteenth and early twentieth centuries—or contemporary forms of liberation theology, which seeks social salvation and the social liberation and empowerment of oppressed peoples through human means.¹⁶ While not all emerging church leaders express this viewpoint, many do.

---

9. See McKnight, *Kingdom Conspiracy*, 237–38.
10. McLaren, *Everything Must Change* 296.
11. Bell, *Love Wins*, 42–43.
12. Bell, *Velvet Elvis*, 149–50.
13. Quoted in Miles, "A Kingdom without a King?," 9.
14. Ibid. 9–10.
15. Bell, *Love Wins*, 77.

16. McKnight observes that "Contemporary progressive Christian thinking in the United States, whether one finds it among Roman Catholics like Elizabeth Johnson at Fordham University or among emergent voices like Brian McLaren, is, in its various forms, a riff on liberation theology where the central drives are justice and peace as manifestations of holistic salvation . . . , Kingdom theology . . . has become a combination of good people doing good things in the public sector and an activistic striving to undo injustices and establish justice against the oppressive systemic forces of, most especially, capitalism and colonialism" (*Kingdom Conspiracy*, 238).

Opposing Penal Substitution

Some within the emerging church movement also strongly oppose the common understanding of the cross as an atonement for sins. In the view of Steve Chalke, an emerging church leader from the United Kingdom, the notion of penal substitution is both offensive and a massive contradiction of the biblical truth of God's love. The cross, he argues, is not "a form of cosmic child abuse—a vengeful Father, punishing his Son for an offence he has not even committed."[17] For Chalke, Christ's sin-bearing act on the cross is "a symbol of love. It is a demonstration of just how far God as Father and Jesus his son are prepared to go to prove that love. The cross is a vivid statement of the powerlessness of love." Further, the cross "stands at the centre of our decaying world—thrust into the dirt to proclaim 'God is here.'"[18] McLaren also suggests that the concept of substitutionary atonement sounds like divine child abuse. While he is largely noncommittal on various theories of the atonement, one that he favors is the "powerful weakness theory":

> It works like this: by becoming vulnerable on the cross, by accepting suffering from everyone, Jews and Roman alike, rather than visiting suffering on everyone, Jesus is showing God's loving heart, which wants forgiveness, not revenge, for everyone. Jesus shows us that the wisdom of God's kingdom is sacrifice, not violence. It's about accepting suffering and transforming it into reconciliation, not avenging suffering through retaliation. So through this window, the cross shows God's rejection of human violence and dominance and oppression that have spun the world in a cycle of crisis from the story of Cain and Abel through the headlines in this morning's *Washington Post*.[19]

While the cross is still important for Chalke and McLaren, it seems to be largely reduced to a moral example of suffering under oppression. That is, similar to the way Christ's death is portrayed in *Jesus Christ Superstar*, the cross is little more than Jesus sharing in the pathos of human suffering and calling us to follow his example of suffering love.[20] This is not to deny that there is an ethical dimension to the cross. As I have argued, this

---

17. Quoted in Carson, *Becoming Conversant with the Emerging Church*, 185.

18. Ibid., 186

19. Ibid., 166–67.

20. One review of Chalke's *The Lost Message of Jesus* states: "In other words, the cross is no more than Jesus identifying with our suffering, sharing in the pathos of it. It is difficult to see how this helps us anymore than my injecting myself with the HIV virus would improve the lot of a friend who has AIDS." See Carson, *Becoming Conversant with the Emerging Church*, 186.

is indeed an important aspect of biblical teaching which is often not sufficiently acknowledged in the church. But the cross cannot be *reduced* to these terms. Moreover, Chalke's and McLaren's portrayal of the concept of substitutionary atonement as "divine child abuse" is a caricature. As D. A. Carson states, "God's love is all the more deeply cherished when the nature of Christ's sin-bearing act on the cross is understood in biblical terms."[21]

Questioning the Exclusivity of Christ

Most leaders in the emerging church are orthodox in their teaching regarding the exclusivity of Christ and the gospel. But this is not always the case. Consider Bell's popular book, *Love Wins*. Bell would deny that he is a proponent of Christian universalism. Yet, there are some things that he says which strongly suggest otherwise:

> As soon as the door is opened to Muslims, Hindus, Buddhists, and Baptists from Cleveland, many Christians become very uneasy, saying that Jesus doesn't matter anymore, the cross is irrelevant, it doesn't matter what you believe, and so forth.
>
> Not true. Absolutely, not true. What Jesus is declaring is that he, and he alone, is saving everybody. And then he leaves the door way, way open. Creating all sorts of possibilities. He is as narrow as himself and as wide as the universe.
>
> He is as exclusive as himself and as inclusive as containing every single particle of creation.[22]

Bell collapses God's saving grace into common grace. Consequently, he downplays the necessity of Christ's vicarious substitution on the cross and the need to personally appropriate God's forgiveness and healing through repentance and belief in Jesus' death and resurrection.

---

21. Ibid., 186. While accepting the view of "penal substitution" as biblical, Bird adds that it would be wise for advocates of the theory to "listen to their critics and ensure they are not theologically bankrolling an atonement theory that legitimates violence or a brutal patriarchy . . . In our atonement theories let us not go beyond what is written" (*Evangelical Theology*, 412). In his *Systematic Theology*, for example, Grudem writes: "God . . . poured out on Jesus the fury of his wrath: Jesus became the object of the intense hatred of sin and vengeance against sin which God had patiently stored up since the beginning of the world" (575). Bird responds: "The concepts here are not entirely wrong, but where does Scripture say that at the cross God hates Jesus or gets revenge on him? Gruden's view becomes liable to some of the criticisms that postconservative, emergent, and liberal theologians raise against penal substitution. More carefully nuanced language should be used" (*Evangelical Theology*, 412, note 166).

22. Bell, *Love Wins*, 155.

How Should We Define the Gospel?

McLaren also embraces religious pluralism and fails to emphasize the fact that the kingdom is realized only through Christ and the indwelling of his Spirit. Todd Miles points out that in his book *The Secret Message of Jesus*, "The Holy Spirit is conspicuously absent . . . The New Covenant is hardly mentioned, if at all. . . . At the end of the day, McLaren's message is essentially a call for humanity to try to be like Jesus by pulling itself up by its own moral bootstraps." The result is a distorted theology of the kingdom.[23]

The gospel is indeed about God reconciling the world to himself. But a comprehensive view of salvation does not nullify the necessity of personal regeneration, which is made possible only through Christ's work on the cross.[24] As Miles asks: "Can there be a kingdom, in the biblical sense, with an impoverished or distorted Christology? . . . When we serve for the advancement of the kingdom while not proclaiming the King who makes the kingdom possible, we are in effect denying the King of the kingdom—making kingdom advancement a matter of human decision and achievement."[25]

Conservative Evangelicals and Religious Individualism

For all of its weaknesses, the emerging church movement does correctly identify some shortcomings within more conservative branches of evangelicalism which are strongly influenced by religious individualism. Historically, evangelicalism has been something of a mixed bag. Mark Noll observes in his masterful study of the origins of evangelicalism in the middle of the eighteenth century that "Evangelicalism was a pietistic movement in which the relationship of the self to God eclipsed all other concerns."[26] Pietism promoted an understanding of the gospel which stressed the personal experience of God's grace. There is, of course, much that is of crucial importance in this orientation. As Noll points out, the pietistic movement did much good in the world. But in focusing its attention on the personal need for a Savior, it tended to edge aside a self-conscious attention to the social, including a concern about the slave system.[27] A number of second-generation evangelicals did became staunch supporters of the abolitionist movements

---

23. Miles points out that in Brian McLaren's *The Secret Message of Jesus* "The Holy Spirit is conspicuously absent . . . The New Covenant is hardly mentioned, if at all . . . At the end of the day, McLaren's message is essentially a call for humanity to try to be like Jesus by pulling itself up by its own moral bootstraps" ("A Kingdom without a King?," 21).

24. See Moore, *The Kingdom of Christ*, 100.

25. Miles, "A Kingdom without a King?," 9, 26.

26. Noll, *The Rise of Evangelicalism*, 233.

27. Ibid., 247–261.

in both England and the United States and advocates of social reform. This is also an important part of our evangelical heritage. But to this day, the pietistic strain continues to exert a powerful influence on evangelicals in America.

Evangelical pietism is evident in the popularity in many of our churches of hymns like "Jesus Paid it All":

> I hear the Savior say,
> "Thy strength indeed is small;
> Child of weakness, watch and pray,
> Find in Me thine all in all."
> Jesus paid it all,
> All to Him I owe;
> Sin had left a crimson stain,
> He washed it white as snow.

Hymns like this highlight the positive aspects of pietism in that they stress the personal appropriation of God's forgiveness of *my* sin. But an overemphasis on the personal dimension of the gospel can cause us to err in translating as singular the plural pronouns of the Bible. Thus, in much pietistic hymnody, Christ died for "me," rather than for "us" or the "world."[28] This makes a big difference in how we present the gospel.

In America, most Christians are deeply influenced by the philosophy of individualism. Briefly, this is the value system which makes the individual central and asserts the primacy of the individual over the group. The roots of this philosophy run deep. For Americans, probably nothing more embodies this ideal than the mental image of the "rugged individual" of the frontier. The concept of the hardworking, self-sufficient, "pull yourself up by your bootstraps" frontiersman is so much a part of the American psyche that we simply take it for granted. This individualistic orientation greatly impacts the way we Americans view the world, and also the way many Christians in American, particularly evangelicals, view salvation.[29] Scot McKnight rightly states that: "*The gospel we preach shapes the kind of churches we create. The kind of church we have shapes the gospel we preach.*"[30]

---

28. A number of hymns couple an individualistic focus on the gospel with the idea of the soul going to heaven. See, for example, "When the Roll Is Called Up Yonder," "The Old Rugged Cross," and "My Jesus I Love Thee." For a fuller discussion, see Middleton, *A New Heaven and a New Earth*, 27–30.

29. For a discussion of this, see Hollinger, *Individualism and Social Ethics*, 13–44; 217–32.

30. McKnight, *A Community Called Atonement*, 5.

There is a sense, of course, in which the gospel can never be "culture-free." The very words that are used to communicate the gospel and give it meaning are embedded in culture. This was true in the very beginning of the Christian faith. And it is true today. However, our task must be to convey the original meaning of the gospel as faithfully as possible. And a weakness of American evangelicalism, in the view of various observers, has been a failure to call into question the ideology of individualism. This has born some unhealthy fruit.[31]

A Self-Centered Gospel

The first consequence of an emphasis on the individual is that we end up with a self-centered gospel. This is evident in summaries of the gospel such as the Four Spiritual Laws and the Romans Road which focus on how God loves *me* and has a wonderful plan for *my* life; how *my* sin has separated *me* from God; how Christ died for *me*; and how if *I* confess *my* sins and believe in Christ *I* will spend eternity with him in heaven. An emphasis on self can also be seen in popular choruses such as "Above All," which contains the following lyrics:

> Like a rose trampled on the ground
> You took the fall
> And thought of me
> Above all.

In addition to conveying a questionable understanding of Christ's atonement for sins, this song errs in making Jesus' death on the cross all about me. Certainly, the gospel *does* involve a personal relationship with Jesus Christ. We must never lose sight of this fact. But the *story* of the gospel does not revolve around me or you. Marc Cortez points out that the New Testament "almost always talks about 'the gospel of Jesus Christ' (Mk 1:1); 'the gospel of God' (Mk 1:14); 'the good news of the kingdom of God' (Lk 4:43), and so on. Only once is it 'the gospel of *your* salvation' (Eph 1:13)."[32] He rightly argues that "the good news of my salvation is only truly good news when I see how it connects to God and the larger story of his glory." In other words, "this story includes good news *for* us; but it's not *about* us."

---

31. See Voskuil, "Individualism and Evangelism in America," 24.
32. Cortez, "The Problem with Our Gospel #1: The Self-Centered Gospel," 4.

Over and over again the Bible makes it clear that this story is about God and *his* kingdom.[33]

Diminishing the Importance of Community

An overly individualistic presentation of the gospel also tends to diminish the importance of community. In the Bible, God's grace is communicated in the context of a relationship between himself and his people as a covenantal community. It's not just "me and God." We can see this in the Genesis creation account where God declares what he has created to be good. At the end of chapter one, he surveys everything he has created and declares it to be "very good" (1:31). But when we come to the second chapter, God looks at Adam in the idyllic setting of the garden and says that it is "not good" (2:18). Why? Because, despite the fact that Adam is in a sinless relationship with the Creator of the universe, he is still "alone." God is not fully satisfied with his creation until he has created another human (Eve) to come alongside Adam. Both humans *together* bear God's image (1:28) and both enjoy God's presence in the temple garden. As we have seen, the book of Revelation beautifully depicts the end of the biblical story with the same picture of God dwelling with his people forever. Scripture makes it clear that God's plan has never been about "me and God." It's always been about "us and God."[34]

However, our churches in America often fail to present the gospel in this fashion. This is particularly the case within more conservative forms of evangelicalism, where evangelism and the "new birth" are almost always spoken of in individualistic terms. Evangelicals, many of whom have been deeply influenced by the pietistic tradition, tend to say: "*You* are saved. *You* are a new person. *You* have been born again." This, of course, *is* true. But if we stop there (as is often the case) we make the church largely optional. It is simply a collection of individuals. This is not biblical. Stanley Grenz reminds us that being a Christian *necessarily* entails "membership in the fellowship of those who have come to know the God of the Bible through Jesus Christ by the Spirit."[35] Biblically, the new birth through Christ is always experienced and shared in the context of community, the *ecclesia* or "people of God" who are under the reign of God and look forward to the eschatological destination of history when *all things* will be made new.[36]

---

33. Ibid., 4–5.
34. Cortez, "The Problem with Our Gospel #2: The Individualistic Gospel," 2.
35. Grenz, *Renewing the Center*, 223.
36. See Webber, *Ancient-Future Faith*, 144.

A Gospel of Self-Fulfillment

A final consequence of an overly individualistic orientation is a tendency by many Christians to view salvation as self-fulfillment. According to theologian David Wells, the modern church's focus on the self, or what he calls "self-piety," has resulted in the "psychologizing" of biblical truths as church leaders attempt to address the "felt needs" of individuals. In many of today's market-driven churches, he argues, there is a "cult of self" which values faith only to the extent that it helps individuals achieve self–understanding, self–improvement, and self-fulfillment.[37] In this privatized and psychologized version of Christianity, sin is often viewed as a personality flaw rather than a moral failing. Sin, in other words, is largely redefined as failure to reach one's full potential as a person created in the image of God. Faith in Christ is regarded as a means to the end of realizing our full human potential.

Wells's critique of contemporary evangelicalism needs to be qualified by the observation that redemption involves a restoration of the image of God, as I will discuss in the next chapter. But when coupled with an ideology of hyper-individualism, the gospel of self-fulfillment can be reduced to a form of religious narcissism that seriously diminishes Christ and the meaning of the cross. Todd Brenneman observes that the primary focus in much of contemporary evangelicalism is on the problems of the individual. In its emphasis on the individual as the center of God's desire, contemporary evangelicalism, he argues, is shaped by American therapeutic and narcissistic culture and pop psychology. The promoters of therapeutic evangelicalism ask their followers to "practice a narcissism that accepts that God is desperately concerned even about their menial quotidian problems." While implicitly acknowledging that there are bigger problems in the world than finding a parking space or having a better job, the focus of many evangelical ministers and writers on the individual's felt needs frequently suggests the opposite: that the universe revolves around the practical problems of day-to-day life and that God has nothing better to do than make sure he fills his children's lives with blessings. "The individual in evangelicalism has become a self-important obsession."[38]

Here, again, maintaining a proper balance is crucial. Many people experience deep pain and are faced with ongoing personal struggles. It is important for them to draw strength and encouragement from an awareness of God's loving care and presence in their lives. The Bible often portrays God as a loving Father who provides for his children. But this should

---

37. Wells, *No Place for Truth*, 176.
38. Brenneman, *Homespun Gospel*, 46–49.

not lead to a syrupy sentimentality or preoccupation with the self that diminishes a concern for the ills of society and God's purposes in the world. Authentic Christian faith is not *merely* a vehicle for self-fulfillment and self-actualization divorced from a call to deny ourselves, take up our cross, and follow Jesus. We therefore need a fuller understanding of why Jesus died, the nature of sin, and our mission in the world. This will be the subject of the next chapter.

Keeping the Kingdom and the Cross Together

Basically, we might say that there are those in the emerging church movement who try to have a kingdom without a King while many within more traditional conservative evangelicalism try to have a King or Savior without a kingdom. The first group errs in working to advance the kingdom while downplaying the exclusivity of Christ as "the way, the truth, and the life." The second group errs in emphasizing the individual's eternal destiny through Christ while downplaying the corporate and social dimensions of the gospel.[39] In response to both of these orientations I would suggest an alternative approach in which the kingdom is defined by the cross (biblically understood) and the cross is defined by the kingdom. If the cross is abstracted from the kingdom of God, then we tend to have forgiveness of sins without a proper regard for Jesus' kingdom ethic. But if we abstract the kingdom from the cross we are left with mere morality without the life-changing power of the cross.[40]

In his recent book *Renaissance: The Power of the Gospel However Dark the Times*, Os Guinness asks the question of whether the power of the gospel is sufficient to overcome the darkness of the present times and whether the church can be renewed to become an effective carrier of the gospel. "Has modernity," he asks, "finally done what no enemy or persecutor has ever succeeded in doing and reduced the authority of the Scriptures to a shifting weather vane and the church to babbling impotence?"[41] Guinness is sharply critical of current "born again" Christianity for its truth-deficient "feel good" theology, sub-Christian politics, mindless evangelism, and trendy chasing after "relevance" which is both transient and worldly.[42] He is also critical of forms of the emerging church which are also trendy, weak on emphasizing biblical orthodoxy, and embrace the postmodern idea that

---

39. See Miles, "A Kingdom without a King?," 25.
40. Russell Moore makes a similar argument in *Onward*, 65.
41. Guinness, *Renaissance*, 13–14.
42. Ibid., 129.

there is no absolute truth.[43] While the church will never be perfect this side of glory, he maintains that it can be revived, reformed, and restored through God's Spirit to be a vibrant witness to the truth and power of the gospel:

> In other words, *when followers of Jesus live out the gospel in the world, we become an incarnation of the truth of the gospel and an expression of the character and shape of the truth. It is this living-in-truth that proves culturally powerful.* It is therefore entirely legitimate to inquire how Christian faithfulness and obedience to the truth serve the purposes and power of God to change the world.[44]

These words by Guinness are a vibrant and urgent call to rethink and redefine the church's engagement with postmodern culture. I share these concerns.[45] In the next chapter I offer a brief proposal for an evangelical politic (our way of life together) based on themes rooted in the Lord's Supper which I believe can help provide a way forward.[46]

---

43. It is important to distinguish between cultural and philosophical forms of postmodernism. The former is an amorphous, pervasive and popular mood characterized by skepticism about grand claims to truth if not the possibility of discovering or knowing truth itself. It is often a nihilistic, anarchic, and individualistic view of truth which states that every individual has his or her own truth and that there is no morality or ethics outside of the individual. As a philosophy, however, postmodernism simply rejects the modern Enlightenment idea that "reason" provides a neutral and disinterested perspective from which to pursue truth and ethics. All knowing takes place from the perspective of some tradition–community or metaphysical vision of reality. There are softer versions of postmodernism that do not entail relativism. As Olson argues, biblical-Christian theism might be seen as a metaphysical vision rooted in the biblical narrative which gives a coherent explanation of reality and the human experience. Olson, *The Essentials of Christian Thought*, 38–9. See also Olson, *The Journey of Modern Theology*, 650–57.

44. Ibid., 73.

45. While I do not agree with all of Guinness's views, I share his concern about evangelical anti-intellectualism—e.g., superficial or bad theology, lack of a serious apology for faith, and lack of a constructive public philosophy—and his call for Christians to define their faith and lives in terms of the announcement of the good news of the kingdom of God by Jesus.

46. I am particularly indebted to the insights of a number of evangelical biblical scholars—including Michael Gorman, Scot McKnight, Ben Witherington, Stanley Grenz, and Timothy Keller—who have broadened and deepened my understanding of the gospel message.

17

The Church as a New Covenant Community

In the movie *Grand Canyon*, the attempt of an immigration attorney to bypass a traffic jam leads to a dark and deserted neighborhood run by street gangs. Then a driver's worst nightmare happens: his expensive car stalls in the middle of an abandoned street. The attorney is able to call for a tow truck, but before it arrives he is surrounded by a group of five thugs who threaten him with considerable bodily harm. Just in the nick of time, the truck driver arrives. As the driver hooks up the disabled car, the group of teenagers react angrily. So, pulling the leader of the group aside, the affable man lectures the teen:

> Man, the world ain't supposed to work like this. Maybe you don't know that, but this ain't the way it's supposed to be. I'm supposed to be able to do my job without askin' you if I can. And that dude is supposed to be able to wait with his car without you rippin' him off. Everything's supposed to be different than what it is here.[1]

The constant message of the Bible, from Genesis to Revelation, is that things in the world aren't the way they are supposed to be. God cares so much about the world he created that he entered it to redeem it. Through the incarnation and the cross he re-established a covenantal relationship with lost humanity to rescue it from the devastating consequences of sin. This is what John means when he states, "From his (Jesus') fullness we have received grace upon grace" (Jn 1:16 RSV). This is radical grace.

In this book I have argued that the gospel is ultimately concerned with the renewal of God's entire creation, not just individual salvation. The

---

1. Plantinga, *Not the Way it's Supposed to Be*, 7.

biblical narrative is, as Craig Bartholomew and Michael Goheen describe it, "a unified and progressively unfolding drama of God's action in history for the salvation of the whole world."[2] This story gives shape to how we live our entire lives, both as individuals and as the church, in the here and now.[3] The Lord's Table (or Eucharist) is itself anchored in this story, and is, in fact, *the story*. "It is," in the words of Michael Bird, "a snapshot of the grand narrative about God, creation, the fall, Israel, the exile, the Messiah, the church, and the consummation."[4] I have tried to demonstrate throughout this book that without an understanding of the full sweep of this story from creation to eschaton we will not fully understand the church's calling or purpose in the world.

In this final chapter my purpose will be to give some concluding observations on what can be described as the church's "political presence" in the world. Here, I am not using the word "political" or "politics" in the usual sense, as referring to the church's political stance on either the left or right of the political spectrum. Rather, by "politics" I mean the church's "politic" in the world—its way of life together, or corporate way of being in the world, including its corporate practices and witness.[5] Properly understood, the gospel expresses what the church as the body of Christ is called to be, say, and do in the world. Within the framework of the Lord's Supper, the church is enjoined by Scripture to be a "new covenant community." Before describing this concept further and what it means for the church, we need to look first at the way the Bible holds sin and grace together.

Sin and Grace

There was a time when there was a common understanding in our culture of the language of sin and grace. But that is no longer the case. As Carl Menninger, a leading psychologist, asks in the title of one of his books, *Whatever Became of Sin?* In this book he states: "When I was a boy, sin was still a serious matter and the word was not a jocular term. But I saw this change; I saw it go. I am afraid I even joined in hailing its going."[6] In our postmodern culture, a theological worldview has been replaced by a therapeutic paradigm. Consequently, the concept of sin has been largely

---

2. Bartholomew and Goheen, *The Drama of Scripture*, 12.

3. Ibid., 206.

4. Bird, *Evangelical Theology*, 777–78.

5. Gorman, *The Death of the Messiah*, 219; see also Fitch, *The End of Evangelicalism?*, xvi.

6. Menninger, *Whatever Became of Sin?*, 24.

replaced by the language of crime and sickness. But this therapeutic model is only symptomatic of a more fundamental problem. With this loss of the deeper meaning and significance of sin, a true understanding of grace has also been lost. It is essential, then, that we recover a biblical understanding of these concepts.

Understanding Sin and its Consequences

Sin is often viewed by Christians in a single dimension, as disobedience or a willful violation of God's moral law. It is the breaking of God's commandments. Alternatively, obedience to God's law is viewed as the basis for a moral and Godly life. But, as Derek Nelson perceptively discusses in *Sin: A Guide for the Perplexed*, the Bible does not give us a single unified "theory" of sin. What we find in the Bible with respect to sin is more like a collage, or a collection of meanings which are as different from each other as they are similar. "All imply something not being right in the complex relationships of oneself to God, oneself to one's neighbor, and oneself to oneself."[7]

At the risk of oversimplification, we might say that there are three basic dimensions to sin. At its root, sin is an idolatrous worship of self instead of the worship of God. It is a prideful attempt to place one's self on the throne instead of God. It is a foolish and pathetic effort to stage a coup d'état against the God of the universe. We might, as Michael Bird suggests, describe it as the "Frank Sinatra Syndrome." It is humanity raising and shaking its puny fist against heaven and declaring, "I did it *my* way."[8] Secondly, sin involves making wrong choices. The Greek word most commonly associated with this dimension of sin is *hamartia*, which signifies a departure from righteousness, a failure to "hit the mark" of God's perfect love and his perfect law.[9] But, thirdly, we can enlarge upon this understanding of sin by saying that it is a violation of *shalom* or the way things are supposed to be. Sin, in other words, is "shalom breaking," a disruption of God's design for creation. As Cornelius Plantinga states, "Sin offends God not only because it bereaves or assaults God directly, as impiety or blasphemy, but also because it bereaves and assaults what God has made."[10]

The concept of sin as "shalom breaking" takes us back again to the story of Adam and Eve, which represents the longings of the human heart for universal flourishing, wholeness, and joy. J.R.R Tolkien diagnoses the

---

7. Nelson, *Sin*, 17.
8. Bird, *Evangelical Theology*, 669.
9. Ibid., 668.
10. Plantinga, *Not the Way It's Supposed to Be*, 14–16.

roots of our longing: "We all long for [Eden], and we are constantly glimpsing it; our whole nature at its best and least corrupted; its gentlest and most humane, is still soaked with a sense of exile."[11] The first chapters of Genesis tell us what God intended for his creation but was lost due to sin.

When reading the account of the fall of Adam and Eve in Genesis 3, our tendency is to focus on their disobedience to God's command (Gen 2:17; 3:11). But at a deeper level, the sin of Adam and Eve involves their decision to trust in the word of the serpent rather than the word of God. In so doing, they no longer reflect the image of God and begin to mirror the serpent's image. Their disobedience ultimately involves the element of self-worship and idolatry in that they think they know what is better for them than God does and autonomously set up their own ethical law.[12]

To summarize sin and its consequences, we can say that Adam and Eve were created to be imagers of God in the sense that they were to be in union with God, in communion with each other, and vice-regents of God in ordering the world and extending God's rule and authority throughout creation. Because the image of God is "multi"-relational or "hyperrelational," sin is also "hyperrelational."[13] Fundamentally, sin is self-worship and rebellion against God. This corruption or distortion of the human relationship with God results in a distortion of all other relationships (with self, others, and the world or creation).

The Healing Power of Grace

Much the same description of sin and its consequences is given by Paul in Romans 1:18–32, where he characterizes those under the power of sin as futile and darkened in their thinking. Pretending to be wise, they become fools; instead of worshipping God, they exchange the glory of the immortal God for images that reflect his creation. As a result, God gives them up to a degrading of their bodies, a depraved mind, and every kind of personal and social evil. Here Paul graphically describes the multidimensional nature of sin as well as its devastating impact on the *imago Dei*. Paul's characterization of the wide variety of evils is intended to show that sin is "comprehensive cancer that has affected not only the body (1:24) but also the human mind

---

11. Beale and Kim, *God Dwells Among Us*, 17.

12. For a fuller discussion of the couple's sin as self-worship and idolatry see Beale, *We Become What We Worship*, 132–35.

13. McKnight, *A Community Called Atonement*, 22–23.

(1:21, 28) and heart (1:24); every dimension of the human person and community needs restoration to health."[14]

But, says Paul, where sin increased, grace increased all the more (Rom 5:20). The ultimate manifestation of God's grace is, of course, the gift of his son culminating in his death on the cross. This radical grace is now a power unleashed in the world (Rom 5:21) that bestows life with God.[15] Paul indicates that Christ's work on the cross is a many-faceted transaction. Scripture in fact hints at a number of "theories" of the atonement.[16] The view which evangelicals most often express is that the cross is a substitutionary sacrifice, or "ransom" for sin. But the New Testament also describes the cross as the means by which Christ defeats and has victory over the powers of sin, evil, and death. It also presents the cross as a profound example or display of sacrificial love. Even further, Christ's atonement through the cross and his resurrection are presented as the means by which we become participants in the divine nature (2 Pet 1:4) by his Spirit. A related understanding of the atonement is that it is God's work of healing and restorative love and justice, which is most fully manifested in and through the church as the body of Christ (1 Cor 12–14).

It is critical that we embrace all of these dimensions of God's grace when we talk about God's redemption through the cross. Sin consists of systemic or universal corruption. Every dimension of the human person and community needs restoration to health. Therefore, the atonement involves the restoration of God's image *in all directions*.[17] In other words, the atonement is a comprehensive work that not only wipes the slate clean of sins but also restores the *imago Dei* through new life in God—a new life which is both *personal and ecclesial*. The church as a community of the new covenant of grace is called to manifest in its relationships God's work of healing, reconciliation, and restorative justice.[18]

---

14. Gorman, *Apostle of the Crucified Lord*, 353.

15. Ibid., 117.

16. Mouw, *When the Kings Come Marching In*, 110; and Gorman, *The Death of the Messiah*, 224–32.

17. McKnight, *A Community Called Atonement*, 24. Witherington likewise argues that in the New Testament the concept of the *imago dei* and its renewal in Jesus Christ is the connecting link between theology and ethics. "By this is meant that all human beings are created in God's image, and after the fall they need to be renewed in that image in order to have an ongoing positive relationship with God. . . . The aim of salvation is not merely to restart a relationship, but to conform a group of people to the image of God's Son, who is the ultimate image of God ever to grace the earth with his presence" (*New Testament Theology and Ethics, Vol. 2*, 10).

18. McKnight, *A Community Called Atonement.*, 71, 126

Rightly understood, this understanding of the atonement does not lead to an anthropocentric reading of the biblical text—or view which places emphasis on human fulfillment and restoration as the ultimate goal of God's plan of salvation. The New Testament is radically theocentric, or God-centered. It focuses on the supremacy of God in Christ. But this concern with God's glory is not in conflict with the redemption of his creation. Rather, God works out his saving plan *so that* he will be magnified in Christ. God is glorified "for his mercy" (Rom 15:8). G. K. Beale sums up the relationship between God's glory and the restoration of the *imago Dei* through Christ in this way: When we try to enlarge ourselves and try to bring glory to ourselves, we not only diminish ourselves. We also ultimately bring about our entire ruin. "But heaping glory on the true God and worshipfully acknowledging his greatness leads to sharing in God's greatness and glory by reflecting his glory, which is reflected back on him. Thus God is seen as the unique and weighty great One of the cosmos."[19] We might add that God is also glorified when his creation (especially humankind, which is created in his image) fulfills the purpose for which it was created.

Recovering the Concept of the "New Covenant" for the Church

Biblical scholars, and even lay Christians, have often engaged in a vigorous debate over which of the above mentioned theories or models of the "atonement" should be given precedence over all the others. Recently, however, some have proposed the need for a more embracive category that incorporates the multiple theories. Scot McKnight uses the following analogy from the game of golf: "We need to use all the clubs in the bag and we need a bag that can hold them all."[20] If that is the case, what over-arching concept will suffice?

As Michael Gorman suggests in *The Death of the Messiah and the Birth of the New Covenant*, a prime candidate is the concept of the "new covenant." After all, in the night before his crucifixion Jesus interprets his death in terms of the "new covenant in my blood" (Lk 22;20; cf. Matt 26:28; Mk 14:24). In the only canonical account of the Last Supper outside of the Gospels, Paul likewise indicates that in both the Last Supper and the church's subsequent act of remembrance, the Lord's Supper, Jesus' death centers on the establishment of a new covenant (1 Cor 11:25). Thus, while the New Testament employs a wide range of images and metaphors to portray God's gracious action through the cross, the most comprehensive understanding

19. Beale, *We Become What We Worship*, 140.
20. Ibid., 114.

of the atonement is the birth of the new covenant through Jesus' death and resurrection.[21]

This means, as Gorman further argues, that Christ's death and resurrection creates a new covenant community—a community whose life in the Spirit of the resurrected Lord is shaped by the faithful, loving, and hope making death of the same crucified Jesus. The atonement, which we celebrate in the Lord's Supper, is about the creation of a liberated, forgiven, loving, and Spirit-infused community that becomes more and more like Christ and thereby regains the glory of God that Adam lost.[22] In this concluding section I will briefly summarize three aspects of this new covenant ideal, which is rooted in the Old Testament and fulfilled in the New: 1) the new covenant spirituality; 2) the theopolitical gospel; and 3) the church as a community of hope.

New Covenant Spirituality

The idea of the "new covenant," which Jesus refers to in the Last Supper and which Paul repeats, is based on the recognition that the purpose of Jesus' coming and death was the restoration (for believing Jews) and the establishment (for believing Gentiles) of a right covenantal relationship between humans and God.[23] This new covenant is connected to the original covenant that God made with Abraham and reaffirmed with the Israelites following the exodus. The covenant with Israel was always based on God's liberating grace, but it also entailed a response from Israel of both love for God and love for neighbor. In the New Testament, the covenant is made new (in fulfillment of the promises of the prophets) by Jesus' shed blood on the cross. This is solely a gift of God's grace which is entered into by faith in Christ.

In Paul's letters, the believer's relationship to Christ is expressed through the metaphor of "being in" Christ and of the risen Christ living in us (Gal 2:20; cf. Rom 8:10) through his Spirit. We might further describe this relationship of being in Christ and Christ being within us as *mutual indwelling*. "It means that Christ (or the Spirit of Christ—Gal 4:6) is not an external mode but an internal power."[24] Paul often defines this relationship in terms of "dying and rising" with Christ and of being conformed to Christ crucified—that is, living a life of *cruciform* or "cross-shaped" faith, hope, and love.

21. Gorman, *The Death of the Messiah*, 14–15.
22. Ibid., 5, 31.
23. Gorman, *Apostle of the Crucified Lord*, 116.
24. Ibid., 120.

Paul's spirituality (and that of New Testament spirituality as a whole) is not merely personal, although it is often described in that fashion. It is also communal and cosmic. Through the cross, we are each reconciled to God; we are reconciled to one another; and we are part of God's larger work of reconciling the world to himself (2 Cor 5:19). All of this is what Paul means by the "new creation." Gorman sums up the significance of this new creation for the believer by pointing out that when we share in the sufferings of the created order in anticipation of its full redemption (and our own), we also share in Jesus' sufferings (Rom 8:17–23). To share in the fellowship of Jesus' sufferings, then, is:

> to know the sufferings of Christ and to be conformed to him in contrast to the surrounding culture, to be comforted and empowered by the Spirit, and to have the hope that the God of Israel, who is the Father of the Lord Jesus, will complete the new creation that has already begun. *The church is the fellowship that speaks and lives that personal, communal, and cosmic story*" (emphasis mine).[25]

A Theopolitical Gospel

A large percentage of Americans say that they made a decision at some point in their lives to "accept Christ." Yet, as Scot McKnight points out, by even the most conservative estimates, *we lose at least 50 percent of those who make decisions.* This trend leads McKnight to observe: "We cannot help but conclude that making a decision is not the vital element that leads to a life of discipleship . . . Our focus on getting young people to make decisions—that is, 'accepting Jesus into our hearts'—appears to distort spiritual formation."[26] Could it be, he continues, that the root problem is a deficient view of the gospel?

Many Christians, McKnight argues, tend to have a "Good-Friday-only" gospel. That is, they begin with the question, "How do I get saved?"—to which the answer is given: "By faith in Jesus, through his atoning death on the cross for forgiveness of sins." Often, only passing reference is made to the resurrection. But, as is clear from passages like 1 Corinthians 15:1–28, *"the story of Jesus Christ is a complete story and not just a Good Friday story."*[27] It is sometimes forgotten that "Christ" is the Greek translation of the Hebrew word "Messiah," which means "anointed King," "Lord," and "Ruler." While

---

25. Ibid., 129.
26. McKnight, *The King Jesus Gospel*, 19–20.
27. Ibid., 53.

Paul speaks of the "gospel" in terms of "forgiveness of sins" through Jesus' death (1 Cor 15:3), he does not stop there. He then focuses on the resurrection of Jesus as the basis of the Christian's hope (15:4-19). And he concludes with a long description of the end (or consummation), when Christ will destroy all dominion, authority, and power and hand over the kingdom to God the Father, who is all in all (15:20-28). This story is much more than a story about me and my own personal salvation, or "who is saved and who is not saved."

This same portrayal of Christ's story of humiliation in his death on a Roman cross and ultimate exaltation as Lord to the glory of God is indicated in Philippians 2:6-11, which may have been an early creed sung in worship.[28] It is this story, as we have seen, that Jesus refers to when during the Last Supper he predicts that he will "drink anew" of the fruit of the vine in his Father's kingdom (Matt 26:29; cf. 1Cor 11:26). And it is the story that is repeated time and again in Luke's account of the founding and growth of the church in the book of Acts (2:14-41; 10:34-43; 13:13-41; 17:1-3, 22-34; 26-1-23).

In the case of both Jesus and Paul, this gospel narrative is not merely religious or theological. It also has strong political connotations. For non-Jews, the word *euangelion* (gospel) or "good news" was closely associated with allegiance to both deified humans (the emperor) and to the Roman Empire. The Caesar's birthday, his ascension to the throne, or a major Roman victory on the battlefield—all were occasions for proclamation of the good news, the gospel.[29] Other terms such as "savior," "salvation," and "Lord" were ascribed to the Roman emperor and employed to authenticate his rule and the rule of the Empire. One ancient inscription from Priene (in present-day Turkey, near Miletus, where Paul gave his farewell address to the Ephesian elders) describes Caesar Augustus as "a savior" who since his birthday "was the beginning of the good news for the world that came by reason of him."[30]

Jews, on the other hand, viewed the prophet's announcement of the "good news" that "your God reigns" (Isa 52:7) as a proclamation of God's sovereignty and rule over creation. The Gospel accounts of Jesus' passion are clear in ascribing this lordship over creation to Christ. When asked by the high priest during his trial if he is the Messiah, the "Son of the Blessed One," Jesus responds positively: "I am. And you will see the Son of Man

---

28. Gorman, *Apostle of the Crucified Lord*, 103.

29. Ibid.,, 15, 107; Crump, *I Pledge Allegiance*, 19;

30. This is based on a conversation I had with my good friend, Jim Baker, who actually saw this inscription.

sitting at the right hand of the Mighty One and coming on the clouds of heaven" (Mk 14:61-62; cf. Matt 26:63-64). The entire ruling council of the Sanhedrin knew that in identifying himself as the "Son of Man," Jesus was alluding to Daniel 7:13-14, which describes the Son of Man as coming from the throne of God to earth in the clouds of heaven to judge the world. Later, at his crucifixion, it is a Roman centurion—a soldier for whom the Caesar was only person a loyal Roman would ever call "Son of God"—who gives this title to Jesus (Mk 15:39; cf. Matt 27:54).[31] One can imagine how scandalous and subversive Jesus' claims about himself must have sounded to the people of his day. The clear subtext for those who heard this message of the early church was that the things that were being said about the Caesar and the Empire were false. In both the Gospels and Paul's Epistles, then, the confession of Jesus as Lord is a *theopolitical* confession. It means that through his death and resurrection Jesus embodies the God of Israel's rightful claim to universal sovereignty and acclamation, and that all other pretenders to what is his (and God's) alone are to be rejected.[32]

At its root—as we have noted—sin is idolatry, or exchanging the glory of God for something else in his creation. In the first century, idolatry was associated with worship of the pagan gods of the Roman Empire as well as with the imperial cult of emperor worship. We are not idolaters in that sense. But in our day there is no shortage of so-called "gods" or "lords" (1 Cor 8:5) which oppose Jesus' lordship, many of which can go unnoticed even within the Christian culture. America is not an "idol-free" zone.[33] In our contemporary society, "idol worship" can take the form of the prideful inflation of our own *personal egos* or desires through lust, pleasure, pride, popularity, greed, ambition, power, violence, hatred and the like; and our *social and national egos* through various sociopolitical ideologies or "isms," such as racism, nationalism, capitalism, socialism, and militarism. Idolatry also occurs when we equate God's kingdom with a "civil religious" worship of the "American way of life." Finally, we can be guilty of idolizing political power and human plans and strategies in our efforts to achieve through these means what can only be achieved through the power of the cross.

If God's glory and lordship is the ultimate purpose and goal of the church's mission, then idolatry is the polar opposite. Chris Wright states in this regard: "Since God's mission is to restore creation to its original purpose of bringing all glory to God himself and thereby enable all of creation to

---

31. See Keller, *King's Cross*, 194-207.
32. Gorman, *Apostle of the Crucified Lord*, 586.
33. See Hostetler, *American Idols*, 4.

enjoy the fullness of blessing that he desires for it, God battles against all forms of idolatry and calls us to join him in that conflict."[34]

The Church as a Community of Hope

What if in our engagement with the world we replaced fear with hope?[35] Fear causes us to look nostalgically to the past and put our faith in those who claim to have the power to restore a world we can never recover. The politics of fear is oriented around the idea of controlling history. In the words of the creators of *An Evangelical Manifesto*, Christians become "useful idiots" for one political party or another and Christian beliefs are used as weapons for political gain and political interests. When faith loses its independence and becomes an ideology it forgets the sage advice: "The first thing to say about politics is that politics is not the first thing."[36] Biblical hope, on the other hand, calls us to place our confidence in God's power to work out his purposes for good. Hope gives both strength and substance to what we are doing, which, in turn, is a sign of where we are going.[37] This is not mere optimism that things will get better if only we could elect the right candidates, but a view of this world as well as the world to come that is forged amid suffering and pain. Hope "draws us into the future" when wrongs will be made right, and in this way "engages us in life."[38]

Various biblical scholars have alerted us to the fact that our culture (often, including the church) is in crisis because the world has "lost its story." It is the church's task to *recover, proclaim, and live out* that narrative before the world in a manner that is consistent with the content of that narrative.[39] Timothy Keller rightly reminds us that "The gospel is the ultimate story that shows victory coming out of defeat, strength coming out of weakness, life coming out of death, rescue from abandonment." Because it is a *true* story, it gives us hope.[40] Stanley Grenz further remarks: "Taken as a whole, the biblical story is directed toward a *telos*. It speaks of the God who is bringing creation to its divinely intended goal."[41] In this age we have not entered into

---

34. Wright, *The Mission of God*, 188.
35. See Fea, *Believe Me*, 182–85.
36. Guinness et al. "An Evangelical Manifesto," 15.
37. Ibid., 6.
38. Fea, *Believe Me.*, 184–85. Fea argues that this biblical hope was exhibited in Martin Luther King and the civil rights movement of the 1960s.
39. Jensen, "How the World Lost Its Story," 19–24.
40. Keller, *King's Cross*, 230.
41. Grenz, *Renewing the Center*, 224.

the fullness of God universal rule. Therefore we must avoid all triumphalism and blind utopianism. Nor should we think that we can produce the kingdom of God within history through our own efforts. At the same time, the radically transcendent kingdom is also radically immanent. Scripture declares that through Christ there is an in-breaking of this new creation into our lives in the here and now (2 Cor 5:17). And "we are invited to be involved in that coming future and in God's historical work in bringing it into the present." This is evident, for example, in Peter's admonition to his readers to live holy and godly lives as they both wait for the day of God *and* hasten its coming (2 Pet 3:11–14).[42]

Insofar as this is a task of the church as a whole, the body of Christ is (or ought to be) a community of hope—or what James Davison Hunter calls a community of "faithful presence" in the world. Faithful presence involves being a different kind of people—a "new creation" (Gal 6:15)—and an alternative culture that is, nevertheless, integrated within the present culture. It is a form of engagement in and with the world that bears witness to and embodies the coming kingdom of God. As such, it challenges all forms of oppression, injustice, enmity, and corruption and, in turn, encourages, harmony, wholeness, joy, security, and well-being.[43] Hunter is not saying that Christians should totally abdicate their political responsibilities; politics is one form of public engagement. What he is proposing, however, is that positive cultural change is more likely to occur through "networks of elites" operating within their spheres of influence (i.e. their families, neighborhoods, voluntary associations, places of work, etc.) *outside* the political maelstrom. Christians should abandon their Constantinian preoccupation with coercion and control through a politics of power. Faithful presence calls us, rather, to offer a counter-narrative of faith, hope, and love. Faith speaks to the fundamental need for meaning. Hope responds to the need for purpose. And love addresses the need for bonds of intimacy and affection. It is also about grace, mercy, and justice. In keeping with this narrative, we should be concerned with offering creative and constructive approaches to social ills and with doing what we can to create conditions in the social structures people inhabit that are conducive to the flourishing of all.[44]

Most importantly, we should not make primary what is secondary. If we make some conception of the good in society the main objective, the very source of good—God himself and intimacy with him—becomes nothing more than a tool that is used to achieve that objective. Yes, we should

---

42. Grenz, *The Millennial Maze*, 197–215.
43. Hunter, *To Change the World*, 95–96; 243–48.
44. Ibid., 247; 262–63; 270–74.

be passionately concerned about issues of justice and peace in the world. "But, for Christians, these are all secondary to the primary good of God himself and the primary task of worshipping him and honoring him in all they do."[45]

Hunter's analysis forces us to think more deeply about the nature and task of the church. The church must actively declare the gospel—the "good news" of God's grace and his presence in the world—so that more people will enter into a saving relationship with him. That is a fundamental and necessary part of the church's mission. But, as a "new creation," the church is the only structure with the spiritual resources capable of offering an alternative to that of the popular culture. Therefore, as Hunter argues, "the church itself must model its alternative, both symbolically (e.g., through the Eucharist) and in actuality, that is, in the conduct of body life."[46] Both elements of proclaiming and living out the gospel need to be integrated into whole-life discipleship. In many cases, this will involve rethinking our mission and church-planting strategies. For example, living out the meaning of the Eucharist will mean forming and nurturing racially, economically, and culturally diverse congregations characterized by servanthood, reconciliation, forgiveness, and mutual love. Participatory remembrance of the atonement through the Lord's Supper also calls us to offer hope and friendship to the most vulnerable and neglected people of our society. Many of these folk live in what have been described as "burned over districts" of "over-evangelized, under-Christianized" communities. They've heard lots of things about Jesus, but often haven't seen him in the lives of Christians.[47] When we truly speak the truth in love and embody the "good news" that is celebrated in the Lord's Supper, we reflect the image of the risen Christ whom we follow and are a foretaste of the great banquet which is yet to come.

I have argued in this book that the Lord's Supper is a ceremony which symbolically proclaims and dramatizes the central beliefs and values of the Christian faith.[48] When we participate in this central rite of the believing community, we are drawn to celebrate in the midst of our present brokenness the promise of a glorious future reality that is already at work in us and in the world by God's Spirit.[49] As we remember Christ's substitutionary death on the cross and look to the hope of his resurrection, we are also called to live out his example of sacrificial service, divine hospitality, and

---

45. Ibid., 285–86.
46. Ibid., 235, 282–83.
47. Heuertz and Pohl, *Friendship at the Margins*, 73.
48. See Witherington, *New Testament Theology and Ethics, Vol. 2*, 64–65.
49. Grenz, *Renewing the Center*, 326.

cruciform love. I realize that not everyone will be convinced by my interpretation or application of particular texts. Our common purpose as followers of Christ, however, is that we might through his Spirit live lives that more faithfully reflect the future new heaven and new earth to his glory, even as we eagerly anticipate his return. My hope is that this book will contribute to that end.

Bibliography

Albright, Madeleine. *Fascism: A Warning.* New York: HarperCollins, 2018.

Alcorn, Randy. *Heaven.* Carol Stream, IL: Tyndale House, 2004.

Alexander, T. Desmond. *From Eden to the New Jerusalem: An Introduction to Biblical Theology.* Nottingham: InterVarsity, 2008.

Allender, Dan B. *To Be Told: God Invites You to Coauthor Your Future.* Colorado Springs: WaterBrook, 2005.

Amstutz, Mark R. *Just Immigration: American Policy in Christian Perspective.* Grand Rapids, MI: Eerdmans, 2017.

Andersen, Kurt. *Fantasyland: How America Went Haywire.* New York: Random House, 2017.

Anderson, Leith, et al. "Open Letter on Immigration Reform." National Association of Evangelicals (Nov. 13, 2012). https://www.nae.net/open-letter-on-immigration-reform/

Anderson, Charles A. "The Business of Busyness: Or, What Should We Make of Martha?" In *Everyday Theology: How to Read Cultural Texts and Interpret Trends*, edited by Kevin J. Vanhoozer, Charles A. Anderson, and Michael J. Sleasman, 155–71. Grand Rapids, MI: Baker Academic, 2007.

Arterbury, Andrew. "Entertaining Angels: Hospitality in Luke and Acts," Center for Christian Ethics at Baylor University (2007). https://www.baylor.edu/content/ services/ document.php/53378.pdf

Bailey, Kenneth E. *Jacob and the Prodigal: How Jesus Retold Israel's Story.* Downers Grove, IL: InterVarsity, 2003.

Baranovski, "The Confessing Church and Antisemitism: Protestant Identity, German Nationhood, and the Exclusion of the Jews." In *Betrayal: German Churches and the Holocaust*, edited by Robert P Erickson and Susannah Heschel, 90–109. Minneapolis, MN: Fortress, 1999.

Barnett, Victoria. *For the Soul of the People: Protestant Protest Against Hitler.* New York: Oxford, 1992.

Bartchy, S. Scott. "Table Fellowship." In *Dictionary of Jesus and the Gospels*, edited by Joel B. Green, Scot McKnight, and I. Howard Marshall, 796–800. Downers Grove, IL: InterVarsity, 1992.

Bartholomew, Craig G. and Michael W. Goheen, *The Drama of Scripture: Finding Our Place in the Biblical Story.* Grand Rapids, MI: Baker Academic, 2004.

Bartholomew, Craig G. "Biblical Theology and Biblical Interpretation: Introduction." In *Out of Egypt: Biblical Theology and Biblical Interpretation*, edited by Craig

Bartholomew, Mary Healy, Karl Moller, and Robin Parry, 1–17. Grand Rapids, MI: Zondervan, 2004.

Beale, G. K. *John's Use of the Old Testament in Revelation*. Bloomsbury: T & T Clark, 2015.

———. *The Temple and the Church's Mission: A Biblical Theology of the Dwelling Place of God*. Downers Grove, IL: InterVarsity, 2004.

———. *We Become What We Worship: A Biblical Theology of Idolatry*. Downers Grove, IL: IVP Academic, 2008.

Beale, G. K. and David Campbell. *Revelation: A Shorter Commentary*. Grand Rapids, MI: Eerdmans, 2015.

Beale, G. K. and Mitchell Kim, *God Dwells Among Us: Expanding Eden to the Ends of the Earth*. Downers Grove, IL: InterVarsity, 2014.

Bell, Rob. *Love Wins: A Book About Heaven, Hell, and the Fate of Every Person Who Ever Lived*. New York: HarperOne, 2011.

———. *Velvet Elvis: Repainting the Christian Faith*. New York: HarperOne, 2005.

Berger, Peter. *Sacred Canopy: Elements of a Sociological Theory of Religion*. New York: Anchor, 1969.

Berger, Peter, Brigitte Berger, and Hansfried Kellner. *The Homeless Mind: Modernization and Consciousness*. Visalia, CA: Vintage, 1974.

Berkhof, Louis. *Systematic Theology*. Grand Rapids, MI: Eerdmans, 1984.

Berry, Daina Ramey. *The Price for Their Pound of Flesh: The Value of the Enslaved from Womb to Grave, in the Building of the Nation*. Boston: Beacon, 2017.

Biema, David Van and Jeff Chu. "Does God Want You to Be Rich?" *Time* (Sept 10, 2006). http://content.time.com/time/magazine/article/0,9171,1533448-1,00.html

Bird, Michael F. *Evangelical Theology: A Biblical and Systematic Introduction*. Grand Rapids, MI: Zondervan, 2013.

Blaiklock, E. M. *The Acts of the Apostles: An Introduction and Commentary*. Grand Rapids, MI: Eerdmans, 1959.

Blaising, Craig A. "Premillennialism." In *Three Views on the Millennium and Beyond*, edited by Darrell L. Bock, 155–227. Grand Rapids, MI: Zondervan, 1999.

Blaising, Craig A. and Darrell L. Bock, *Progressive Dispensationalism: An Up-to-Date Handbook of Contemporary Dispensational Thought*. Wheaton, IL: BridgePoint, 1993.

Blim, Michael. *Equality and Economy: The Global Challenge*. Walnut Creek, CA: UltaMira, 2005.

Bloesch, Donald G. *Essentials of Evangelical Theology, Vol. 2: Life, Ministry & Hope*. San Francisco: Harper and Row, 1982.

Blomberg, Craig. *1 Corinthians: The NIV Application Commentary*. Grand Rapids, MI: Zondervan, 1994.

Bock, Darrell L. *Luke: The NIV Application Commentary*. Grand Rapids, MI: Zondervan, 1996.

———. "The Reign of the Lord Christ." In *Dispensationalism, Israel and the Church: The Search for Definition*, edited by Craig A. Blaising and Darrell L. Bock, 37–67. Grand Rapids, MI: Zondervan, 1992.

Boersma, Hans. *Violence, Hospitality, and the Cross: Appropriating the Atonement Tradition*. Grand Rapids, MI: Baker Academic, 2004.

Borg, Marcus J. and John Dominic Crossan, *The Last Week: A Day-by-Day Account of Jesus's Final Week in Jerusalem*. San Francisco: Harper, 2006.

Bouma–Prediger, Steven. "Eschatology Shapes Ethics: New Creation and Christian Ecological Virtue Ethics." *Canadian Theological Review* 2 (2013) 15–32. https://cetactr.files.wordpress.com/2015/12/ctr-2013-v2-2–bouma-prediger.pdf

Boyd, Gregory A. *The Myth of a Christian Nation: How the Quest for Political Power is Destroying the Church.* Grand Rapids, MI: Zondervan, 2005.

Brenneman, Todd M. *Homespun Gospel: The Triumph of Sentimentality in Contemporary Evangelicalism.* New York: Oxford University Press, 2014.

Broome, Deborah. "Who's at the Table? Inclusiveness in the Gospel of Luke." http://wn.anglican.org.nz/files/docs/inclusion-in-luke.pdf

Brown, Mark. "Study Finds 10,000 Families in Chicago Experienced Homelessness Last Year." *Chicago Sun Times* (June 15, 2018). https://chicago.suntimes.com/news/homeless-cps-families-study-10000/

Brown, Michael L. *A Queer Thing Happened to America.* Concord, NC: EqualTime, 2011.

Brueggemann, Walter. *The Prophetic Imagination: Prophetic Voices in Exile.* Philadelphia: Fortress, 1986.

———. *Worship in Ancient Israel: An Essential Guide.* Nashville: Abingdon, 2005.

Bruinius, Harry. "Why Evangelicals are Trump's Strongest Travel-ban Supporters." *Christian Science Monitor* (March 3, 2017). https://www.csmonitor.com/USA/Politics/2017/0303/Why-Evangelicals-are-Trump-s-strongest-travel-ban-supporters

Brustein, William. *The Logic of Evil: The Social Origins of the Nazi Party, 1925–1933.* New Haven, CT: Yale University Press, 1996.

Budde, Michael L. and Robert W. Brimlow, *Christianity Incorporated: How Big Business is Buying the Church.* Grand Rapids, MI: Brazos, 2002.

Burke, John. *Imagine Heaven: Near-Death Experiences, God's Promises, and the Exhilarating Future that Awaits You.* Grand Rapids, MI: Baker, 2015.

Burnett, Jane. "The Average Millennial Expects to Become a Millionaire at Some Point and Retire at Age 56." *Ladder* (June 12, 2018). https://www.theladders.com/career-advice/the-average-millennial-expects-to-become-a-millionaire-and-retire-at–age-56

Burton, Tara Isabella. "68% of White Evangelicals Think America Shouldn't House Refugees." *Vox* (May 29, 2018). https://www.vox.com/identities/2018/5/29/17405704/white-evangelicals-attitudes-refugees

Butler, Karen. "John Legend: 'Jesus Christ Superstar' is all about Love." *UPI* (March 30, 2018). https://www.upi.com/John-Legend-Jesus-Christ-Superstar-is-all-about-love/ 3621522087223/

Byrne, Brandan. *The Hospitality of God: A Reading of Luke's Gospel.* Collegeville, MN: Liturgical, 2000.

Cahn, Jonathan. *The Harbinger: The Ancient Mystery that Holds the Secret of America's Future.* Lake Mary, FL: Front Line, 2011.

Camosy, Charles C. *Beyond the Abortion Wars: A Way Forward for a New Generation.* Grand Rapids, MI: Eerdmans, 2015.

Carroll R., M. Daniel. *Christians at the Border: Immigration, the Church, and the Bible.* Grand Rapids, MI: Baker Academic, 2008.

Carson, D. A. *Becoming Conversant with the Emerging Church: Understanding a Movement and Its Implications.* Grand Rapids, MI: Zondervan, 2003.

Carter, Warren. *John and Empire: Initial Explorations.* New York: T & T Clark, 2008.

Charlesworth, Martin and Natalie Williams. *The Myth of the Undeserving Poor: A Christian Response to Poverty in Britain Today.* Surbitan, UK: Grosvenor House, 2014.

Chattaway, Peter T. "NBC Resurrects 'Jesus Christ Superstar.'" *Christianity Today* (March 28, 2018). https://www.christianitytoday.com/ct/2018/march-web-only/nbc-jesus-christ-superstar-live.html

Chester, Tim. *A Meal with Jesus: Discovering Grace, Community, and Mission around the Table.* Wheaton, IL: Crossway, 2011.

Clarke, Rosiland S. "Canonical Interpretations of the Song of Songs." *Tyndale Bulletin* 65.2 (2014) 305–308. https://legacy.tyndalehouse.com/Bulletin/65=2014/07_Clarke-4.pdf

Cleveland, Christena. *Disunity in Christ: Uncovering the Hidden Forces that Keep Us Apart.* Downers Grove, IL: InterVarsity, 2013.

Cole, Graham A. *God the Peacemaker: How Atonement Brings Shalom.* Downers Grove, IL: InterVarsity, 2009.

Coloe, Mary L. *Dwelling in the Household of God: Johannine Ecclesiology and Spirituality.* Collegeville, MN: Liturgical, 2007.

Coleman, Emily K. "Controversy Over PADS Lake County Inspires Art Exhibit Featuring Photos by Gurnee Pastor." *Lake County News-Sun* (Nov. 29, 2018). https://www.chicagotribune.com/suburbs/lake-county-news-sun/ct-lns-waukegan-pads-art-exhibit-st-1130-story.html

Cook, Robert W. "Eschatology in John's Gospel." *Criswell Theological Review* 3.1 (1988) 79–99. https://faculty.gordon.edu/hu/bi/ted_hildebrandt/NTeSources/NTArticles/CTR-NT/Cook-JohnsEschatology-CTR.htm

Copan, Paul. *Is God a Moral Monster?: Making Sense of the Old Testament God.* Grand Rapids, MI: Baker, 2011.

Copan, Paul and Matthew Flannagan, *Did God Really Command Genocide? Coming to Terms with the Justice of God.* Grand Rapids, MI: Baker, 2014.

Corbett, Steve and Brian Fikkert. *When Helping Hurts: How to Alleviate Poverty Without Hurting the Poor or Yourself.* Chicago: Moody, 2009.

Cortez, Marc. "The Problem with Our Gospel #1: The Self–Centered Gospel." *Transformed* (Nov. 14, 2011). https://www.westernseminary.edu/transformedblog/2011/11/14/problem-1-the-self-centered-gospel/

———. "The Problem with Our Gospel #2: The Individualistic Gospel." *Transformed* (Nov. 21, 2011). https://www.westernseminary.edu/transformedblog/2011/11/21/the-problem-with-our-gospel-2-the-individualistic-gospel/

Crouse, Andy. *Culture Making: Recovering Our Creative Calling.* Downers Grove, IL: InterVarsity, 2008.

Crump, David. *I Pledge Allegiance: A Believer's Guide to Kingdom Citizenship in 21st-Century America.* Grand Rapids, MI: Eerdmans, 2018.

Dallas, Kelsey. "Faithfully Engaging the Immigration Debate in the Age of Trump." *The Herald News* (March 15, 2017). https://www.heraldnews.com/news/20170315/faithfully-engaging-immigration-debate-in-age-of-trump

Das, A. Andrew. "1 Corinthians 11:17–34 Revisited." *Concordia Theological Quarterly* 62.3 (July 1998) 187–208. http://www.ctsfw.net/media/pdfs/dasacorinthiansrevisited.pdf

Davis, Ellen F. *Proverbs, Ecclesiastes, and Song of Songs.* Louisville, KY: Westminster John Knox, 2000.

Delistraty, Cody C. "The Importance of Eating Together." *The Atlantic* (July 18, 2014). https://www.theatlantic.com/health/archive/2014/07/the-importance-of-eating-together/374256/

deSilva, David A. *Seeing Things John's Way: The Rhetoric of the Book of Revelation.* Louisville, KY: Westminster John Knox, 2009.

DeYoung, Curtiss Paul, Michael O. Emerson, and George Yancey. *United by Faith: The Multiracial Congregation as an Answer to the Problem of Race.* New York: Oxford University Press, 2003.

DeYoung, Kevin and Greg Gilbert. *What is the Mission of the Church? Making Sense of Social Justice, Shalom, and the Great Commission.* Wheaton, IL: Crossway, 2011.

Donaldson, Alistair W. *The Last Days of Dispensationalism: A Scholarly Critique of Popular Misconceptions.* Eugene, OR: Wipf & Stock, 2011.

Duguid, Iain M. *The Song of Songs: An Introduction and Commentary.* Downers Grove, IL: InterVarsity, 2015.

Ehioghae, Efe M. "A Theological Evaluation of the Utopian Image of Prosperity Gospel and the African Dilemma." *IOSR Journal of Humanities and Social Science* 20.8 (August 2018) 69–75. https://pdfs.semanticscholar.org/ed15/086d2484489364bf37a6781c4c85bc0d6a6c.pdf

Elliott, Michael. *Why the Homeless Don't Have Homes and What to Do about It.* Cleveland, OH: Pilgrim, 1993.

Emerson, Michael O. and Christian Smith, *Divided by Faith: Evangelical Religion and the Problem of Race in America.* New York: Oxford University Press, 2000.

Emerson, Matthew Y. *Christ and the New Creation: A Canonical Approach to the Theology of the New Testament.* Eugene, OR: Wipf & Stock, 2013.

Enns, Peter. *The Evolution of Adam: What the Bible Does and Doesn't Say about Human Origins.* Grand Rapids, MI: Brazos, 2012.

Estes, Douglas. *SimChurch: Being the Church in the Virtual World.* Grand Rapids, MI: Zondervan, 2009.

Fahmy, Miral. "Super-sizing the 'Last Supper.'" *Reuters* (March 23, 2010). https://www.reuters.com/article/us-food-lastsupper/super-sizing-the-last-supper-id USTRE62M1HG20100323?type=lifestyleMolt

Fea, John. *Believe Me: The Evangelical Road to Donald Trump.* Grand Rapids, MI: Eerdmans, 2018.

Finger, Rita Halteman. *Of Widows and Meals: Communal Meals in the Book of Acts.* Grand Rapids, MI: Eerdmans, 2007.

Fitch, David E. *The End of Evangelicalism? Discerning a New Faithfulness for Mission: Towards an Evangelical Political Theology.* Eugene, OR: Wipf & Stock, 2011.

Fitzpatrick, Elyse. *Home: How Heaven and the New Earth Satisfy Our Deepest Longings.* Minneapolis, MN: Bethany House, 2016.

Fox, Robin. "Food and Eating: An Anthropological Perspective." Social Issues Research Center. http://www.sirc.org/publik/foxfood.pdf

Fulford, Robert. *The Triumph of Narrative: Storytelling in the Age of Mass Culture.* New York: Broadway, 2001.

Gaede, S. D. *When Tolerance is No Virtue: Political Correctness, Multiculturalism and the Future of Truth and Justice.* Downers Grove, IL: InterVarsity, 1993.

Gehring, Roger W. *House Church and Mission: The Importance of Household Structures in Early Christianity.* Peabody, MA: Hendrickson, 2004.

George, Abraham and Nikki A. Toyama-Szeto, *God of Justice*. Downers Grove, IL: InterVarsity, 2015.
Glasser, Arthur F., with Charles E. Van Engen, Dean S. Gilliland, and Shawn B. Redford. *Announcing the Kingdom: The Story of God's Mission in the Bible*. Grand Rapids, MI: Baker, 2003.
Goheen, Michael W. *A Light to the Nations: The Missional Church and the Biblical Story*. Grand Rapids, MI: Baker Academic, 2011.
Gorman, Michael J. *Apostle of the Crucified Lord: A Theological Introduction to Paul and His Letters*. Grand Rapids, MI: Eerdmans, 2004.
―――. *Becoming the Gospel: Paul, Participation, and Mission*. Grand Rapids, MI: Eerdmans, 2015.
―――. *Cruciformity: Paul's Narrative Spirituality of the Cross*. Grand Rapids, MI: Eerdmans, 2001.
―――. *Reading Revelation Responsibly. Uncivil Worship and Witness: Following the Lamb into the New Creation*. Eugene, OR: Cascade, 2011.
―――. *The Death of the Messiah and the Birth of the New Covenant*. Eugene, OR: Cascade, 2014.
―――. "What Has the Spirit Been Saying?: Theological and Hermeneutical Reflections on the Reception/Impact History of the Book of Revelation." ResearchGate (January 2012). https://www.researchgate.net/publication/292255214_What_has_the_spirit_been_saying_Theological_and_hermeneutical_reflections_on_the_receptionimpact_history_of_the_ book_of_Revelation
Gospell, Louise A. *The Poor, the Crippled, the Blind, and the Lame: Physical and Sensory Disability in the Gospels of the New Testament*. Tubingen: Mohr Siebeck, 2018.
Grassi, Joseph A. *Informing the Future: Social Justice in the New Testament*. Mahwah, NJ: Paulist, 2003.
Green, Joel B. *The Gospel of Luke*. Grand Rapids, MI: Eerdmans, 1997.
Grenz, Stanley J. *Renewing the Center: Renewing Theology in a Post-Theological Era*. Grand Rapids, MI: Baker Academic, 2006.
―――. *The Millennial Maze: Sorting Out Evangelical Options*. Downers Grove, IL: InterVarsity, 1992.
Griffin, Mark and Theron Walker, *Living on the Borders: What the Church Can Learn from Ethnic Immigrant Culture*. Grand Rapids, MI: Brazos, 2004.
Grigg, Viv. "The Spirit of Christ and the Postmodern City." Ph.D. dissertation. http://www.urban-leadership.org/PhD.htm
Grudem, Wayne. *Systematic Theology: An Introduction to Biblical Doctrine*. Grand Rapids, MI: Zondervan, 1994.
Guder, Darrell L. *Be My Witnesses: The Church's Mission, Message, and Messengers*. Grand Rapids, MI: Eerdmans, 1985.
Guinness, Os. *A Free People's Suicide: Sustainable Freedom and the American Future*. Downers Grove, IL: InterVarsity, 2012.
―――. *Last Call for Liberty: How America's Genius for Freedom Has Become its Greatest Threat*. Downers Grove, IL: InterVarsity, 2018.
―――. "Making the World Safe for Diversity: Religious Liberty and Social Harmony in a Pluralistic Age." ERIC. https://eric.ed.gov/?q=%22%22&ft=on&ff1= pubInformation+Analyses&ff2=lawUnited+States-Constitution&id=ED352277
―――. *Renaissance: The Power of the Gospel However Dark the Times*. Downers Grove, IL: InterVarsity, 2014.

———. *The Case for Civility: And Why Our Future Depends On It*. New York: HarperOne, 2008.

———. "The Golden Triangle of Freedom." RZIM. https://www.rzim.org/read/just-thinking-magazine/the-golden-triangle-of-freedom.

Guinness, Os et al. "An Evangelical Manifesto: A Declaration of Evangelical Identity and Public Commitment." The Gospel Coalition (May, 2008). http://osguinness.com/wp-content/uploads/2016/02/Evangelical-Manifesto-2.pdf

Gundry, Robert H. *Matthew: A Commentary on His Handbook for a Mixed Church under Persecution*. Grand Rapids, MI: Eerdmans, 1994.

Gushee, David P. *The Future of Faith in American Politics: The Public Witness of the Evangelical Center*. Waco, TX: Baylor University Press, 2008.

Gushee, David P. and Glen H. Stassen, *Kingdom Ethics: Following Jesus in Contemporary Context*. Downers Grove, IL: InterVarsity, 2003 and 2016.

Guthrie, Donald. "The Lamb in the Structure of the Book of Revelation." *Vox Evangelica* 12 (1981) 64–71.

Hagee, John. *Four Blood Moons: Something is about To Change*. Brentwood, TN: Worthy, 2013.

Hamilton, James M. "The Lord's Supper in Paul: An Identity-Forming Proclamation of the Gospel." In *The Lord's Supper: Remembering and Proclaiming Christ Until He Comes*, edited by Thomas R. Schreiner and Matthew R. Crawford, 68–102. Nashville, TN: B & H, 2010.

Hasson, Kevin Seamus. *The Right to Be Wrong: Ending the Culture War over Religion in America*. San Francisco: Encounter, 2005.

Hays, Daniel J. *From Every People and Nation: A Biblical Theology of Race*. Downers Grove, IL: InterVarsity, 2003.

Hays, Richard B. *First Corinthians: Interpretation: A Bible Commentary for Preaching and Teaching*. Louisville, KY, 1997.

———. *The Conversion of the Imagination: Paul as Interpreter of Israel's Scripture*. Grand Rapids, MI: Eerdmans, 2005.

———. *The Moral Vision of the New Testament: A Contemporary Introduction to New Testament Ethics*. San Francisco: Harper, 1996.

Henne, Peter S. "Superstar Christianity." *Patheos* (March 28, 2018). https://www.patheos.com/blogs/christiansingeneral/2018/03/superstar-christianity-jesus-christ–superstar/

Hesselgrave, Ronald P. *The JustMissional Church: Pursuing God's Path for Justice*. Createspace, 2014.

Heuertz, Christopher L and Christine D. Pohl. *Friendship at the Margins: Discovering Mutuality in Service and Mission*. Downers Grove, IL: InterVarsity, 2010.

Hilber, John W. "Theology of Worship in Exodus 24." *Journal of the Evangelical Theological Society* 39 (1996) 177–89.

Hilton, Allen. *A House United: How the Church Can Save the World*. Minneapolis, MN: Fortress, 2018.

Hollinger, Dennis P. *Individualism and Social Ethics: An Evangelical Syncretism*. Lanham, MD: University Press of America, 1983.

Holmes, Barbara A. *Joy Unspeakable: Contemplative Practices in the Black Church*. Minneapolis, MN: Augsburg, 2004.

Horsley Richard and Tom Hatcher. *John, Jesus, and the Renewal of Israel*. Grand Rapids, MI: Eerdmans, 2013.

Hostetler, Bob. *American Idols: Worship of the American Dream.* Nashville, TN: Broadman and Holman, 2006.

Humes, James C. *Churchill: The Prophetic Statesman.* Washington, DC: Regnery History, 2012.

Hunt, Zack. *Unraptured: How End Times Theology Get It Wrong.* Harrisonburg, VA: Herald, 2019.

Hunter, James Davison. *To Change the World: The Irony, Tragedy, and Possibility of Christianity in the Late Modern World.* New York Oxford University Press, 2010.

Isaac, Gordon L. *Left Behind or Left Befuddled: The Subtle Dangers of Popularizing the End Times.* Collegeville, MN: Liturgical Press, 2008.

James, Steven L. *New Creation Eschatology and the Land: A Survey of Contemporary Perspectives.* Eugene, OR: Wipf & Stock, 2017.

Jensen, Robert W. "How the World Lost Its Story." *First Things* (October 1993). https://www.firstthings.com/article/1993/10/how-the-world-lost-its-story

Jethani, Skye. *The Divine Commodity: Discovering a Faith Beyond Consumer Christianity.* Grand Rapids, MI: Zondervan, 2009.

Jipp, Joshua W. *Saved by Faith and Hospitality.* Grand Rapids, MI: Eerdmans, 2017.

Johnson, Alan F. *1 Corinthians.* Downers Grove, IL: InterVarsity, 2004.

Johnson, Luke T. *Sharing Possessions: Mandate and Symbol of Faith.* Philadelphia, PA: Fortress, 1981.

Johnson, Paul. *A History of the Jews.* New York: Harper & Row, 1987.

Julier, Alice P. *Eating Together: Food, Friendship, and Inequality.* Urbana, IL: University of Illinois Press, 2013.

Kaiser, Walter C. Jr. *Toward Old Testament Ethics.* Grand Rapids, MI: Zondervan, 1983.

Katz, Michael B. *Undeserving Poor: From the War on Poverty to the War on Welfare.* New York: Pantheon, 1989.

Keener, Craig S. *Acts: An Exegetical Commentary, Vol 2.* Grand Rapids, MI: Baker Academic, 2014.

———. *The Gospel of John: A Commentary, Vol. Two.* Peabody, MA: Hendrickson, 2003.

———. *The Historical Jesus of the Gospels.* Grand Rapids, MI: Eerdmans, 2009.

Keller, Timothy. *Generous Justice: How God's Grace Makes Us Just.* New York: Penguin, 2010.

———. *King's Cross: The Story of the World in the Life of Jesus.* New York: Dutton, 2011.

———. *The Prodigal God: Recovering the Heart of the Christian Faith.* New York: Dutton, 2008.

Klink, Edward W. III and Darian R. Lockett, *Understanding Biblical Theology: A Comparison of Theory and Practice.* Grand Rapids, MI: Zondervan, 2012.

Koenig, John. *New Testament Hospitality: Partnership with Strangers as Promise and Mission.* Eugene, OR: Wipf & Stock, 1985.

Koester, Craig R. *Revelation and the End of All Things.* Grand Rapids, MI: Eerdmans, 2001.

———. "Revelation's Visionary Challenge to Ordinary Empire." Digital Commons, Luther Seminary. https://digitalcommons.luthersem.edu/cgi/viewcontent.cgi?referer=https://www.google.com/&httpsredir=1&article=1008&context=faculty_articles

———. *Symbolism in the Fourth Gospel: Meaning, Mystery, Community.* Minneapolis, MI: Augsburg Fortress, 2003.

———. *Word of Life: A Theology of John's Gospel.* Grand Rapids, MI: Eerdmans, 2008.

Kostenberger, Andreas J. *A Theology of John's Gospel and Letters: Biblical Theology of the New Testament*. Grand Rapids, MI: Zondervan, 2009.

Kraybill, J. Nelson. *Apocalypse and Allegiance: Worship, Politics, and Devotion in the Book of Revelation*. Grand Rapids, MI: Brazos, 2010.

Ladd, George Eldon. *Theology of the New Testament (Revised Edition)*. Grand Rapids, MI: Eerdmans, 1993.

LaHaye, Tim. *Revelation Unveiled*. Grand Rapids, MI: Zondervan, 1999.

LaVerdiere, Eugene. *Dining in the Kingdom of God: The Origins of the Eucharist in the Gospel of Luke*. Chicago, IL: Liturgy Training, 1994.

Lawson, "The Gospel According to Safeway." In *Everyday Theology: How to Read Cultural Texts and Interpret Trends*, edited by Kevin J. Vanhoozer, Charles A. Anderson, and Michael J. Sleasman, 63–79. Grand Rapids, MI: Baker Academic, 2007.

Leithart, Peter J. *Blessed Are the Hungry: Meditations on the Lord's Supper*. Moscow, ID: Canon, 2000.

Lemons, J. Derrick. "Communitas at the Tables: Jesus, the Marginalized, and the Modern Church." *Asbury Journal* 70.1 (2015) 157–70. https://place.asburyseminary.edu/cgi/viewcontent.cgi?article=1300&context=asburyjournal

Leong, David P. *Race and Place: How Urban Geography Shapes the Journey to Reconciliation*. Downers Grove, IL: InterVarsity, 2017.

Levitsky, Steven and Daniel Ziblatt. *How Democracies Die*. New York: Crown, 2018.

Lewis, C. S. *Mere Christianity*. New York: HarperOne, 2001.

———. *The Screwtape Letters*. New York: Touchstone, 1996.

———. *Weight of Glory*. New York: HarperOne, 2001.

Long, Phillip J. *Jesus the Bridegroom: The Origin of the Eschatological Feast as a Wedding Banquet in the Synoptic Gospels*. Eugene OR: Pickwick, 2013.

Longenecker, Bruce W. *Remember the Poor: Paul, Poverty, and the Roman Empire*. Grand Rapids, MI: Eerdmans, 2010.

Longenecker, Richard N. *New Testament Social Ethics for Today*. Grand Rapids, MI: Eerdmans, 1984.

Lorenz, Glenn Virgil. "Leading from the Margins: Recovering the Christian Tradition of Hospitality in Church Leadership." PhD Dissertation. https://place.asburyseminary.edu/cgi/viewcontent.cgi?referer=https://www.google.com/&httpsredir=1&article=1236&context=ecommonsatsdissertations

Lutzer, Erwin W. *Hitler's Cross: How the Cross Was Used to Promote the Nazi Agenda*. Chicago: Moody, 1995.

———. *One Minute After You Die: A Preview of Your Final Destination*. Chicago: Moody, 1997.

MacArthur, John. *Because the Time is Near*. Chicago: Moody, 2007.

Marshall, I Howard. *Luke: Historian and Theologian*. Grand Rapids, MI: Zondervan, 1970.

Martin, Francis and William M. Wright IV. *The Gospel of John*. Grand Rapids, MI: Baker Academic, 2015.

McGill, Rachael L. "God's Getting Married: The Wedding at Cana as a Dramatization of Covenant Fulfillment." *The Hilltop Review* 8 (2015). https://scholarworks.wmich.edu/cgi/viewcontent.cgi?referer=https://www.google.com/&httpsredir=1&article=1152&context=hilltopreview

McGuire, Paul and Troy Anderson. *The Babylon Code: Solving the Bible's Greatest End-Times Mystery.* New York: FaithWords, 2015.

McKnight, Scot. *A Community Called Atonement.* Nashville, TN: Abingdon, 2007.

———. *Kingdom Conspiracy: Returning to the Radical Mission of the Local Church.* Grand Rapids, MI: Brazos, 2014.

———. *The Heaven Promise: Engaging the Bible's Truth About Life to Come.* Colorado Springs, Co: Waterbrook, 2015.

———. *The Jesus Creed: Loving God, Loving Others.* Brewster, MA: Paraclete, 2004.

———. *The King Jesus Gospel: The Original Good News Revisited.* Grand Rapids, MI: Zondervan, 2011.

McLaren, Brian D. *Everything Must Change: Jesus, Global Crisis, and a Revolution of Hope.* Nashville, TN: Thomas Nelson, 2007.

McNeil, Brenda Salter. *Roadmap to Reconciliation: Moving Communities into Unity, Wholeness and Justice.* Downers Grove, IL: InterVarsity, 2015.

Menninger, Karl A. *Whatever Became of Sin?* New York: Hawthorne, 1973.

Middleton, J. Richard. *A New Heaven and a New Earth: Reclaiming Biblical Eschatology.* Grand Rapids, MI: Baker Academic, 2014.

———. "A New Heaven and a New Earth: The Case for a Holistic Reading of the Biblical Theology of Redemption." *Journal for Christian Theological Research* 11 (2006) 73–97. https://digitalcommons.luthersem.edu/cgi/viewcontent.cgi?article=1031&context=jctr

Middleton, J. Richard and Brian J. Walsh. *Truth Is Stranger Than It Used to Be: Biblical Faith in a Postmodern Age.* Downers Grove, IL: InterVarsity, 1995.

Miles, Todd L. "A Kingdom Without a King? Evaluating the Kingdom Ethic(s) of the Emerging Church," ETS National Conference (2007). https://www.monergism.com/thethreshold/ sdg/Miles,%20Todd%20-%20A%20Kingdom%20without%20a%20King.pdf

Moore, Russell D. "Moving Forward with a Kingdom Consensus." Crossway interview (July 16, 2005). http://www.angelfire.com/tn/steveweaver/Russell_Moore_Interview.pdf

———. *Onward: Engaging the Culture without Losing the Soul.* Nashville, TN: B & H, 2015.

———. *The Kingdom of Christ: The New Evangelical Perspective.* Wheaton, IL: Crossway, 2004.

———. "What's the Real Issue behind the Abortion Debate?" *National Review* (Oct. 29, 2018) 1-4. https://www.nationalreview.com/2018/10/abortion-debate-real-issue/

Morris, Leon. *The First Epistle of Paul to the Corinthians: An Introduction and Commentary.* Grand Rapids, MI: Eerdmans, 1973.

Mott, Stephen Charles. *A Christian Perspective on Political Thought.* New York: Oxford University Press, 1993.

———. *Biblical Ethics and Social Change.* New York: Oxford University Press, 1982.

Motyer, J. Alec. *Isaiah: An Introduction and Commentary.* Downers Grove, IL: InterVarsity, 1999.

Mouw, Richard J. *When the Kings Come Marching In: Isaiah and the New Jerusalem.* Grand Rapids, MI: Eerdmans, 2002.

Nelson, Derek R. *Sin: A Guide for the Perplexed.* New York: T & T Clark, 2011.

Newman, Elizabeth. *Untamed Hospitality: Welcoming God and Other Strangers.* Grand Rapids, MI: Brazos, 2007.

Noll, Mark A. *The Rise of Evangelicalism: The Age of Edwards, Whitefield and the Wesleys*. Grand Rapids, MI: InterVarsity, 2003.

O' Day, Gail R. "I Have Called You Friends." Center for Christian Ethics at Baylor University (2008). https://www.baylor.edu/content/services/document.php/61118.pdf

Olson, Roger E. *How to Be Evangelical without Being Conservative*. Grand Rapids, MI: Zondervan, 2008.

———. *The Essentials of Christian Thought: Seeing Reality through the Biblical Story*. Grand Rapids, MI: Zondervan, 2017.

———. *The Journey of Modern Theology: From Reconstruction to Deconstruction*. Downers Grove, IL: IVP Academic, 2014.

Oswalt, John N. *The Bible among the Myths: Unique Revelation of Just Ancient Literature?* Grand Rapids, MI: Zondervan, 2009.

Ott, Bernhard. *God's Shalom Project: An Engaging Look at the Bible's Sweeping Story*. Intercourse, PA: Good, 2004.

Pao, David W. *Acts and the Isaianic New Exodus*. Grand Rapids, MI: Baker Academic, 2000.

Pennington, Jonathan T. "The Lord's Last Supper in the Fourfold Witness of the Gospels." In *The Lord's Supper: Remembering and Proclaiming Christ until He Comes*, edited by Thomas R. Schreiner and Matthew R. Crawford, 31–67. Nashville, TN: B & H, 2010.

Pew Research Center. "Fairness of the Economic System, Views of the Poor, and the Social Safety Net." (June 26, 2014). http://www.people-press.org/2014/06/26/section-3-fairness-of-the-economic-system-views-of-the-poor-and-the-social-safety-net/

———. "Few Say Religion Shapes Immigration, Environment Views." (September 17, 2010). http://www.pewforum.org/2010/09/17/few-say-religion-shapes-immigration-environment-views/

Piper, John. *Future Grace*. Sisters, OR: Multnomah, 1995.

Pitre, Brant. *Jesus and the Jewish Roots of the Eucharist: Unlocking the Secrets of the Last Supper*. New York: Image, 2011.

———. *Jesus and the Last Supper*. Grand Rapids, MI: Eerdmans, 2017.

———. *Jesus the Bridegroom: The Greatest Love Story Ever Told*. New York: Image, 2014.

———. "Jesus, the Messianic Banquet, and the Kingdom of God." *Letter and Spirit* 5 (2009) 145–166. https://static1.squarespace.com/static/569543b4bfe873607 95306d6/t/ 57f548c4cdof68c 740aa7d15/1475692745347/Jesus-MesBanquet-KingdomofGod.pdf

Plantinga, Cornelius Jr. *Not the Way It's Supposed to Be: A Breviary of Sin*. Grand Rapids, MI: Eerdmans, 1995.

Pohl, Christine D. *Making Room: Recovering Hospitality as a Christian Tradition*. Grand Rapids, MI: Eerdmans, 1999.

Richard, Lucien. *Living the Hospitality of God*. Mahwah, NJ: Paulist, 2000.

Robinson, Anthony B. and Robert W. Wall. *Called to Be Church: The Book of Acts for the Church Today*. Grand Rapids, MI: Eerdmans, 2006.

Rocke, Kris and Joel Van Dyke. *The Geography of Grace: Doing Theology from Below*. Tacoma WA: Center for Transforming Mission, 2012.

Ross, Josh and Jonathan Storment. *Bringing Heaven to Earth: You Don't Have to Wait for Eternity to Live the Good News*. Colorado Springs, CO: Waterbrook, 2015.

Routledge, Robin. "Replacement or Fulfillment? Re-applying Old Testament Designations to the Church." *Southwestern Theological Review* 4.2 (Winter 2014) 137–54. https://static1.squarespace.com/static/58485b63440243698143794a/t/58a1ffd215d5db9ab57ba282/1487011795483/STR_4_2_Routledge.pdf

Rowe, C. Kavin. *World Upside-Down: Reading Acts in the Graeco-Roman Age.* New York: Oxford University Press, 2009.

Sanders, Michael J. *Justice: What's the Right Thing to Do?* New York: Farrar, Straus, and Giroux, 2009.

Sanders, Ron. *After the Election: Prophetic Politics in a Post-Secular Age.* Eugene, OR: Cascade, 2018.

Schaeffer, Steve. *Living in the Overlap: How Jesus' Kingdom Proclamation Can Transform Your World.* Enumclaw, WA: Wine, 2010.

Shults, F. LeRon and Steven J. Sandage. *The Faces of Forgiveness: Searching for Wholeness and Salvation.* Grand Rapids, MI: Baker Academic, 2003.

Sider, Ronald J. *Just Politics: A Guide for Christian Engagement.* Grand Rapids, MI: Brazos, 2012.

Skillen, James W. *The Good of Politics: A Biblical, Historical, and Contemporary Introduction.* Grand Rapids, MI: Baker Academic, 2014.

Smith, Samuel. "Pro-Trump Billboard Quotes John 1:14, 'The Word Became Flesh,' 'Make America Great Again.'" The Christian Post (November 6, 2018). https://www.christianpost.com/news/pro-trump-billboard-quotes-john-114-the-word-became-flesh-make-gospel-great-again.html

Smith, Gary Scott. *Heaven in the American Imagination.* New York: Oxford University Press, 2011.

Snyder, Howard. "Church Growth Must be Based on a Biblical Vision of the Church as the Vital Community of the Kingdom of God." In *Evaluating the Church Growth Movement: Five Views*, edited by Gary L. McIntosh, 209–31. Grand Rapids, MI: Zondervan, 2004.

Stearns, Richard. *The Hole in Our Gospel.* Nashville, TN: Thomas Nelson, 2009.

Stevenson, Gregory. *A Slaughtered Lamb: Revelation and the Apocalyptic Response to Evil and Suffering.* Abilene, TX: Abilene Christian University Press, 2013.

Stott, John W. *The Cross of Christ.* Downers Grove, IL: InterVarsity, 2006.

Sweetman, Brendan. *Why Politics Needs Religion: The Place of Religious Arguments in the Public Square.* Downers Grove, IL: InterVarsity, 2006.

Tasker, R. V. G. *The Gospel According to St. John: An Introduction and Commentary.* Grand Rapids, MI: Eerdmans, 1977.

Thomson-DeVeaux, Amelia. "Why Rank-And-File Evangelicals Aren't Likely to Turn on Trump Over Family Separation." FiveThirtyEight (June 21, 2019). https://fivethirtyeight.com/features/why-rank-and-file-evangelicals-arent-likely-to-turn-on-trump-over-family-separation/

Turner, George Allen. "Soteriology in the Gospel of John." *Journal of the Evangelical Theological Society* 19.4 (Fall 1976) 271–77. https://www.etsjets.org/files/JETS-PDFs/19/19-4/19-4-pp271-278_JETS.pdf

Twenge, Jean M. and W. Keith Campbell. *The Narcissist Epidemic: Living in the Age of Entitlement.* New York: Atria, 2009.

Twitchell, James B. *Living it Up: Our Love Affair with Luxury.* New York: Columbia University Press, 2002.

U Chicago Urban Labs, *Ending Family Homeless Report: Understanding the Scale and Needs of Families Experiencing Homelessness in Chicago.* Urban Labs (June 1, 2018). https://urban labs.uchicago.edu/projects/linking-housing-and-education-data-to-help-end-family-homelessness-in-chicago

Vanhoozer, Kevin J. *Faith Speaking Understanding: Performing the Drama of Doctrine.* Louisville, KY: Westminster John Knox, 2014.

———. *Pictures at a Theological Exposition: Scenes of the Church's Worship, Witness and Wisdom.* Downers Grove, IL: IVP Academic, 2016.

———. *The Drama of Doctrine: A Canonical Linguistic Approach to Christian Doctrine.* Louisville, KY: Westminster John Knox, 2005.

Volf, Miroslav. "From Exclusion to Embrace: Reflections on Reconciliation." http://ce-un.org/resources/speeches/20010911-exclusion-to-embrace.pdf

Voskuil, Dennis N. "Individualism and Evangelism in America." *Reformed Review* 41.1 (1987) 21–28. https://repository.westernsem.edu/pkp/index.php/rr/article/view/1088

Wainwright, Geoffrey. *Eucharist and Eschatology.* New York: Oxford University Press, 1981.

Waldman, Steven. *Founding Faith: How Our Founding Fathers Forged a Radical New Approach to Religious Liberty.* New York: Random House, 2008.

Wallis, Jim. *On God's Side: What Religion Forgets and Politics Hasn't Learned About Serving the Common Good.* Grand Rapids, MI: Brazos, 2013.

Walton, John H. *Genesis: The NIV Application Commentary.* Grand Rapids, MI: Zondervan, 2001.

———. *Old Testament Theology for Christians: From Ancient Context to Enduring Belief.* Downers Grove, IL: IVP Academic, 2017.

———. *The Lost World of Adam and Eve: Genesis 2–3 and the Human Origins Debate.* Downers Grove, IL: IVP Academic, 2015.

———. *The Lost World of Genesis One: Ancient Chronology and the Origins Debate.* Downers Grove, IL: IVP Academic, 2009.

Walton, John H. and J. Harvey Walton. *The Lost World of the Israelite Conquest: Covenant, Retribution, and the Fate of the Canaanites.* Downers Grove, IL: IVP Academic, 2017.

Webber, Robert. *Ancient-Future Faith: Rethinking Evangelicalism for a Postmodern World.* Grand Rapids, MI; Baker, 1999.

Webster, Douglas D. *Follow the Lamb: A Pastoral Approach to the Revelation.* Eugene, OR: Wipf & Stock, 2014.

Weigel, George. *The Fragility of Order: Catholic Reflections in Turbulent Times.* San Francisco, CA: Ignatius Press, 2018.

Wells, David F. *No Place for Truth: Or Whatever Happened to Evangelical Theology?* Grand Rapids, MI: Eerdmans, 1995.

Wilbanks, Dana W. *Re-Creating America: The Ethics of U.S. Immigration and Refugee Policy in a Christian Perspective.* Nashville, TN: Abingdon, 1996.

Wilkinson, Alissa. "The Last Jedi is a Magnificent Next Step for the Star Wars Universe." *Vox* (December 16, 2017). https://www.vox.com/culture/2017/12/12/16765308/last–jedi–star–wars–review–rey–carrie-fisher-poe-finn-kylo-ren

Williamson, Peter S. *Revelation.* Grand Rapids, MI: Baker Academic, 2015.

Wilsey, John D. *One Nation Under God? An Evangelical Critique of Christian America.* Eugene, OR: Wipf & Stock, 2011.

Wilson–Hartgrove, Jonathan. *Reconstructing the Gospel: Finding Freedom from Slaveholder Religion.* Downers Grove, IL: InterVarsity, 2018.

Witherington, Ben III. *Making a Meal of It: Rethinking the Theology of the Lord's Supper.* Waco, TX: Baylor University Press, 2007.

———. *New Testament Theology and Ethics (Vols. One and Two).* Downers Grove, IL: InterVarsity, 2016.

Wood, Todd Charles and Darrel R. Falk. *The Fool and the Heretic: How Two Scientists Moved Beyond Labels to a Christian Dialogue About Creation and Evolution.* Grand Rapids, MI: Zondervan, 2019.

Wright, N. T. *Evil and the Justice of God.* Downers Grove, IL: InterVarsity, 2006.

———. *Following Jesus: Biblical Reflections on Discipleship.* Grand Rapids, MI: Eerdmans, 1994.

———. *How God Became King: The Forgotten Story of the Gospels.* New York: HarperOne, 2012.

———. *John for Everyone, Part 1: Chapters 1–10.* London: SPCK, 2004.

———. *Simply Christian: Why Christianity Makes Sense.* New York: HarperCollins, 2006.

———. *Surprised by Hope: Rethinking Heaven, the Resurrection, and the Mission of the Church.* New York: HarperOne, 2008.

———. *The Day the Revolution Began: Rethinking the Meaning of Jesus's Crucifixion.* New York: HarperOne, 2016.

———. *The Lord and His Prayer.* Grand Rapids, MI: Eerdmans, 1996.

———. *The Meal Jesus Gave Us: Understanding Holy Communion.* Louisville, KY: Westminster John Knox, 2015.

———. "The Royal Revolution: Fresh Perspectives on the Cross." N. T. Wright Page (January 24, 2017). http://ntwrightpage.com/2017/01/30/the-royal-revolution-fresh-perspectives-on-the-cross/

Wright, Christopher J. H. *The Mission of God: Unlocking the Bible's Grand Narrative.* Downers Grove, IL: IVP Academic, 2006.

———. *The Mission of God's People: A Biblical Theology of the Church's Mission.* Grand Rapids, MI: Zondervan, 2010.

Yancey, Philip. *Vanishing Grace: What Ever Happened to the Good News?* Grand Rapids, MI: Zondervan, 2014.

Yoder, John H. *The Original Revolution: Essays on Christian Pacifism.* Scottdale, PA: Herald, 1971.

www.ingramcontent.com/pod-product-compliance
Lightning Source LLC
Chambersburg PA
CBHW070237230426
43664CB00014B/2333